Disarming Beauty

CATHOLIC IDEAS FOR A SECULAR WORLD

O. Carter Snead, *series editor*

The purpose of this interdisciplinary series is to feature authors from around the world who will expand the influence of Catholic thought on the most important conversations in academia and the public square. The series is "Catholic" in the sense that the books will emphasize and engage the enduring themes of human dignity and flourishing, the common good, truth, beauty, justice, and freedom in ways that reflect and deepen principles affirmed by the Catholic Church for millennia. It is not limited to Catholic authors or even works that explicitly take Catholic principles as a point of departure. Its books are intended to demonstrate the diversity and enhance the relevance of these enduring themes and principles in numerous subjects, ranging from the arts and humanities to the sciences.

Disarming Beauty

ESSAYS ON FAITH, TRUTH, AND FREEDOM

JULIÁN CARRÓN

Foreword by Javier Prades

University of Notre Dame Press

Notre Dame, Indiana

University of Notre Dame Press
Notre Dame, Indiana 46556
www.undpress.nd.edu

English Language Edition Copyright © 2017
Fraternità di Comunione e Liberazione

Translated from *La bellezza disarmata*, by Julián Carrón, published by Rizzoli,
Milan, 2015. Italian edition © 2015 RCS Libri S.p.A., Milano.

Published in the United States of America

Library of Congress Cataloging-in-Publication Data

Names: Carrón Pérez, Julián, author.
Title: Disarming beauty : essays on faith, truth, and freedom / Julián
    Carrón ; foreword by Javier Prades.
Description: Notre Dame : University of Notre Dame Press, 2017. | Series:
    Catholic ideas for a secular world | Includes bibliographical references
    and index.
Identifiers: LCCN 2016058493 (print) | LCCN 2017009531 (ebook) | ISBN
    9780268101978 (hardcover : alk. paper) | ISBN 0268101973 (hardcover : alk.
    paper) | ISBN 9780268101992 (pdf) | ISBN 9780268102005 (epub)
Subjects: LCSH: Catholic Church—Doctrines. | Christianity and culture.
Classification: LCC BX1751.3 .C372413 2017 (print) | LCC BX1751.3
    (ebook) | DDC 282—dc23
LC record available at https://lccn.loc.gov/2016058493

∞ *This paper meets the requirements of ANSI/NISO Z39.48-1992*
(Permanence of Paper).

CONTENTS

FOREWORD

Javier Prades

In a Connected World

I recently had the opportunity to travel to Angola for reasons related to my work at the university. My hosts took advantage of the moments of rest to tell me about some educational and charitable works in so-called *barrios*, the dry and dusty suburbs of the city of Benguela.

For a European like me, every opportunity to travel in Africa or Latin America generates a wide range of sensations. Certainly I feel nostalgia towards the freshness of a simpler way of life, free from the adulteration of what Augusto Del Noce has called our affluent society. I also envy the simplicity of a faith rooted in everyday life, able to sustain the effort and the suffering of so many privations, so different from the tormented and problematic faith that we know well. In people, especially in children, you can perceive the echo of a joy that is not easy to recognize in European societies.

On the other hand, and with the same force, the precariousness of this life provokes a feeling of injustice. It is undeniable that without the necessary human, cultural, economic, and social resources, these forms of society, exposed to profound and rapid changes, can get lost or become further impoverished. The solidity and density of Europe's social, cultural, and economic life—even with all its wounds—seems to demonstrate its unique strength in human history. Indeed, the fresh and moving faith of these people is quite exposed to the antihumanist currents that exert so much influence in the West and from the West, the effects of which can already be seen in their societies.

These contrasts, which strike us when we travel outside Europe, recall the distinguished thinkers that have concluded that our culture has lost its way and cannot find effective remedies to recover the path. From Glucksmann to Habermas or Manent, they draw our attention to a divided West, fighting with itself, exhausted. Perhaps that is why, in the course of the twentieth century, many Europeans have come to question the value of the fruits of the civilization into which they were born. Nonetheless, we note a desire to not lose this precious European heritage of civilization and humanity, whose richness is almost unparalleled in history, a heritage that permits us, among other things, to speak today of "the person."

We Europeans now seem to glimpse the end of an economic crisis that has been both profound and painful for millions of our fellow citizens. On the one hand, it has brought out with particular intensity that feeling of weariness and exhaustion I mentioned, as if a deep malaise were lodged in our hearts. Secondly, the same crisis offers us the opportunity to begin again, to change, to try to improve. It is up to us to discern the situation in which we find ourselves, together with the possible solutions. What is happening to Europeans? And, especially, what is happening to European Christians? I never stop posing these questions to the churchmen, academics, and people of culture, both believers and agnostics or atheists, whom I meet. It is not easy to translate the answer into a fully determined path, but the trail map that we hear Julián Carrón propose in the first part of this book will lead us along the "interrupted paths"—in the words of Martin Heidegger—of our society.

The European Malaise

Our starting point is that in Western society a real malaise has surfaced. What is the task that lies ahead, imposed upon us by the episodes that strike us most painfully? It is precisely to properly interpret this malaise, which is expressed in ambiguous and often ideological ways. If we do not wish to close ourselves off from reality, we must seriously take this condition into account.

In my opinion, this malaise cannot be explained simply by the economic factors of the crisis, as serious as they have become in recent years. Think, for example, of the deep demographic crisis in Europe, with the dramatic decline in birth rates and the obvious difficulties in integrating immigrants. As known observers—from Böckenförde to Pérez Díaz—have lucidly noted, there is a moral and cultural subtext to the crisis in institutional participation we are experiencing. In addition, in order to identify the nature of the crisis we must understand it as a symptom of the ultimately infinite set of needs and evidence that constitute the common elementary experience of all people, needs and evidence whose full realization reveals man's foundational religious experience. The fact that young second- and third-generation Europeans succumb to the lure of Islamic fundamentalism should cause us to think about the lack of ideals that also touches the religious sphere.

The malaise of European society, and of European Christians, is not limited to superficial aspects, as plentiful as they are. Its roots are deep. It is a difficulty that we may describe, in the words of María Zambrano, as a crisis of "relationship with reality." But how so? It is a sort of loss of trust in our own life experience. It shows itself in the struggle to simply recognize and embrace reality as it appears, that is, full of attraction, as a manifestation of a foundation that is within everything and to which everything refers beyond itself.[1]

If, on the contrary, everything is reduced to mere appearances, our relationship with the real enters into crisis. We cannot ensure that knowledge of ourselves, of others, and of the world remains a sign of the foundation, of that good mystery that—in the words of Saint Thomas Aquinas—"everyone understands to be God."[2] The risk is not small, because the way we use reason and freedom, and thus our intelligence about reality, about its ultimate foundation, is undermined. When reason, freedom, and reality are questioned, there is cause for alarm in any society. In the medium and long term it is impossible—or at least far more uncertain and risky—to work, to establish bonds of affection, enjoy rest, and build a peaceful society. Thus the malaise we are experiencing gives rise to an existential weakness in humanity as humanity.

Examples of this process of weakening can be multiplied in each of the concrete orders of elementary experience to which we have alluded: love, work, leisure. Referring to young people in particular, Fr. Giussani coined the highly descriptive term "the Chernobyl effect," referring to an effect that threatens humanity today. He described the Chernobyl effect in these words: "It is as if today's youth were all penetrated by . . . the radiation of Chernobyl. Structurally, the organism is as it was before, but dynamically it is no longer the same. . . . People are . . . abstracted from the relationship with themselves, as if emptied of affection [without the energy of affection to adhere to reality], like batteries that last for six minutes instead of six hours."[3] Carrón uses these same words as a criterion for judgment, to understand the current situation of our pluralistic societies, precisely in formulating the question about what it means to be a Christian today (see chapter 5). The nature of this weakening process is not primarily ethical or psychological, though it also includes these factors; rather, it concerns the dynamics of knowledge and freedom in relationship to reality in its totality.

If this is so, and therefore the crisis is not only an economic, cultural, or moral one, but a fundamentally anthropological and religious one, then in order to foster coexistence and peace in Western society, it is necessary to analyze this category of issues. It is evident that what is happening in the West inevitably reflects on other cultures, and thus the road that the societies of and the Church in Europe ultimately take will also affect the rest of the world.

The Cultural Interpretation of Faith

How have we managed to reach this weakened human condition?

In a television interview at the end of his life, Giussani responded to the famous question of T. S. Eliot, "Has the Church failed mankind, or has mankind failed the Church?"[4] His response—perhaps surprising to some—was that both had happened. I believe that one of the aims of this collection of essays by Carrón is to carefully explore the ways in which the religious experience has been proposed to contemporary people, born into a pluralistic, multicultural society, a society, to a large extent, without Christ. Let us enter the field of what we might call the cultural interpretation of the faith.

Pope John Paul II made a now-classic contribution to defining the value of dialogue between the Christian faith and pluralistic society when he stressed that "the synthesis between culture and faith is not only a demand of culture but also of faith. . . . A faith that does not become culture is a faith not fully accepted, not entirely thought out, not faithfully lived."[5] This indication highlights the need of faith to be converted into culture, into a concrete way of living. Pope John Paul II does not suggest, of course, a process in which faith is diluted to the point of becoming mere culture, according to the "horizontalist" or "humanist" tendencies that prevailed at certain times after the Second Vatican Council. On the contrary, he claims that faith is capable of profoundly changing human dynamics, because it results in a concrete way of living and addresses the major issues that touch people's lives. If this process is not accomplished, we are faced with that separation between faith and life whose deleterious effects for the Christian tradition and for a fully human civilization were denounced by Vatican II and the postconciliar magisterium. A result of this separation is the inability to communicate the faith to people of different cultures and religious traditions.

On the contrary, when there is this indispensable "cultural translation," the faith acquires a public dimension and retains its living capacity for transmission, for building society and a new way of facing reality. We should note that this formula does not directly suggest a particular social or political profile of the faith. I am referring instead to a concrete way, born of faith, to realize human life, a way that by its nature must involve all life's personal and social dimensions. In the process different perspectives find space, not all of equal value, but all forced to measure themselves against the original nature of the Christian event, as it has been transmitted and confirmed by apostolic succession. If you do not accept this task of discernment, Eliot's question is destined to remain unanswered.

Cardinal Angelo Scola has offered a useful reading of two widespread interpretations of the faith in Europe, bearing in mind national differences.[6]

A first interpretation sees Christianity as a "civil religion," that is, as the ethical glue capable of generating social unity in the face of the widespread problems of coexistence in society. In this interpretation, the public implementation of Christianity means the defense and promotion of ethical values that underpin an increasingly faltering society. More specifically, the deterioration of the social fabric in its aspects most directly linked to moral life—of which we have countless examples—favors identification of a public implementation of the faith with efforts to recover the social validity of those values perceived to be more and more threatened. This conception can be promoted both by practicing Christians and by agnostics or nonbelievers, who expect just such an attitude from Christians. It is not hard to argue that this position reflects the tendency to identify the faith with a universal ethics, to ensure that some rational dignity is accorded to its public presence in the West.

Then there is a second interpretation, which tends to reduce Christianity to a "pure proclamation of the cross for the salvation of the world." On this interpretation, for example, a concern with bioethics or biopolitics would mean a distancing from the authentic message of Christ's mercy—as if the Christian message was ahistorical and had no social, anthropological, and cosmological implications. This interpretation asserts that the strength of Christian proclamation consists in a "pure" proposal of the mystery of the cross. In contrast to the first position, this one diverts attention from the ethical aspects, whether of the individual or of society, to emphasize the paradoxical strength of a Christian message, which, from the perspective of this world, is offered covertly, secretly; thus the strength of the divine power that is manifested in weakness is emphasized. It is perhaps possible to identify in this position the background influences of certain positions—originally Protestant, but later also Catholic—that reduce the universality of reason in favor of a faith life more dominated by sentiment or emotion.

What can we say about these two cultural interpretations of the faith? Both are based on elements that are, in themselves, essential for a full understanding of the role of Christian faith in the pluralistic society: on the one hand, the importance of the cross of Christ for salvation, on the other, the obvious ethical and cultural implications of the Christian message. Nonetheless, neither of them comprehensively expresses the true nature of Christianity and the way it should be present in society. More importantly, neither is able to adequately respond to the anthropological weakness that lies at the origin of the fatigue and confusion of our European society.

The first interpretation would reduce the Catholic faith to its secular dimension, separating it from the force that is born in the Christian as a gift of the encounter with Jesus Christ in the Church. Moreover, the attempt to provide a universal ethics while bracketing off the event of Christ, for historical reasons that all can understand, has already failed to ensure perpetual peace, as Pope Benedict XVI keenly pointed out in his judgment on the European Enlightenment. Carrón has examined this phenomenon in detail in the first part of this book.

The second interpretation deprives the faith of its incarnated and historical depth, reducing it to an inner inspiration and the expectation of a fullness in the hereafter. This "eschatological" interpretation also fails to understand the anthropological weakening process with its historical consequences, nor does it offer an answer that is adequate to the situation.

To overcome the limitations of both of these positions we need an understanding of Christianity in which the advent of Christ—irreducible to any human interpretation—is shown in its originality and its supercreaturely origin. On the other hand, we need an understanding of the reasonableness of this singular event in history, an event that transcends any measure reason is capable of imposing. Christianity claims to offer nothing less than a kind of experience that corresponds to what is human in any culture, because it springs from an event unique in history, one that opens all cultures to come face-to-face with a transcendent truth. This is one of the keys to intercultural and interreligious dialogue.

There is, then, a third position, which we call "the personalization of faith." Briefly, it comes down to choosing an understanding of the Catholic faith that implies its necessary existential verification, both on a personal and communitarian level, as a way to become a Church that is fully human within the conditions of a postsecular and post-Christian society. If I'm not mistaken, this is precisely the thread that runs through Julián Carrón's educational and cultural approach, as reflected in his presentations in very different fields, from which this book was born.

Personalizing Faith: Existential Verification

The Christian message claims to generate an "unprecedented newness" that "gives life a new horizon and a decisive direction." This famous statement of Benedict XVI, taken up by Pope Francis, gives us an adequate understanding of the originality of Christianity.[7] If we look at the life of Christian communities, especially in the southern regions of Europe, the initial impact of the newness is apparent in many places; indeed we often come across episodes of moving conversions, sometimes with almost miraculous consequences. We must thank God for all of that. So it is not the initial impact of the Christian message that is most lacking in Europe, although it is urgent that that impact multiply exponentially according to the Lord's mandate to reach all people. What is necessary, instead, is a type of education in the faith that can preserve, renew, and transmit this unexpected newness in all the circumstances of daily life. Christian experience, even when it is received with sincerity and generosity, often does not generate a human maturity sufficiently founded on its corresponding certainties so as to be able to work and love in the present and also keep the prospect of eternal life alive. Among those aware of this were some of the most acute observers of European Christianity, such as Newman in the nineteenth century and Guardini, Schlier, or Giussani in the last century, to cite the figures I am most aware of.

The anthropological weakness of Christians thus points to a weakness in the way we live and transmit the faith, one we could define as a "lack of verification" of the faith within Christian education. Faith is "verification" when it shows its ability to illuminate and bring to fullness the typically human dynamics of reason, affection, and freedom, and so increases the existential certainty essential to an adult in all of life's circumstances. In the other, opposite sense of "verification," faith "cannot cheat because it is tied to your experience in some way; essentially, it is summoned to appear in a court where you, through your experience, are the judge,"[8] to echo Giussani's bold expression taken up by Carrón in this book (on experience verifying faith, see chapter 6). If we skip this verification, we simply assume that faith is a rational and free adherence to the event of God in history, and the Church's action slips into the generous practice of its social, political, cultural, or charitable consequences, but does not effectively and profoundly form the Christian adult.[9]

If we wish to follow the indications of the magisterium and to consider the profound interconnection between faith, religion, and culture, the most serious methodological issue is that of the "personalization of faith," which is necessary in order to bring forth persons and communities capable of regenerating the Christian community. So we must more deeply understand the "circularity" between elementary human experience and faith.[10] On one hand, the encounter with Christ awakens our relationship with reality in its original breadth; on the other hand, the vitality of human experience—including its fundamental questions about love, pain, death, and beauty, and its search for the meaning of life—protects it from a formalistic and ultimately rigid expression of faith itself. These are the decisive factors needed to accompany and address, over time and with the necessary patience, the human fragility of so many Church members. From a standpoint of method, this implies the art of knowing how to recognize the expressions of the quest for meaning reflected in many questions, frustrations, searches, and efforts of our contemporaries in the postsecular culture, thanks to the light that comes from the truth freely manifested in Jesus.

Only a faith subject to verification can address the root of the West's crisis, which strikes at our relationship with reality not in generic terms but in the concreteness of human life's basic dimensions, as the "Chernobyl effect" demonstrates. Let us return to this question of method, because its importance is crucial for achieving the sought-after goal of a faith that is neither formalistic nor spiritualistic, but which perfects what is human. To achieve this goal, it is necessary for Christian education to have an effective impact on the understanding and maturing of each person's elementary experience, so that that experience, in turn, gives life to the believer's human position. Thus faith will, according to the famous gospel parable, show its value for every person "one hundredfold."

In this process, how we refer back to the elementary experience that is at the heart of the understanding of the religious sense is crucial. In fact, we can directly identify it in its formal characteristics, so to speak, abstracted from any concrete content, or we can describe a given situation or a particular action and recognize the elementary experience by its formal features and by the criteria for acting that result from it. In my opinion, the genius of education lies in not allowing these levels of understanding of the human experience to be separated. The irresistible force of an educational position emerges when one takes into account all the factors. It is not enough to accumulate examples, placing each of them in the category of "experience," as if this makes education more concrete. If you do not get to the "why," that is, a judgment in formal—universal—terms, the path is culturally less fruitful.

On the other hand, the criterion of judgment is not reached by deduction, but by starting from the description of concrete lived experience. So a good teacher is not one who simply repeats formulas, even excellent ones.

A "Culture of Encounter"

The primary task of the Church, from the dusty *barrios* of Angola to the corridors and classrooms of our European universities, from attending to those most affected by the crisis to participating in the daily lives of friends and families, is what I described briefly as personalization of faith. Only a lively adult, one whose experience is enhanced and transformed by the encounter with Christ, will be able to dialogue with others, whatever their cultural or religious position, within a pluralistic society.

Our world "asks Christians to be willing to seek forms or ways to communicate in a comprehensible language the perennial newness of Christianity."[11] These words of Pope Francis in his beautiful message to the Rimini Meeting of 2014 continue to show us the way. In a society so marked by change as to be defined by Bauman as a "liquid society," we need adults who can communicate the radical novelty of Christianity, without being paralyzed by changes in forms that might have been useful in the past. Francis's message can be a contemporary echo of the words of Saint Paul commented on by Josef Zvérina. "Do not conform! *Me syschematizesthe!* How well this expression reveals the perennial root of the verb: schema. In a nutshell, all schemas, all exterior models are empty. We have to want more, the apostle makes it our duty, 'change your way of thinking, reshape your minds'— *metamorfoûsthe tê anakainósei toû noós.* Paul's Greek is so expressive and concrete! He opposes *schêma* or *morphé*—permanent form, to *metamorphé*—change in the creature. One is not to change according to any model that in any case is always out of fashion, but it is a total newness with all its wealth (*anakainósei*)."[12] Only then can the "culture of encounter" to which the pope tenaciously invites us spread. Dialogue then becomes an exciting opportunity for critical reception of the truth present in every human experience and of passionately communicating one's own experience, transformed by the newness of the Christian fact. It is a fundamental issue that is before—or beyond—the wearisome debates between liberalism and conservatism.

"Disarming Beauty"

In the light of the analysis that Carrón offers in the first part of the book, you will better understand the range of proposals for a cultural and educational work appropriate to the crisis in which we are living in Europe. Carrón shows us the path he has taken in recent years, starting from his numerous talks in university, cultural, media, social, and business venues, almost as a type of program for the moment we are living in. Often his reflections are the result of an open dialogue with stakeholders from different backgrounds and cultural sensitivities, without any other weapon than the "disarming" beauty of the mystery of Christ. He offers us some examples of his passionate quest to glimpse the basic outlines of elementary experience within all the spheres of human life, illuminated by the Christian event.

His concern to propose to us criteria for judgment, and thus for action, within the different dimensions of life—education, family, social and charitable works, and even politics—puts in our hands a very valuable tool for understanding and loving our European society on the basis of a positive hypothesis that makes us protagonists of the era in which we live, and therefore open to the realities of all continents. We will be protagonists only if along the path of our actions we mature because we understand what we are living.

I hope this book will provoke in readers the same gratitude and the same desire to encounter the author that it inspired in me.

Madrid, July 15, 2015

PART I

THE CONTEXT AND THE CHALLENGES

———•◆•———

CHAPTER 1

Is a New Beginning Possible?

What Is at Stake?

Europe was born around a few great words, like "person," "work," "matter," "progress," and "freedom." These words achieved their full and authentic depth through Christianity, acquiring a value they did not previously have, and this determined a profound process of "humanization" of Europe and its culture. For example, just think about the concept of person. "Two thousand years ago, the only man who had all human rights was the *civis romanus*, the Roman citizen. But who decided who was a *civis romanus*? Those in power. One of the greatest Roman jurists, Gaius, defined three levels of tools which the *civis* [*romanus*], who had full rights, could possess: tools which do not move and do not speak; those which move and do not speak, which is to say, animals; and those which move and speak, the slaves."[1]

But today all of these words have become empty, or they are gradually losing their original significance. Why?

Through a long and complex process, from which we cannot exempt the mortification of words like "freedom" and "progress" by the very Christianity that had helped create them, at a certain point along the European trajectory, the idea took hold that those fundamental achievements ought to be separated from the experience that had allowed them to fully flourish.

In a memorable talk he gave years ago in Subiaco, Italy, then-Cardinal Ratzinger said, referring to Enlightenment thinkers, that as a result of a troubled historical trajectory, "in the situation of confessional antagonism and in the crisis that threatened the image of God, they tried to keep the essential moral values outside the controversies and to identify an evidential quality in these values that would make them independent of the many divisions and uncertainties of the various philosophies and religious confessions." At that time, this was thought to be possible, since "the great fundamental convictions created by Christianity were largely resistant to attack and seemed undeniable."[2] Thus developed the Enlightenment attempt to affirm those "great convictions," whose evidence seemed able to support itself apart from lived Christianity. What was the result of this attempt? Have these great convictions, which have laid the foundation for our coexistence for centuries, withstood the test of time? Did their evidence hold up before the vicissitudes of history, with its unforeseen elements and its provocations? The answer is in front of all of us. Cardinal Ratzinger continued: "The search for this kind of reassuring certainty, something that could go unchallenged despite all the disagreements, has not succeeded. Not even Kant's truly stupendous endeavors managed to create the necessary certainty that would be shared by all. The attempt, carried to extremes, to shape human affairs to the total exclusion of God leads us more and more to the brink of the abyss, toward the utter annihilation of man."[3]

To grasp the evidence of that setting aside, it suffices to consider the effect this process has had on two of the things that we modern Europeans hold most dear: freedom and reason.

"This Enlightenment culture," Cardinal Ratzinger wrote, "is substantially defined by the rights to liberty. Its starting point is that liberty is a fundamental value and the criterion of everything else: the freedom of choice in matters of religion, which includes the religious neutrality of the state; the liberty to express one's own opinion, on condition that it does not call precisely this canon into question; the democratic ordering of the state, that is, parliamentary control of the organs of state; . . . and finally, the protection of the rights of man and the prohibition of discrimination." Nevertheless, the ongoing evolution of these concepts already reveals the other side of the coin, the consequences of an insufficient definition of freedom that characterizes Enlightenment culture. On the one hand, any exercise of the principle of individual freedom or self-determination must take stock of the opposition between certain human rights, for example, the conflict between a woman's desire for freedom and the right of the unborn to live. And on the other, the concept of discrimination is constantly extended, without denying the inalienable benefits associated with it, with the result that "the prohibition of discrimination can be transformed more and more into a limitation on the freedom of opinion and on religious liberty. . . . The fact that the Church is convinced that she does not have the right to confer priestly ordination on women is already seen by some as irreconcilable with the spirit of the European Constitution." Therefore, Ratzinger continues, indicating the ultimate results of the trajectory: "A confused ideology of liberty leads to a dogmatism that is proving ever more hostile to real liberty." Thus we witness a singular and significant reversal. "The radical detachment of the Enlightenment philosophy from its roots ultimately leads it to dispense with man."

Secondly, we need to ask ourselves if the type of reason that Enlightenment philosophy hinges upon can legitimately be said to have reached a "complete self-awareness" so as to be able to give the final word on human reason as such. Ratzinger therefore invites us to remember that Enlightenment reason is itself conditioned by history, the result of a "self-limitation of reason that is typical of one determined cultural situation, that of the modern West." Enlightenment philosophy "expresses not the complete reason of man, but only one part of it. And this mutilation of reason means that we cannot consider it to be rational at all." It is not a matter of denying the importance of the achievements of this philosophy, but of objecting to its self-absolutization, its pitting itself with a sense of superiority against "humanity's other historical cultures." Thus, Ratzinger can conclude: "The real antagonism typical of today's world is not that between diverse religious cultures; rather, it is the antagonism between the radical emancipation of man from God, from the roots of life, on the one hand, and the great religious cultures, on the other."[4]

This does not mean assuming a prejudicially "anti-Enlightenment" position. "The Enlightenment has a Christian origin," writes Ratzinger, "and it is not by chance that it was born specifically and exclusively within the sphere of the Christian faith."[5] In a memorable speech from 2005, Benedict XVI recalls the "fundamental 'yes' to the modern era" announced by the Second Vatican Council—without, however, underestimating "the inner tensions as well as the contradictions." He thus emphasizes the overcoming of that situation of "clash," in which "it seemed that there was no longer any milieu open to a positive and fruitful understanding" between faith and the modern era, as was typical of the Church in the nineteenth century.[6]

A few years after his address at Subiaco, Benedict XVI returned to the "real opposition" that cuts across the present day and treated the subject in more depth. "The problem Europe has in finding its own identity consists, I believe, in the fact that in Europe today we see two souls." This is how he describes the two souls: "One is abstract anti-historical reason, which seeks to dominate all else because it considers itself above all cultures. It is like a reason which has finally discovered itself and intends to liberate itself from all traditions and cultural values in favor of an abstract rationality." A clear example was the Strasbourg Court's first verdict on crucifixes (in Italian classrooms), as "an example of such abstract reason which seeks emancipation from all traditions, even from history itself. Yet we cannot live like that and, moreover, even 'pure reason' is conditioned by a certain historical context, and only in that context can it exist." What is Europe's other soul? "We could call Europe's other soul the Christian one. It is a soul open to all that is reasonable, a soul which itself created the audacity of reason and the freedom of critical reasoning, but which remains anchored to the roots from which this Europe was born, the roots which created the continent's fundamental values and great institutions, in the vision of the Christian faith."[7]

At this point, in light of what he have discussed, we can better understand Europe's problem, the root of its crisis and what is truly at stake. What is at risk today is precisely man, his reason, his freedom, and the freedom of critical reasoning. "The greatest danger," said Fr. Giussani years ago, "is not the destruction of peoples, killing and murder, but the attempt by the reigning power to destroy the human. And the essence of the human is freedom, i.e., the relationship with the Infinite." Therefore, the battle that must be fought by the man who feels himself to be a man is "the battle between authentic religiosity and power."[8]

This is the nature of the crisis, which is not primarily economic. It has to do with the foundations. It is therefore clear that we need to recognize that, "in terms of the underlying anthropological issues, what is right and may be given the force of law is in no way simply self-evident today. The question of how to recognize what is truly right and thus to serve justice when framing laws has never been simple, and today in view of the vast extent of our knowledge and our capacity, it has become still harder."[9] Without the clear awareness that what is at stake is the evidence of those foundations, the absence of which would make stable coexistence impossible, we distract ourselves in the debate over the consequences, forgetting that their origin lies elsewhere, as we have seen. Regaining the foundations is of the utmost urgency for us.

Responding to this urgency does not mean returning to a religious state or to a Europe that is based on Christian laws—a sort of new edition of the Holy Roman Empire—as if this were the only possibility to defend the person, his freedom, and his reason. That would be against the very nature of Christianity. "As a religion of the persecuted, and as a universal religion, . . . [Christianity] denied the government the right to consider religion as part of the order of the state, thus stating the principle of the liberty of faith." Therefore, it is important to add that "where Christianity, contrary to its own nature, had unfortunately become mere tradition and the religion of the state . . . it was and remains the merit of the Enlightenment to have drawn attention afresh to these original Christian values and to have given reason back its own voice."[10] Therefore, what is necessary is not to return to a time gone by, but rather to undertake a path in which true dialogue about foundations is possible.

Given these new conditions, where can we begin again?

Man's Heart Does Not Surrender

Despite all of the prodigious attempts to set man aside, to reduce the needs of his reason (by reducing the scope of his question) and the urgency of his freedom (which cannot help but express itself in his every move as a desire for fulfillment), man's heart continues to beat, irreducible. We can discover this in the most varied efforts—sometimes confused, but no less dramatic and somehow sincere—that contemporary Europeans make to attain that fullness that they cannot help but desire, fullness that sometimes hides beneath contradictory disguises.

An example can help us understand the nature of the problem, the reductions with which we normally live reason and freedom. "Tonight," a friend writes me,

> I went to dinner with two high school classmates of mine who are engaged and living together. After dinner we sat and talked for a while, and the topic of whether or not to have children came up. My friend said, 'I will never bring a child into this world. Where would I get the courage to condemn another wretch to unhappiness? I will not take on that responsibility.' Then he added, 'I'm afraid of my freedom. At best it's useless, and at worst I can only cause someone harm. What I expect from life is to try to do the least damage possible.' We talked for a long time, and they told me about a great many fears they have, and about how at this point they feel that they can't hope for anything more from life. And they are just 26 years old."

Behind the refusal to have children lies nothing but the fear of freedom, or perhaps the fear of losing freedom understood in a reduced way, that is, the fear of giving up oneself and one's own space. But how much will that set of fears that paralyzes the young man described in the letter determine his life? To talk about "great convictions" is to talk about the foundations, that is, the foothold that makes the experience of freedom possible, makes freedom from fear possible, and allows reason to look at reality in a way that does not suffocate us.

This episode demonstrates that "the bewilderment about the 'fundamentals of life'" does not eliminate questions. Rather, it makes them more acute, as Cardinal Angelo Scola says: "What is sexual difference; what is love; what does it mean to procreate and to educate; why should we work; why may a pluralistic civil society be richer than a monolithic society; how can we meet one another to reciprocally build a working communion among all Christian communities and the good life in civil society; how can we renew finance and the economy; how can we face the fragilities of illness and death, and moral fragility; how can we seek justice; how can we constantly learn and share the needs of the poor? All of this must be re-written in our times, reconsidered and, therefore, re-lived."[11] Rewritten, reconsidered, and therefore relived.

This is the nature of the provocation addressed to us by the crisis in which we are immersed. "A crisis," Hannah Arendt wrote, "forces us back to the questions themselves and requires from us either new or old answers, but in any case direct judgments. A crisis becomes a disaster only when we respond to it with preformed judgments, that is, prejudices. Such an attitude not only sharpens the crisis but makes us forfeit the experience of reality and the opportunity for reflection it provides."[12]

Therefore, rather than being a pretext for complaints and closure, all of these problematic points in European coexistence represent a grand occasion to discover or rediscover the great convictions that can ensure this coexistence. That these great convictions may fade should not surprise us. Benedict XVI reminds us of the reason. "Incremental progress" is possible only in the material sphere. In the field of "ethical awareness and moral decision-making, there is no similar possibility of accumulation for the simple reason that man's freedom is always new and he must always make his decisions anew. These decisions can never simply be made for us in advance by others—if that were the case, we would no longer be free. Freedom presupposes that, in fundamental decisions, every person and every generation is a new beginning." The ultimate reason for which a new beginning is always necessary is that the very nature of the evidence of those convictions is different from that of "material inventions. The moral treasury of humanity is not readily at hand like tools that we use; it is present as an appeal to freedom and a possibility for it."[13]

But what are these "fundamental decisions" about?

The Focus Is Always Man and His Fulfillment

Behind every human effort there is a cry for fulfillment. Listening to this cry is in no way taken for granted; it is the first choice of freedom. Rilke reminds us of the temptation to hush it up, which is always lurking within us: "And all things conspire to keep silent about us, half out of shame perhaps, half as unutterable hope."[14]

Those who do not give in to this temptation find themselves seeking forms of fulfillment, but are always exposed to the risk of taking shortcuts that seem to let them reach this goal more quickly and in a more satisfying way. This is what we see today, for example, in the attempt to obtain fulfillment through so-called new rights. The discussion that has grown up around them shows what the debate about foundations means and what its possible outcomes are.

Since the mid-1970s, the "new rights" have become increasingly numerous, with a strong acceleration in the last fifteen or twenty years. Their origin is that same yearning for liberation that was the soul of the 1960s protest movement—it was not by chance that abortion was legalized for the first time in 1973 in the United States, and laws regarding divorce and abortion began to appear in Europe around the same time, as well. Today we hear about the right to marriage and adoption for same-sex couples, the right to have a child, the right to one's own gender identity, the rights of transsexuals, the right of an unhealthy child not to be born, the right to die, . . . The list goes on and on.

Many people feel these new rights to be an affront, a true attack on the values on which Western—and particularly European—civilization has been founded for centuries. To say it better: these new rights exert a great attraction on many people—and, for this reason, they spread very easily—while others fear them as factors of the destruction of society. The deepest social rifts and most intense political controversies are today created around these themes of "public ethics," not only in Italy but in all of Europe and around the world.

Why this strange mix of appeal and aversion? Let us try to ask ourselves where the so-called new rights originate.

Each of these ultimately springs from deeply human needs. The need for affection, the desire to be a mother or a father, fear of pain and death, the quest for one's own identity, and so on. Each of these new rights has its roots in the constitutive fabric of every human existence: hence their attraction. The multiplication of individual rights expresses the expectation that the juridical system can resolve these human dramas and ensure satisfaction of the infinite needs that dwell in the human heart.

Their common trait is that they are centered on an individual subject who lays claim to absolute self-determination in every circumstance of life: he wants to decide if he lives or dies, if he suffers or not, if he has a child or not, if he is a man or a woman, and so on. This is a person who conceives of himself as absolute freedom, without limits, and does not tolerate any sort of conditioning. Absolute self-determination and nondiscrimination, along with this cultural background, are, therefore, the key words of the new rights culture.

> The contemporary self—like an eternal adolescent— . . . does not want to hear about limits. To be free means, then, to put oneself in the condition of always being able to access new possibilities . . . claiming to be able to reduce desire to enjoyments . . . to be pursued and seized, primarily in the form of socially organized consumption: of goods, of course, but also of ideas, experiences, and relationships. And yet, immediately after attaining them we perceive their insufficiency. Nevertheless, we start over again every time, focusing on another object, another relationship, another experience . . . , continuing to invest our psychological

energies in things that, when put to the test, cannot but reveal themselves to be disappointing.[15]

This culture carries within itself the conviction that the attainment of more and more new rights constitutes the path to the fulfillment of the person. In this way, it believes that it can avoid or render superfluous any debate about the foundations, which can be summed up in Giacomo Leopardi's question, "And what am I?"[16] But not asking what the individual is, what the "I" is, is like trying to cure a disease without making a diagnosis! So, since debating about foundations is considered too abstract with respect to life's needs, we entrust ourselves to techniques and procedures. This approach gave rise to the race to obtain recognition of new rights from lawmakers and judges.

But the critical point of contemporary culture lies in the myopia with which it looks at the profound needs of man: not grasping the infinite scope of man's constitutive needs, it proposes—on both the material plane and the emotional and existential one—the infinite multiplication of partial answers. Partial answers are offered in response to reduced questions. But, as Cesare Pavese reminds us, "What a man seeks in his pleasures is that they should be infinite, and no one would ever give up hope of attaining that infinity."[17] And a multiplication, even to the nth degree, of "false infinities" (to use Benedict XVI's term)[18] will never be able to satisfy a need that is infinite in nature. It is not the quantitative accumulation of goods and experiences that can satisfy man's "restless heart."

The drama of our culture, therefore, lies not so much in the fact that man is allowed everything, but in the false promises and illusions that such permissiveness carries with it. Each person can verify in their own experience whether the attainment of ever-more-new rights is the path to their fulfillment or whether it actually produces the opposite result, because the failure to understand the infinite nature of desire, the failure to recognize the fabric of the self, leads to a de facto reduction of the person to a gender, to a set of biological or physiological factors, and so on. Here we can clearly see the contradiction inherent to a certain conception of man that is so widespread in our advanced societies: we exalt, in an absolute manner, a self without limits in its new rights and, at the same time, implicitly affirm that the subject of these rights is basically a "nothing," because he or she dissolves in antecedent factors, whether material, natural, or accidental.

What does all of this tell us about the situation of man today? What we have said also judges those efforts that oppose this tendency, but without bringing into question the common framing of the problem. Indeed, some of those who have put forth these efforts expect contrary legislation to solve the problem, and thus they, too, avoid the discussion about foundations. Of course, a just law is always better than a wrong one, but recent history demonstrates that no just law has succeeded in preventing the drift we see happening before our eyes.

Both sides share the same framework. For both, T. S. Eliot's words ring true: "They constantly try to escape / From the darkness outside and within / By dreaming of systems so perfect that no one will need to be good."[19] This applies to one group as much as the other.

But the attempt to resolve human questions with procedures will never be sufficient. Again it is Benedict XVI who says it best: "Since man always remains free and since his freedom is always fragile, the kingdom of good will never be definitively established in this world. Anyone who promises the better world that is guaranteed to last forever is making a false promise; he is overlooking human freedom." Rather, "If there were structures which could irrevocably guarantee a determined—good—state of the world, man's freedom would be denied, and hence they would not be good structures at all. . . . In other words: good structures help, but of themselves they are not enough. Man can never be redeemed simply from outside."[20]

Is there another way?

Examining the Nature of the Subject

Only by focusing on man and the yearning for fulfillment that constitutes him, his profound need, will we be able to rewrite, rethink, and relive values. In fact, "man's religious sense appears as the root from which values spring. A value is ultimately that perspective of the relationship between something contingent and totality, the absolute. Man's responsibility, through all the kinds of provocations that reach him in the impact with reality, commits itself in answering those questions that are posed by man's religious sense (or man's 'heart' as the Bible calls it)."[21] It is the religious sense, it is the complex of those ultimate needs that defines the depths of every human being—needs for truth, for beauty, for goodness, for justice, for happiness—that measures what a "value" is. Only the awareness of the factor common to all men can open the path to the search for shared certainties.

Fr. Giussani said years ago that the solution to the problems life poses to us every day "does not come from addressing the problems directly, but from exploring more deeply the nature of the individual who faces them." In other words, "You resolve the details by better understanding the essential."[22]

This is the great challenge that Europe is facing. The great educational emergency demonstrates the reduction of man, his dismissal, the lack of awareness of what man truly is, of what the nature of his desire is, and of the structural disproportion between what he expects and what he can achieve with his efforts. We have already recalled the reduction of reason and of freedom; to these we now add the reduction of desire. "The reduction of desires or the censure of some needs, the reduction of desires and needs is the weapon of power," Fr. Giussani said. What surrounds us, "the dominant mentality, . . . power, achieves [in us] an extraneousness from ourselves."[23] It is as though our being were stripped away from us. We are thus at the mercy of many reduced images of desire, and we delude ourselves into expecting that the solution to the human problem will come from rules.

Faced with such a situation, we ask ourselves: Is it possible to reawaken the subject so that he can truly be himself, become entirely aware of himself, further understand his nature, and thus free himself from the dictatorship of his "little" desires and all the false answers? Without this reawakening, man will not be able to avoid domination by all sorts of tyrannies that are unable to give him the longed-for fulfillment.

But how can desire be reawakened? Not through a line of reasoning or some psychological technique, but only by encountering someone in whom the dynamic of desire has already been activated. To this effect, let us return to the dialogue between the young letter writer and the friends of his who were afraid of their freedom. The young man, after having listened to the tale of all of his friends' fears, replied: "'You're right to be afraid. You're smart, and you realize that freedom is something great and difficult, and that life is a serious thing. But don't you want to be able to enjoy your freedom? And don't you want to be able to desire happiness?' I told them that I am not able to rid myself of this desire! They remained silent for a few seconds, and then told me: 'That's what we envy the most about you, that you're not afraid.' And, when we were saying our good-byes at the end of the evening, he said, 'Let's get together more often, because when I'm with you, I'm less afraid, too.'"

No one more than Fr. Giussani was able to see the value of this experience, an experience as simple as it was radical and culturally powerful, as an answer to the question about how to reawaken the "I." Giussani wrote: "What I am about to give is not an answer [that applies only] for our present situation . . . ; what I am saying is a rule, a universal law, as old as man's existence: a person finds himself or herself again in a living encounter [like the one we just heard described: "That's what we envy the most about you, that you're not afraid. . . . Let's get together"], that is, in a presence that he comes across and that releases an attractiveness, . . . provokes us to acknowledge the fact that our hearts, with what they are made of . . . are there, that they exist."[24] The heart is oftentimes asleep, buried beneath a thousand pieces of debris, a thousand distractions, but then it is reawakened and provoked to make a recognition: it exists; the heart exists; your heart exists. You have a friend; you find, on the street, a friend for life when this happens to you with him, when you find yourself in front of one who reawakens you to yourself. This is a friend—all of the rest leaves no trace.

"Our greatest need in the present historical moment," said Benedict XVI, "is people who make God credible in this world by means of the enlightened faith they live. . . . We need men who keep their eyes fixed on God, learning from him what true humanity means. We need men whose intellect is enlightened by the light of God, men whose hearts are opened by God, so that their intellect can speak to the intellect of others and their hearts can open the hearts of others."[25]

In this way one can understand the good that the other person constitutes for him. Without an encounter with the other person—with that particular other—an "I" that opens itself to the fundamental questions of life, that does not content itself with partial responses, could never emerge or stay alive. The relationship with the other is an anthropologically constitutive dimension.

The Other Is a Good

It is on this foundation—that is, the awareness that the other is a good, as the dialogue between these friends demonstrates—that Europe can be built. Without recovering the elementary experience that the other is not a threat, but rather a good for the realization of our "I," it will be difficult to emerge from the crisis of human, social, and political relationships in which we find ourselves. From here derives the need that Europe be a space in which different subjects, each with his or her own identity, can encounter one another in order to help each other to walk toward the destiny of happiness for which we all yearn.

Defending this space of freedom for each and every person is the definitive reason to work for a Europe where nothing is imposed by anyone, and neither is anyone excluded on the basis of preconceptions or affinities different from one's own: a Europe in which each person can freely contribute to its construction, offering his own witness, which is recognized as a good for everyone, without any European being forced to renounce his own identity to belong to the common home.

Only in an encounter with the other will we be able to develop together what Habermas called a "process of argumentation sensitive to the truth."[26] In this sense, we can become even more aware of the significance of Pope Francis's statement that "truth is a relationship. As such, each one of us receives the truth and expresses it from within, that is to say, according to one's own circumstances, culture, and situation in life, etc."[27] "Our commitment does not consist exclusively in activities or programs of promotion and assistance; what the Holy Spirit mobilizes is not an unruly activism, but above all an *attentiveness* which considers the other 'in a certain sense as one with ourselves.'"[28] Only in this renewed encounter will the few great words that generated Europe be able to come to life once more. Because, as Benedict XVI reminds us, "Even the best structures function only when the community is animated by convictions capable of motivating people to assent freely to the social order. Freedom requires conviction; conviction does not exist on its own [nor can it be generated by law], but must always be gained anew by the community."[29] This recovery of the fundamental convictions does not happen unless in a relationship. The method through which the "fundamental convictions" (the significance of the person, the absolute value of the individual, the freedom and dignity of every human being, etc.) fully emerged is the same method through which they can be recovered. There is no other way.

We Christians are not afraid to enter into this wide-ranging dialogue, without privileges. For us this is a precious occasion to verify the capacity of the Christian event to hold up in the face of new challenges, since it offers us the opportunity to witness to everyone concerning what happens in existence when man intercepts the Christian event along the road of life. Our experience, in the encounter with Christianity, has shown us that the lifeblood of the values of the person is not Christian laws or juridical structures and confessional politics, but the event of Christ. For this reason, we do not place our hope, for ourselves or for others, in anything but the recurrence of the event of Christ in a human encounter. This does not at all mean that we consider this event to be opposed to the legal sphere, but merely that we recognize a genetic order among them. Indeed, it is the recurrence of the Christian event that reopens the human being to self-discovery and allows the intelligence of faith to become the intelligence of reality, so that Christians can offer an original and meaningful contribution by bringing to life those convictions that can be introduced into the human community.

This is the clarification at the heart of *Evangelii Gaudium*: the observation that, in the Catholic world, the battle for the defense of values has become, over time, so important that it has ended up being more important than the communication of the newness of Christ and the witness of his humanity. This exchange of antecedent and consequent demonstrates the "Pelagian" error of much of today's Christianity: the promotion of a "Christianist" Christianity (according to the definition of Rémi Brague),[30] deprived of grace. The alternative is not found, as some people complain, in a "spiritualistic" escape from the world. Rather, the true alternative is the Christian community—when not emptied of its historical substance—which offers its original contribution "by awakening in men, through faith, the forces of genuine liberation."[31]

Those who are engaged in public life, in the cultural or political field, have the duty, as Christians, to oppose today's anthropological drift. But this undertaking cannot involve the entire Church as such, since it has the obligation, today, to encounter all people, independently of their ideology or political affinity, in order to witness the "attraction of Jesus." The engagement of Christians in politics and in the realm of decision making about the common good remains necessary. Indeed, the Church, through its model of social doctrine, indicates the formulas for shared coexistence that Christian experience has tested and verified over time. Today this is more important than ever, though we must never forget that, in the present circumstances, such an undertaking assumes, in the Pauline sense, more of a *kate-chontic* value: one that is critical and resistant, within the limits of possibility, toward the negative effects of mere procedures and of the mentality that creates them. This undertaking cannot presume, however, that, from its action, no matter how praiseworthy, the ideal and spiritual renewal of the city of man can mechanically arise. Such renewal arises from "what comes before," what *primerea* ("comes first" in the Spanish term often used by Pope Francis): a new humanity generated by love for Christ, by Christ's love.

It is this awareness that allows us to see the limits of the positions of those who believe that they can resolve everything through procedures or laws, and thus think that defending a space of freedom is not enough. Many would like politics to ensure the granting or restriction of rights. In this way, they would be spared "being good," as Eliot said. What can we learn from the fact that "not even Kant's truly stupendous endeavors managed to create the necessary certainty that would be shared by all"? What does our recent history teach us, given that good laws were not enough to keep the great convictions alive? The road to "shared certainty" is a long one.[32]

The long journey that the Catholic Church has traveled in order to clarify the concept of "religious freedom" can help us to understand that defending the space of this freedom is not such a small thing, after all. After much labor, the Church came to declare in the Second Vatican Council that "the human person has a right to religious freedom," even while it continues to profess Christianity as the only "true religion." The recognition of religious freedom is not a sort of compromise, like saying, "Since we were unable to convince mankind that Christianity is the true religion, let's at least defend religious freedom." No, what pushed the Church to modify an approach that had been in place for many centuries was a deeper understanding of the nature of truth and of the path to reach it: "The truth cannot impose itself except by virtue of its own truth."[33] This was the firm belief of the Church in the first centuries, the great Christian revolution founded on the distinction between the two cities, between God and Caesar. This belief was destined to weaken after the Edict of Thessalonica (AD 380), thanks to the emperor Theodosius. In a return to the patristic spirit, Vatican II could affirm that "all men are to be immune from coercion . . . in such wise that no one is to be forced to act in a manner contrary to his own beliefs, whether privately or publicly, whether alone or in association with others, within due limits." If this is true for the most important of values, then it is even more so for all the others! And finally, "This right of the human person to religious freedom is to be recognized in the constitutional law whereby society is governed and thus it is to become a civil right."[34]

Only if Europe becomes a space of freedom, where each person can be immune from coercion, make his or her own human journey, and share it with those he or she meets along the way, will an interest in dialogue be reawakened, an interest in an encounter in which each person offers the contribution of his or her experience in order to reach that "shared certainty" that is necessary for communal life.

Our desire is that Europe become a space of freedom for the encounter among truth seekers. This is worth working for.

———•◦•———

CHAPTER 2

Truth and Freedom: A Paradigm

The radical nature of the challenge to which we are subject, and the rate at which the change in attitudes is now occurring in European countries and in the West generally, are impressive.

What I am about to say has no claim to be complete or exhaustive. I will simply offer some food for thought in order to come to grips with the time we are in, following the perception, the true awareness, shared with us by Benedict XVI and Pope Francis.

History and the Self-Evident

First we must reckon with the "collapse of the self-evident," to sum up the situation I described in the previous chapter. Cardinal Ratzinger spoke of the "collapse of ancient religious certainties" and the subsequent "collapse of humane values."[1] What is it? How can the self-evident collapse? It almost seems to be a contradiction in terms. And what do we mean when we say something is self-evident?

The starting point of the phenomenon we'd like to become aware of is to be found in the Enlightenment attempt to remove the core values that have sustained and animated Europe until a few decades ago from the religious sphere, and in particular the Christian sphere, from which they emerged historically. In the age of "confessional antagonism," Ratzinger observed, there was a quest for "an evidential quality in these values that would make them independent of the many divisions and uncertainties of the various philosophies and religious confessions." It was an understandable effort. After the split brought about by the Reformation and the resulting conflicts, with the so-called wars of religion between Christians, Christians wanted to "guarantee the basis of life in society and, in more general terms, the bases of humanity," beyond any reference to Christianity, on "neutral territory" that was seemingly more secure, safe from the strife. At that time this seemed possible, since "the great fundamental convictions created by Christianity were largely resistant to attack and seemed undeniable."[2] The idea was that they would remain valid even if God did not exist.

What was the outcome of such an attempt? Ratzinger points out bluntly, "The search for such a reassuring certainty, which could remain uncontested beyond all differences, failed." Those beliefs have not stood the test of their "autonomy," even though no one would have imagined how quickly they would be eclipsed. "Not even Kant's truly stupendous endeavors managed to create the necessary certainty that would be shared by all." If Kant, in denying the intellect's ability to know God in the context of pure reason, kept God's role as a postulate of practical reason, implied in moral behavior, after him an effort developed "to shape human affairs doing completely without God." Contrary to what was thought, this separation seems to lead us ever more to the "edge of the abyss, towards the total elimination of man."[3]

Romano Guardini clearly understood the root of the phenomenon, noting the historic and genetic nexus between the affirmation of fundamental human values and a lived Christianity.

At many points in our study we have noted how this non-Christian culture commenced its growth at the very outset of the modern age. At first, the attack upon Christianity was directed against the content of Revelation. It was not made against those ethical values, individual or social, which had been perfected under the inspiration of the faith. At the same time modern culture claimed those very values as its own foundation. Due largely to its changes in historic study, the modern world dedicated itself to the theory that it had discovered and developed ethical values. It is true, indeed, that the modern age did further the intrinsic worth of personality, of individual freedom, of responsibility and dignity, of man's inherent potentiality for mutual respect and help. These human values begin their development, however, during earliest Christian times, while the Middle Ages continued their nurture by its cultivation of the interior and religious life. But the modern era suffered the invasion of consciousness by personal autonomy; human perfection became a cultural acquisition independent of ethics or of Christianity. This point of view was expressed in many ways by many groups, preeminently in the voicing of the "Rights of Man" during the French Revolution.[4]

Kant compares the historical trajectory that led to the Enlightenment to the growth stages of an individual from childhood to adulthood. Humanity is first like a child, who needs a father and mother, for he has no autonomy of thought and does not make choices on his own. But in becoming an adult he can do without this bond and live independently. It is the end of his status as a minor. All of history until the time of the Enlightenment therefore corresponds to humanity's great childhood and adolescence. All this implies that once humanity has reached clarity, the autonomous use of reason, we can do without what made that autonomy possible.

In other words, the attempt was to affirm values independently from what made them germinate, develop, and grow. In this perspective, if the Church was useful for humanity to reach a certain level of self-awareness, then once this had been achieved, it could—or must— leave her behind.

But the attempt failed, as we have seen. Guardini invites us to come to terms with the fact that those fundamental values that are "related uniquely to Revelation" have entered history with Christ, by the power of his testimony and his ability to awaken reason and human freedom. Through Christianity "'natural' human powers would be freed for full development, a development impossible outside a Christian Order."[5] Here is the key: values that are "evident in themselves" (as the value of life, or the value of the person) "take on visible manifestation" only by virtue of Christ and "under the *aegis*"[6] of the Christian faith and remain evident within it. The concept of person, for example, considered in its fullness, came into the world with Jesus, through the testimony of a way of relating to people that was previously unknown, so that those who came across it exclaimed, "We have never seen anything like this!"[7] "The fundamental factor of Jesus Christ's outlook is the existence in man of a reality superior to any other reality subject to time and space. The whole world is not worth the most insignificant human person. Nothing in the entire universe can compare with a person, from the first instant of her conception until the last step of her decrepit old age. Every person possesses within himself a principle by which he depends on no one, the foundation of inalienable rights, a fount of values.[8]

It all started from there, through a witness, in a given cultural and social environment. Therefore, Guardini adds, "Those who maintain that these values and cultural attitudes are simply one with the autonomous development of human nature misunderstand the essential role of a Christian economy of Revelation, Faith and Grace. In fact the misunderstanding leads—permit me to speak plainly—to a kind of dishonesty which, as anyone who takes a clear-eyed view can see, is integral to the contemporary world itself."[9] It is this "dishonesty" which may explain why continuing to affirm those values while severing the link with what historically allowed their appearance was considered possible.

This issue has to do with our relationship to our context. If we do not sufficiently grasp the foundational link between a lived Christianity and values, we think we can insist on defending certain values as though they were evident to everyone. It is no longer so—and it was not so before Christianity. Developing this train of thought,

Guardini concludes, "The knowledge of what it means to be a person is inextricably bound up with the Faith of Christianity. An affirmation and a cultivation of the personal can endure for a time perhaps after Faith has been extinguished, but gradually they too will be lost."[10] Therefore, if we insist on saying that certain values are evident by the fact that we affirm them, we end up considering other people bad because they do not accept them.

In this sense I am thinking of a group of African women with AIDS whom I met in Kampala. Is there anything more evident than the value of health and life (not to mention the survival instinct itself)? Yet these women were not interested in taking the latest generation of drugs that could have given them a wider prospect of survival. Those values seemed absent, vanished. It was the encounter with a nurse that allowed them to "see" again. She communicated to them a passion for life. Her testimony reawakened a desire to live that was dormant, reopening their reason to the consideration of motives and the recognition of values. Only when, by virtue of that encounter, they rediscovered the value of their person did they have compelling motives for taking medication. Values that in themselves are evident became truly visible, comprehensible, clear, only within the atmosphere produced by the encounter with that nurse.

Think of the story of Eluana Englaro. Just saying "Life has an absolute value" was not sufficient, because it is a value that can become obscure. At the time we said—citing an interview of Enzo Jannacci—that we need "a caress of the Nazarene"[11] to discover that life has value always and everywhere. This need is evident in the daily witness offered by many doctors and nurses who enter the rooms of the terminally ill, where almost no one has the courage to enter, bringing with them the look that they have received and continue to receive in the Christian encounter. Without the caress of the Nazarene, certain values, which are evident in themselves, are obscured, clouded, and in this way collapse.

The collapse of the self-evident sums up the current crisis, the human condition in the West today. Faced with the cultural challenges that arise, you cannot take for granted what is no longer taken for granted. In this regard, I have often quoted this passage of Benedict XVI, from his speech to the German Parliament: "In terms of the underlying anthropological issues, what is right and may be given the force of law is in no way simply self-evident today. The question of how to recognize what is truly right and thus to serve justice when framing laws has never been simple, and today in view of the vast extent of our knowledge and our capacity, it has become still harder."[12] How surprising it is that the one to utter this statement is not an avid relativist, but a pope. Within the current cultural and political context, in order for Christians to make a contribution, it is decisively important that they grasp what has happened over the last decades, as a result of a long trajectory, and what are the real stakes. We are faced with a collapse of the certainties that for centuries were the basis of our coexistence, and the question that arises is what is the path towards a positive rediscovery of what belongs to the truth of human experience. We must respond to this question if we are to renew the foundation of shared life in our plural society.

These acknowledgments of the situation we find ourselves in allow us to better understand what Pope Francis means by calling for a focus on the essential, stressing that we cannot insist only on issues related to personal and social morality.

> The dogmatic and moral teachings of the church are not all equivalent. The church's pastoral ministry cannot be obsessed with the transmission of a disjointed multitude of doctrines to be imposed insistently. Proclamation in a missionary style focuses on the essentials, on the necessary things: this is also what fascinates and attracts more, what makes the heart burn, as it did for the disciples at Emmaus. We have to find a new balance; otherwise even the moral edifice of the church is likely to fall like a house of cards, losing the freshness and fragrance of the Gospel. The proposal of the Gospel must be more simple, profound, radiant. It is from this proposition that the moral consequences then flow.[13]

Don Giussani focused our attention on the urgency to rediscover and communicate Christianity in its original elements, as an event full of attractiveness, which seizes human beings with its beauty by its correspondence to the heart's needs.

Along with the first and crucial point related to the collapse of the self-evident, we should now consider a second, closely connected factor: the dominant role played by freedom in today's culture. "This Enlightenment culture is substantially defined by the rights to liberty. Its starting point is that liberty is a fundamental value and the criterion of everything else."[14] "In the consciousness of mankind today, freedom is largely regarded as the greatest good there is, after which all other good things have to take their place."[15] These two statements of Ratzinger are meant, on the one hand, to recognize freedom as the distinguishing feature of today's culture and, on the other, to denounce a certain absolutism—which we will not deal with here—and the problems it brings with it.

Freedom is a gift. It is a basic feature of the human being. It is almost *the* fundamental feature: "freedom to," "freedom from," and "freedom for." Our relationship with reality on each and every level is characterized by freedom, and structurally implies that freedom is at stake. Each of us can choose to realize ourselves or to lose ourselves. We can say yes or no to what fulfills us. This is the risk that the Mystery wished to take by creating man free, and that is what so often causes us vertigo, fear, and even scandal. Just think of parents when they see a child misusing freedom, or adults witnessing the mistakes of children in whose education they are involved. We often suffer the scandal of freedom. Therefore, as in the well-known parable, we would like to remove the "weeds" from the field, because they are dangerous for freedom. The owner of the field has, instead, a very different way of thinking. He allows everything to grow, because he knows that positivity will triumph. This is Jesus' certainty: the power of the seed will be greater. This also applies to us today. How much certainty is necessary in order to not tear away that which could put the harvest at risk!

The combination of these two factors, the collapse of what is self-evident and freedom, might suggest that because the exercise of freedom is risky, the surest way to defend values would be to impose them, so freedom would not go astray. But the ability to decide is in the nature of man; it cannot be erased. In order to do so it would be necessary to change the very structure of the self. This is, in a nutshell, what we are all immersed in, each of us with everyone else, parents with children, teachers with students, we with ourselves, at home, in relationships: the drama of freedom.

In this context it may be useful to consider the experience of the Church, because from the beginning she was faced with the question of values and freedom. The early Christians were forced to live the newness of the gospel in a pluralistic world, in which the values they carried were not recognized and accepted. Some quick examples may help. These episodes show immediately how a new development broke into history with Christianity and how it was communicated.

The first example is slavery. Saint Paul ends up in jail and is in a cell with a slave, Onesimus, who was arrested because he tried to run away from his master. Slavery at the time was a normal practice. What then did Paul do? He wrote a note to the slave's master—the Letter to Philemon is exactly this—to persuade him to forgive Onesimus and welcome him back:

> I appeal to you for my child, Onesimus, whose father I have become in my imprisonment. (Formerly he was useless to you, but now he is indeed useful to you and to me.) I am sending him back to you, sending my very heart. I would have been glad to keep him with me, in order that he might serve me on your behalf during my imprisonment for the gospel; but I preferred to do nothing without your consent in order that your goodness might not be by compulsion but of your own free will. Perhaps this is why he was parted from you for a while, that you might have him back for ever, no longer as a slave but more than a slave, as a beloved brother, especially to me but how much more to you, both in the flesh and in the Lord. So if you consider me your partner, receive him as you would receive me.[16]

Saint Paul's gesture seems like nothing in the infinite ocean of slavery, nothing compared to all the weeds around. Who would have bet on this simple fact? Instead it was a beginning that, over time, according to an unforeseeable plan, led to the elimination of slavery.

A second example is abortion. The Letter to Diognetus, one of the most beautiful writings of early Christianity, dedicates a line, or better, half a line, to the issue. What does it say? "Like others, [Christians] marry and have children, but they do not expose them."[17] That's it. Nothing more. The beginning of the affirmation of certain values, like that of life from birth, followed the same process.

These are two examples among the many that we could bring forward the show how the cultural atmosphere of the beginning of the Christian era was very similar to the present.

But the early Christians also had to bear witness to the newness they experienced within a context of intolerance and persecution. Although they prayed for the emperors, they refused to worship them. And they defended the freedom to profess their faith, and their freedom of conscience, vis-à-vis the empire and power, even at the cost of their lives and martyrdom, until the great Edict of Milan in 313, which granted freedom of worship to all, even to those who, like the Christians, had been denied it until then.[18]

In less than a century, however, the situation changes and the right to freedom of worship is called into question. The temptation of hegemony—to put it in terms closer to us—was lurking in the shadows. In 380, in fact, with the Edict of Thessalonica, the emperor Theodosius says that Christianity is the only legitimate religion. Although the application of the act at that time concerned only the situation of Constantinople, it was an act whose consequences contrasted with the stated belief of Christianity of the first centuries that religion, and Christianity in particular, could not be spread by force.

The travail of this step is reflected in the position of Augustine, who, as we know, had a great influence on later Christianity. Until 405 he shows himself opposed to the use of secular power to force the schismatics into ecclesiastical communion. "For originally my opinion was, that no one should be coerced into the unity of Christ, that we must act only by words, fight only by arguments, and prevail by force of reason, lest we should have those whom we knew as avowed heretics feigning themselves to be Catholics."[19] Yet after repeated and brutal violence perpetrated by the Donatists,[20] he changed his mind and said that to avoid evil, it is permissible to use force.[21] It is true that later Saint Augustine, in *The City of God*, which is a more mature work, he revises his position. But historically in his work these two models remain present and detectable. In his letters Augustine admits the necessity of compulsion to recognize truth; in *The City of God*, freedom prevails over power. And yet "later Christian thought, from the Carolingian period on, re-read the *De Civitate Dei* in the light of his letters";[22] that is, it read the work as legitimizing efforts to compel acceptance of truth, and that—given Augustine's authority—was not without consequences.

For many centuries, with ups and downs, there would be no explicit rethinking of the issue of religious freedom. Even with Luther's Reformation, during the dispute between Catholics and Protestants, both sides held to the idea that a Christian society cannot tolerate heretics and schismatics. Indeed, the developments of the Protestant Reformation (considered in its various expressions: Lutheran, Calvinist, Waldensian, and also Anglican), rather than enlarge the area of religious freedom, restricted it, as it further consolidated the link between political power and religious power, leading to the so-called wars of religion. The Peace of Westphalia of 1648, which was to be a response to the confrontational situation that had arisen, finally established the principle *cuius regio, eius et religio*, which obliged subjects to comply with the religion of their prince. The state thus imposed its preferred faith, and the boundaries of nation states also coincided with those of the citizens' religious beliefs.[23]

Through a path which we cannot fully trace here, at the intersection between events and historical changes, especially through the developments of modernity, the Church's self-awareness grew until the breakthrough achieved by the Second Vatican Council, which solemnly stated that each and every person has the right to religious freedom. The council did not adopt this position because the Church, having lost ground, decided to renounce its prior stance. This happened instead thanks to a development of the Church's self-awareness.

This Vatican Council declares that the human person has a right to religious freedom. This freedom means that all men are to be immune from coercion on the part of individuals or of social groups and of any human power, in such wise that no one is to be forced to act in a manner contrary to his own beliefs, whether privately or publicly, whether alone or in association with others, within due limits. The council further declares that the right to religious freedom has its foundation in the very dignity of the human person as this dignity is known through the revealed word of God and by reason itself. This right of the human person to religious freedom is to be recognized in the constitutional law whereby society is governed and thus it is to become a civil right.[24]

Nikolaus Lobkowicz has precisely identified the scope of this turning point. "The extraordinary quality of the declaration *Dignitatis humanae* consists in the fact that it shifted the issue of religious freedom from the notion of truth to the notion of the rights of a human person. Although error may have no rights, a person has rights even when he or she is wrong. This is, of course, not a right before God; it is a right with respect to other people, the community and the State."[25]

In a historic 2005 speech to the Roman Curia, Benedict XVI underlines the importance of the step taken by Vatican II. He focuses on the three major issues that the council had had to face, namely, the relationship between the Church and the modern age, between Church and state, and between Christian faith and other religions, all within the horizon of religious tolerance. In reference to the third issue, religious freedom, he speaks of the Church's journey in terms of "innovation in continuity" and "a discontinuity in which . . . the continuity of principles proved not to have been abandoned." What does the route taken by the Church teach?

It is precisely in this combination of continuity and discontinuity at different levels that the very nature of true reform consists. In this process of innovation in continuity we must learn to understand more practically than before that the Church's decisions on contingent matters—for example, certain practical

forms of liberalism or a free interpretation of the Bible—
should necessarily be contingent themselves, precisely because
they refer to a specific reality that is changeable in itself. It
was necessary to learn to recognize that in these decisions it is
only the principles that express the permanent aspect, since
they remain as an undercurrent, motivating decisions from
within. On the other hand, not so permanent are the practical
forms that depend on the historical situation and are therefore
subject to change. Basic decisions, therefore, continue to be
well-grounded, whereas the way they are applied to new contexts can change.[26]

The relationship between the principles and contingent decisions
is most paradigmatic in the field of religious freedom.

Thus, for example, if religious freedom were to be considered an expression of the human inability to discover the truth
and thus become a canonization of relativism, then this social
and historical necessity is raised inappropriately to the metaphysical level and thus stripped of its true meaning. Consequently, it cannot be accepted by those who believe that the
human person is capable of knowing the truth about God and,
on the basis of the inner dignity of the truth, is bound to this
knowledge. It is quite different, on the other hand, to perceive
religious freedom as a need that derives from human coexistence, or indeed, as an intrinsic consequence of the truth that
cannot be externally imposed but that the person must adopt
only through the process of conviction.[27]

This is the crucial point. Freedom of religion comes from
a consciousness of the nature of truth and the relationship between
it and freedom. The truth cannot be imposed from the outside; it
must be embraced and appropriated by man in freedom. But precisely in this renewed awareness of the relationship between truth and
freedom the council links itself to the original experience of the
Church.

The Second Vatican Council, recognizing and making its own an essential principle of the modern State with the Decree on Religious Freedom, has recovered the deepest patrimony of the Church. By so doing she can be conscious of being in full harmony with the teaching of Jesus himself (cf. Mt 22:21), as well as with the Church of the martyrs of all time. The ancient Church naturally prayed for the emperors and political leaders out of duty (cf. 1 Tm 2:2); but while she prayed for the emperors, she refused to worship them and thereby clearly rejected the religion of the State. The martyrs of the early Church died for their faith in that God who was revealed in Jesus Christ, and for this very reason they also died for freedom of conscience and the freedom to profess one's own faith—a profession that no State can impose but which, instead, can only be claimed with God's grace in freedom of conscience.

There was thus a correction, but relative to historical and contingent judgments, not to principles. "The Second Vatican Council, with its new definition of the relationship between the faith of the Church and certain essential elements of modern thought, has reviewed or even corrected certain historical decisions, but in this apparent discontinuity it has actually preserved and deepened her inmost nature and true identity."[28]

In this deepening of her self-awareness, the Church also rethought her relationship with the modern age. Moving away from "a temptation that one could encounter both in nineteenth century Romanticism with its nostalgia for the Middle Ages and also in Catholic circles between the two world wars,"[29] the Church recovered a correct vision of the Enlightenment contribution, in the light of a renewed awareness of the original contribution of Christianity as well. The latter, in fact, "as religion of the persecuted, and as universal religion that was wider than any one state or people, . . . denied the government the right to consider religion as a part of the order of the state, It [i.e., Christianity] has always defined men—all men without distinction—as creatures of God made in his image, proclaiming the principle that they are equal in dignity, though of course within the given limits of societal order. In this sense, the Enlightenment has a Christian origin, and it is not by chance that it was born specifically and exclusively within the sphere of the Christian faith." On the other hand, since "Christianity, contrary to its own nature, had unfortunately become mere tradition and religion of the state," it has been a principal "merit of the Enlightenment to have drawn attention afresh to these original Christian values and . . . given reason back its own voice. In its Constitution on the Church in the Modern World, the Second Vatican Council restated this profound harmony between Christianity and Enlightenment, seeking to achieve a genuine reconciliation between the Church and modernity."[30]

The maturation process led the Church to recognize as more faithful to her truth the affirmation and respect for religious freedom, and to admit the times throughout the centuries when she acted in ways not consistent with it.

> In faithfulness therefore to the truth of the Gospel, the Church is following the way of Christ and the apostles when she recognizes and gives support to the principle of religious freedom as befitting the dignity of man and as being in accord with divine revelation. Throughout the ages the Church has kept safe and handed on the doctrine received from the Master and from the apostles. In the life of the People of God, as it has made its pilgrim way through the vicissitudes of human history, there has at times appeared a way of acting that was hardly in accord with the spirit of the Gospel or even opposed to it. Nevertheless, the doctrine of the Church that no one is to be coerced into faith has always stood firm.[31]

Thus, for a long time the meaning of religious freedom has been obscured. How was it possible? The reason is no different from the reason why the other values were obscured. Their recognition implies the necessary and dramatic relationship with freedom, a relationship in which every generation is called to live again and again. The heritage of values that a generation receives from the previous one is an "appeal to freedom." It can, therefore, take it on or reject it, "because it can never be self-evident in the same way as material inventions."[32]

Here, then, is the necessary question if we want to the face current challenges without ideological debates and without becoming closed in on ourselves: How can freedom again be "won over for the good," since "free assent to the good never exists simply by itself"? Only through witness, as happened at the beginning. It is necessary for values to be alive in someone, as an active consequence of their lived roots, so that the values can again be "seen" and engage freedom. Only the witness of truth can reach man's heart. As Lobkowicz keenly observes regarding the subject of religious freedom, "Though it took the Church a considerable time to sort out what in the modern call for religious freedom was legitimate and what could not be accepted, *Dignitatis humanae* is an expression of something like the 'spirit' of the *Vaticanum secundum*: though it unambiguously insisted on truth, the Church no longer wanted to lay any claim to any form of power but only to reach the hearts of people, just as Jesus Christ had done."[33]

In this situation we can, therefore, make a contribution starting from the nature of faith. By living within reality, living our jobs, living the answer to life's challenges starting from the encounter with the event of Christ, we can give proof of the difference that it introduces into our approach to everything. We can be like a seed. "In a society like this, you cannot create something new, if not with life. There is no structure or organization or initiative that can do this. Only a new and different life can revolutionize structures, initiatives, relationships, everything."[34] How long will it take for the seed to bear fruit? We do not know. Just think of the examples of Saint Paul on slavery or the Letter to Diognetus on abortion. Nor is it up to us to decide. But there is no other way, because what is self-evident becomes obscure if it is separated from its living root, from the experience that allowed it to fully emerge.

———•◦•———

CHAPTER 3

In the Collapse of the Self-Evident, a Subject Is Generated

Without recognizing how things really are, without a sufficient awareness of what is happening, even if we take initiative—because in any case all of us move because we perceive things in one way or another, because we catch sight of a need—what we do will fail to have an impact. For this reason, helping each other to have a true gaze on reality, on the circumstances we are living in, is the first gesture of friendship we can offer each other for living like human beings in the presence of the needs of the world.

A Different Perception of Reality

The first gift Fr. Giussani gave us, through which he began to generate the history to which we all belong, was his perception of reality. I am thinking of his dialogue with the young people on the train, or with the high school students who came to him for confession, when he went to the parish on Lazio Avenue in Milan on the weekends in the early 1950s.[1] Dialoguing and hearing confessions, he had a clear perception of what the situation was, and so he decided to change everything, even his own academic prospects, even though, to some extent, doing this disrupted what his superiors had in mind for him: he did it to respond to an urgent need that had clearly appeared to him. This was his point of departure.

In a situation like that of the Catholic Church in Milan in the 1950s, in which there were no particular problems of orthodoxy and everything was transmitted peacefully, his gaze caught—by grace—a crucial issue, with a capacity for truly reading the signs of the times, those signs that almost nobody saw. What is evident to everyone now, because of the consequences we have seen and see, was recognized by only a few at the beginning, as always happens. Genius requires only a few clues to draw a general conclusion. This is the genius of the Spirit, who can give a person the grace to begin to understand. During his life, Fr. Giussani offered us many signs of this different gaze, different from that of the others and from ours as well, so much so that we, too, were surprised.

What was the problem in those years? The doctrine that was transmitted in an orthodox way no longer penetrated life; it did not become new experience. Fr. Giussani gave life to a movement, getting involved with the Catholic youth groups of Milan, to begin to respond to that urgent need. He began anew by focusing on experience, because without it—that is, if doctrine does not enter into life and one does not have an experience of it—we cannot understand the nature of faith. From the beginning, he put experience at the center: "I'm not here so that you can take my ideas as your own, but to teach you a true method that you can use to judge the things I will tell you."[2] In other words, I have not come to convince you about something, but to give you the instrument you need in order to experience it and convince yourselves, so that your personality is generated through the constant comparison between what you live and the criteria that you discover within yourselves, engaging yourselves in the verification of the proposal you receive.

In the Collapse of the Self-Evident, a Subject Is Generated   37

A Weakness of Awareness:
"As If There Were No Longer Anything Self-Evident"

But at a certain point, many years after the movement began, Fr. Giussani realized that, especially in the life of young people, something new was happening again that did not manifest itself—as we might expect—in a sort of ethical inconsistency. This would be nothing. He understood that the weakness of the young people of the 1980s was not merely a matter of acting consistently, or of moral fragility: "It seems to me that the difference lies in a greater weakness of awareness people have today, a weakness that is not ethical, but rather pertains to the energy of our awareness. . . . It is as if [today] nothing were really self-evident except fashion, because fashion is a project of power."[3]

This disappearance of what is self-evident grew exponentially in the following years and continues to grow. In fact, as then-Cardinal Ratzinger wrote in 1998, "The collapse of old religious certainties, which seventy years ago still seemed stoppable, has in the meantime to a great extent become reality. Thus the fear of a collapse of human values . . . has itself become more widespread and intense."[4] Therefore, when we speak of a "collapse of the self-evident," we are indicating something that profoundly characterizes our historical context. Giussani did not let himself be confused by consequences. As a matter of fact, this collapse causes a whole series of ethical and moral consequences, but what Giussani intended to clearly identify was the origin: there is no longer anything truly evident. The fact that we find it difficult to realize this shows just how far we participate in this situation. Its origin, according to Giussani, is a reduction of the human person, of our fundamental capacities, which leads us to no longer recognize what is self-evident.

This reduction is asserted through the influence of power. Its fundamental attack is against the self; it is a reduction of the self, of desire, of reason's capacity to recognize reality. Perhaps we, too, are defined more than we think by power, and our difficulty in recognizing the type of collapse that characterizes our time is the first sign of this fact. Therefore, power can allow us to get distracted by other things because, deep down—since we do not grasp and strike the origin of everything, whence come all the negative consequences we see—our activity does not constitute a problem.

In this regard, a friend reminded me of a line of Chesterton's: "The sages, it is often said, can see no answer to the riddle of religion. But the trouble with our sages is not that they cannot see the answer, it is that they cannot even see the riddle."[5] In other words, they do not realize the problem, do not see the evidence, and so it is difficult for them to understand all the rest. And this, by the way, is not a problem of ecclesiastical alignments, of progressives or conservatives, but of a gaze on reality, and it regards everyone. For that matter, Jesus had the same problem with the Pharisees. Why did they insist so fiercely on ethics? Because they did not understand the nature of the problem and could consequently settle for an insistence on ethics. The Pelagianism we often find within depends on the fact that we do not realize the nature of the human problem. For this reason, we can hustle and bustle to activate many attempts at a solution, without in the least challenging the foundation of the issue. At times, Jesus appears naive to our eyes, and we are scandalized. When he says, "Look, deep down, this is not the problem," he scandalizes everyone. "What? How is it possible that Jesus thinks it is more important to eat at Zacchaeus's house than to give him a lesson on morality?" Jesus' attitude blows everyone away. "But how is it possible?"

Jesus has a different perception of the human problem, a true perception. How long until we understand this? Something similar already happened to us. In fact, Fr. Giussani saw certain things from the very beginning, but it took a long time for it to become clear to us, too, and now to everyone. It is not a problem of alignments, of discussions or debates. Thinking the problem can be resolved with debates is already part of the inability to recognize the evidence, the "most evident" evidence—excuse the play on words. It is already part of the inability to grasp what is happening, what the collapse in front of us is. If we do not realize this, we cannot hope to respond to the challenge adequately, even if we hustle and bustle about in a thousand ways.

A Reduction of the Capacity to Look

What is reduced is a perception of the human condition as a whole, of the human as such. If we do not realize it, it is because of the influence of power, the way it reduces our capacity to look at reality. This influence does not primarily reduce our ethical capacity, our capacity for consistency, but our capacity to look. The consequence is a reduced awareness of what is happening and what is necessary to face it.

> If we are so shamefully divided [within ourselves], so fragmented that even unity between man and woman is impossible and we can trust no one, if we are so cynical towards everyone and everything and so out of love with ourselves [as if we were detached from ourselves], how can we extract something from this mire in order to reconstruct the battered walls of our person—the cement for building new walls? . . . Given this, our wounded situation, we cannot then say: 'Let's set ourselves to work to reconstruct humanity.' If we are so defeated, how can we possibly win? . . . Someone needs to come from outside—*can only come from outside* [from outside our thoughts, outside our reduced capacity to look, our reduced capacity to see. Someone must come from outside for us now, not for us before we began living Christianity, not for those who still are not Christians, but for us who are already Christians]—who sees our battered dwelling place and re-builds the walls. . . . This is the major difficulty as far as . . . authentic Christianity is concerned: it is through *something other*—that comes from outside—that man becomes himself."[6]

We do not like this. We see a resistance in ourselves, because each of us claims he already has a clear idea of the situation, each person already has her own judgment on the situation, on what should be done. We already know! For this reason, we do not like it that someone else must come from outside to rebuild our shattered walls. We do not like it because . . . it welcomes something that does not correspond to our imagination or to our image of experience, and it appears abstract in its claim. [Thus] . . . we come to a halt [we should write this line across our foreheads so we see it whenever we look in the mirror!] . . . in an impotent aspiring to find a remedy, or, in *a fraudulent, lie-filled claim.* In other words, we *identify the remedy with our own image* [whatever image each of us forms] and according to our own desire to make good. [We form an image and entrust ourselves to our will to fix things, carrying out whatever we have in mind.] . . . Thus is born the "discoursing" on moral values, because discoursing on moral values suggests that the remedy to the dissolution lies in man's power of imagination and will: "Let's work together. Together we can fix it!"[7]

Christ Came to Reawaken Our Capacity to Know Reality

The situation that we have described is the same one the Church has reminded us of throughout the course of her history: "The precepts of natural law [that is, the greatest evidence for the human person] are not perceived by everyone clearly and immediately [because of the reduction of our "I," which we, too, experience]. In the present situation sinful man needs grace and revelation so moral and religious truths [that is, the evidences] may be known 'by everyone with facility, with firm certainty and with no admixture of error.'"[8] This is the situation: it was described by the First Vatican Council back in the 1800s, speaking of the knowledge of God, and then it was discussed again in the catechism. Therefore, the International Theological Commission, in a document on the same theme, declared: "We must therefore be modest and prudent when invoking the 'obviousness' of natural law precepts."[9] This condition worsened with the influence of secularization, and for this reason the condition of contemporary man is characterized precisely by the collapse of evidences.

Thus Fr. Giussani was not distracted when, to respond to the disorientation of humankind in our age, he communicated Christianity to us not to convince us of his ideas, but so that we could see anew reality as it is. He told us that Christ came precisely to reawaken the religious sense in us, to reawaken our capacity to know reality. If we do not realize this, we will end up plugging leaks, consequences, here and there, but without truly helping people to see. The situation has changed radically: it is not that people see the evidence and deny it because they are bad or closed-minded; they do not see it at all. This is part of the reduction of the human that we have constantly before us. If we can say we see, it is only because we are Christians, because the fact of Christ puts us in the condition to see. Otherwise we would think like everyone else. So there is no use scolding people because they do not see—we could do it, but it is useless! We need to give others a real contribution, helping them to come out of this blocked situation and to see reality again.

I was struck by an observation Cardinal Scola made in an interview for the Italian newspaper *La Repubblica* during the days of the Synod on the Family. I think it is very valuable, and so I want to call it to your attention today. Speaking of the today in which the Church finds herself, he says: "Facing the sexual revolution [as the ultimate attempt of individuals to save themselves by themselves, according to all the images that each person can construct] is perhaps no less of a challenge than that issued by the Marxist revolution."[10] They are two attempts, on the social and individual level, to save oneself by oneself.

Let us see how Fr. Giussani faced the challenge of the Marxist revolution of 1968 and how he judged our attempt to respond to it.

An Existential Insecurity That Makes Us Seek Our Foundation in the Things We Do

Behind our efforts during those years, all desirous of responding to the situation generated by the student uprising, there was, as the first consequence of a certain attitude, "'an [efficiency-based] conception of Christian commitment, with accentuations of moralism.' Not accentuations—wholesale reduction to moralism! [Because deep down we did not understand what it was about.]. . . . Second consequence: . . . the incapacity to 'culturalize' the words, to bring one's Christian experience to the level in which it becomes systematic and critical judgment, and thus a prompt for a method of action. . . . Third consequence: the theoretical and practical underestimation of the authoritative experience, of authority."[11]

Why did this happen? Because of naivety, "the naivety of a man who says, 'Get out of the way and let me set things right.' . . . How very sad!"[12] How sad, truly, because, as we can note today as well, many of those efforts were born and are born "of an existential insecurity, that is, from a deep fear that makes us seek our foundation in our own expressions. This observation, which we have made before, is of supreme importance. Those who are full of insecurity, or who are dominated by profound fear and existential anxiety, seek security in things they do: culture and organization. . . . It is an existential insecurity, a deep-rooted fear, which makes us view the things we do culturally and organizationally as our foundation, as the reason that gives us substance." But the most terrible thing is what he observes next: all the things we do, "all the cultural activity and all the organizational activity do not become an expression of a new physiognomy, of a new person." "If they were the expression of a new person," Fr. Giussani continues, "they could also not exist, when circumstances did not permit them, but that person would still stand. Instead, for many of our people present here today, if there were not these things, they would not stand; they would not know what they are here for; they would not know what to belong to: they do not stand, they have no substance, because the substance of my person is the presence of an Other."[13]

If we do not take this history to heart, even if we continue with our initiatives, our activism, our hustle and bustle, we will never touch the ultimate origin of the question, and we will remain naive.

Examining More Deeply the Nature of the Self

Drawing upon the experience of the gospel, Fr. Giussani underlines that the person who is reduced by the powers that be "rediscovers herself [only] in a living encounter, that is, in a presence she runs up against and that attracts her."[14] If this does not happen, none of our attempts to respond to the new challenges—to this reduction that makes people settle for all the images they build of themselves, according to a modality that can be different from that of the preceding revolution—will bear fruit. If people do not rediscover themselves, they will only emerge further reduced by their efforts to resolve the problem. We already see just how much the attempts of our contemporaries fail to grasp the nature of the "I" and thus to respond to its ultimate needs.

What does Jesus do to reawaken men and women, to raise them up from this situation of disorientation and alienation? He meets people, puts before them a human presence that is not reduced—his own. Only the impact with him—with his presence, with the clear awareness that he has of himself, with his capacity to understand the density and expectation of the heart—can reawaken their humanity, their perception of the importance of their need, and consequently enable them not to waste time seeking solutions that cannot respond adequately. For this reason, the solution of the problems life sets before us every day "does not come from addressing the problems directly, but from examining more deeply the nature of the subject who faces them,"[15] by exploring more deeply, in other words, the nature of the self, the nature of one's desire. Only if a person becomes self-aware to this level will he be able to free himself from all his presumed solutions and imaginings, as happens with us as well.

What is the mission of Christ? Christ did not come to solve the problems of the human person, but to educate the religious sense, that is, to reawaken the self, putting it in the right position for facing those problems. "Jesus Christ did not come into the world as a substitute for human effort, human freedom, or to eliminate human trial—the existential condition of freedom. He came into the world to call man back to the depths of all questions, to his own fundamental structure, and to his own real situation. . . . It is not the task of Jesus to resolve all the various problems, but to harken man back to the position where he can more correctly try to resolve them. This toil is a rightful part of every individual's commitment, whose function in existing lies precisely in that search for solutions."[16]

"No One Generates Unless He Has Been Generated"

Therefore, when we are facing the collapse of evidences, the whole issue is whether subjects are generated that are able to have such an awareness of their own nature, of their own human need, that they do not let themselves be overwhelmed by reduced images and partial solutions that give no satisfaction. The Christian experience, truly lived, frees the self from all the partial efforts, makes it overflow with joy and fullness, setting before everyone a truly desirable humanity. Indeed, it is not having a different opinion about things that strikes people, but rather the impact with a true and full humanity. This different humanity is irresistible to people, no matter what latitude their home, as recounted by a young man who lived a few months in Texas. The people who had contact with him told him: "We have never seen a humanity like this." Today we see repeated the same reaction that the first people had to Jesus. What moves people is not religious opinions, but a true, full humanity. Later it will be necessary to give all the reasons for this diversity, but the first repercussion comes from the encounter with a true humanity, one that is not reduced.

What must we live—what must we experience—in order to be able to educate a subject capable of facing reality? "No one generates unless he has been generated,"[17] that is, unless you allow yourself to be generated by that history in which Christ became an important reality for your life, by the path that constantly offers us all the tools for journeying toward maturity. It was a grace for us that Fr. Giussani's sole concern was this generation, as if he had foreseen the situation in which we find ourselves living today more and more. All the others were concerned about other things, even the right things, but they took for granted the subject that would have to face the problems. The one who gave his whole life for this generation of the self was Fr. Giussani. He gave himself in order to generate adults like himself, so overflowing with the presence of Christ, so joyful because of their experience of Christ, that they can testify to everyone about who Christ is. There is no other road, Pope Francis always tells us, than the testimony of a life overflowing with Christ's presence, so that anyone who meets us can participate in this fullness that was given to us by grace, but that we must always have the simplicity to accept, to receive, and without which we would lose our relationship with reality.

The light that comes from our history is a contribution that should lead us back to our origins. Only in this way can we live in this historical context with a difference in our gaze and according to an original way of being present in reality. As Pope Francis told us that without a foundation on something essential—and the essential is Christ—we will only be frightened in the face of new challenges. The essential, the return to the essential, to which Fr. Giussani always called us and to which now Pope Francis invites us, is crucial for us. If we do not return to it, we will find it difficult to be sufficiently free to seek new forms and ways of communicating the truth encountered, as the pope wrote in the message to the Meeting of Rimini in 2014.[18]

Gestures of New Humanity That Evoke Interest

Only by always returning to the essential will we be able to set before everyone a presence, a new way of staying in reality. Through encountering this presence people can overcome the profound unease that prevents them from taking personal responsibility within their circumstances. In order for them to face the current challenges, something must happen that reawakens all of the "I" in such a way that it can begin to look at things again with sufficient clarity and adhere to what it once again recognizes as evident. If we do not communicate, by living it, that essentialness that is alone able to attract and move the self, we will not be able to respond or give a real contribution to the current situation of weakness and emptiness that people are thrown into today.

Our original contribution, that for which Fr. Giussani began everything, consists in rebuilding a subject able to recognize the truth, the evidence of things, and adhere to it. This is what makes the historical moment we are living in so exciting: the fact that when people see the evidence of something true in certain gestures, even in the midst of general indifference (which is a symptom of the reduction of the subject), they begin to become interested and are attracted. How does a possibility for new life spread? "A new reality is not built by speeches or organizational projects, but by living gestures of new humanity in the present"[19]—that is, gestures in which people can see and touch what makes them more themselves. When people discover this, they begin to change. Gestures of new humanity, that is, of friendship: they are features that belong to an original presence.

If we want to make a real contribution to the present situation, we have to become even more aware of the nature of the challenge. Otherwise, we will try to plug the leaks, the circumstances, which may even be useful for some time, but this will not be what truly changes things. This means that we will need time: we plant olive trees knowing that perhaps we will not see the fruit, except in certain moments, in certain people. Precisely for this reason it is even more crucial that we know how to identify well the purpose for which we are in the world. Fr. Giussani understood it very well, much earlier than others: Christ came to reawaken the human person, and his presence is revealed in the fact that those who acknowledge him relate differently with reality, live intensely in every circumstance that is given to them. Only if we experience this can we communicate it to others, giving the reasons for our faith, and thus moving something in the reason of those we encounter. Otherwise, our contribution will be equal to zero.

---◆·◆·◆---

CHAPTER 4

The Challenge of True Dialogue after the Charlie Hebdo Attacks

Since the events in Paris happened, there has been a great deal of discussion;[1] nobody has been spared a sense of bewilderment or fear. The numerous analyses offered have brought forth interesting points for reflecting on and understanding such a complex phenomenon. But a month later, now that the routine of daily life has taken over again, what remains? What can keep these disturbing events from rapidly being erased from our memory? To help us remember, it is necessary to discover the true nature of the challenge posed by the Paris attacks.

We Europeans have what our forebears desired: Europe as a space of freedom where each person can be what she or he wants. The Old Continent has become a crucible of the most varied cultures, religions, and visions of the world.

The events of Paris document how this space of freedom should not be taken for granted as self-perpetuating: it can be threatened by those who fear freedom and are willing to impose their own vision of things with violence. What response is required for such a threat? It will be necessary to defend this space with all the legal and political means possible—starting with dialogue with the Arab nations disposed to impede a disaster that would hurt them as well—and to build a juridical framework that guarantees authentic religious freedom for all. But this is not enough, and the reason is obvious. Those who carried out the massacre in Paris did not come from abroad; they were second-generation immigrants, born in Europe, educated and formed as European citizens, like a great many others who have long dwelt in our countries. It is a phenomenon *in fieri*, in virtue of the constant flows of migration and the demographic growth of the populations who reach here from all parts of the world, driven by hardship and poverty.

For this reason, the problem is primarily within Europe, and the most important part is played here at home. The true challenge is cultural, its terrain daily life. When those who abandon their homelands arrive here in search of a better life, when their children are born and become adults in the West, what do they see? Can they find something able to attract their humanity, to challenge their reason and their freedom? The same problem exists for our children: do we have something to offer them that speaks to their search for fulfillment and meaning? In many young people who have grown up in the so-called Western world there reigns a great nothingness, a profound void that constitutes the origin of the desperation that ends up in violence. Just think of the Europeans who go to fight in the ranks of terroristic organizations, or of the lost and disoriented life of many young people of our cities. This corrosive void, this far-spreading nothingness, requires a response.

In the wake of the events of Paris it is sterile to mount opposition in the name of an idea, no matter how right it may be. We have learned after a long journey that the only way to truth is through freedom. Therefore, we have decided to reject the violence that has marked moments of our past. Today none of us nurtures the dream of responding to the challenge of the other with the imposition of a truth, whatever it may be. For us, Europe is a space of freedom; this does not mean an empty space, void of proposals for life, because nothing can live off of nothingness. Nobody can stand, have a constructive relationship with reality, without something that makes life worth living, without a hypothesis of meaning.

So then, this is the true element that will decide the future of Europe: whether she will finally be the place of a real encounter between proposals of meaning, different and numerous as they may be, as happened for centuries in some countries of the Middle East where different cultures and religions were able to live in peace, but where Christians now are forced to abandon their homeland because the situation has made their life impossible. In this way, however, the problem is not resolved, only shifted aside.

Now the verification for Europe begins. Space for freedom means space for saying in front of everyone, individually or together, who we are. Each makes available for everyone his or her vision and way of living. This sharing will enable us to encounter each other on the basis of the real experience of each person, and not on the basis of ideological stereotypes that make dialogue impossible. As Pope Francis said, "Dialogue, thus, begins with encounter. The first knowledge of the other is born from it. Indeed, if one begins from the premise of the common affiliation in human nature, one can go beyond prejudices and fallacies and begin to understand the other according to a new perspective."[2]

This historical situation offers an exceptional opportunity to everyone, Christians included. Europe can constitute a great space for us, space for the testimony of a changed life, full of meaning, capable of embracing that which is different and of awakening its humanity with gestures rich in generosity.

Inviting all Christians to nurture the desire for testimony, Pope Francis underlined that "in this way alone can the liberating message of the love of God and the salvation that Christ offers be proposed in its strength, beauty and simplicity. One can only move forward in this way, with an attitude of respect for people."[3] Do we Christians still believe in the capacity of the faith we have received to attract those we encounter, and do we believe in the living fascination of its disarming beauty?

PART 2

AN EVENT OF REBIRTH

CHAPTER 5

———•◦•———

Christianity Faced with the Challenges
of the Present

"Can one believe while being civilized, i.e., a European?, believe without reservation in the divine nature of Jesus Christ, the Son of God?"[1]
This passage by Dostoevsky identifies the challenge that faith in Jesus
Christ faces today. It is not a generic question about whether absolute
faith in Christ is possible. The decisive aspect of the Russian writer's
question lies in his reference to a specific context: contemporary Europe. It was addressed to what Dostoevsky termed a civilized person:
a cultured, educated European, who does not renounce the exercise of
his reason with all its demands, who brings into play all his need for
freedom, all its affective potential, that is, a person who does not give
up any aspect of his humanity. For a human being with such characteristics, is it possible to believe in Jesus Christ? "Believe without
reservation?" insists Dostoevsky, as if wanting to emphasize that it is
a faith that truly rises to the level of the nature and demands of reason.

Dostoevsky's insistence on the circumstances in which—for over a century now!—we are called to live the faith shows to what extent he rightly considers them decisive. Indeed, "the circumstances God has us pass through are an essential, and not secondary factor of our vocation, of the mission to which He calls us. If Christianity is the announcement that the Mystery became incarnate in a man, the circumstance in which one takes a stand on this, in front of the whole world, is important to the very definition of witness."[2]

We know very well the circumstances in which we Christians are living the faith today. They can be summed up in the realization that we live in a pluralistic world, where Christianity—and the conception of man and life that comes from it—has become one option among many. We are called to live the faith without a context to protect us; not only without privileges, but sometimes even persecuted. More and more often we see a view of the human being taking shape in legislative form that is entirely opposite to the one that to us seems more human, and which until recently was shared by all, even by those without Christian faith.

We can live in this new situation with anger, because the tide is going in a direction that we do not agree with, or we can accept the challenge. This challenge does not allow us to take for granted the survival of what was once our common heritage; it calls us to show the relevance of the faith to the needs of personal and social life. Faced with this unprecedented challenge, Christians, not surprisingly, develop different interpretations about how to deal with it. These positions range from retreating into one's shell, refusing to witness the public importance of faith, to believing that the only way to defend Christian values is to take a reactive position, without bothering to give reasons for the positivity of those values within the culturally pluralistic context in which we live.

We all see how inadequate these attitudes are. But in order to be free of them it is not enough to show our desire to discard them or to wish not to succumb to them. In order to overcome them, we need to find a way of living the faith, within this social reality and pluralistic culture, such that others can perceive our presence not as something to defend themselves from, but as a contribution to the common good and their own personal good. We need a way of being present without a will to dominate or oppress, and at the same time *with* a commitment to living the faith in reality, in order to show the human benefit of belonging to Christ.

Years ago Pope John Paul II explained the magnitude of the challenge to us. "Many Europeans today think they know what Christianity is, yet they do not really know it at all. . . . Many of the baptized live as if Christ did not exist. . . . The great certainties of the faith are being undermined in many people by a vague religiosity lacking real commitment. . . . 'When the Son of man comes, will he find faith on earth?' (Lk 18:8)."[3] Pope Benedict XVI confirmed that the situation has not changed over the years. "Often we are anxiously preoccupied with the social, cultural and political consequences of the faith, taking for granted that faith is present, which unfortunately is less and less realistic. Perhaps we have placed an excessive trust in ecclesial structures and programs, in the distribution of powers and functions; but what will happen if salt loses its flavor?"[4] In many cases one cannot speak of a lack of faith or its explicit denial, but rather a reduced faith, lived more like a habit or a devotional practice, where the existence of the faith itself is taken for granted, as a free and reasonable choice. We see this by the fact that it does not withstand the shocks of present reality, demonstrated by the number of those who leave the faith or live it with indifference or disinterest.

This makes the urgency of an education in the faith more and more evident, an education that shows its relevance to the needs of life, so that it becomes able to resist the impact of adverse circumstances. *Gaudium et Spes* already affirmed this in the mid-1960s. "The remedy which must be applied to atheism, however, is to be sought in a proper presentation of the Church's teaching as well as in the integral life of the Church and her members. . . . This result is achieved chiefly by the witness of a living and mature faith, namely, one trained to see difficulties clearly and to master them."[5]

Dostoevsky's question thus maintains all its seriousness. In this situation, does the faith have a chance to fascinate, attract, and be embraced by the people of our time? At a conference in 1996, then-Cardinal Ratzinger replied to this question by saying that faith can still make inroads and be accepted "because it corresponds to the nature of man. . . . The longing for the infinite is alive and unquenchable within man."[6] With this he pointed out the necessary condition for that experience of correspondence: to show its full potential, all its truth, Christianity needs to meet the human—the unquenchable aspiration—that vibrates within each of us. That is precisely why Fr. Giussani emphasized so strongly that "it would be impossible to become fully aware of what Jesus Christ means if one did not first become fully aware of the nature of that dynamism which makes man human. Christ proposes himself as the answer to what 'I' am and only an attentive, tender and impassioned awareness of my own self can make me open and lead me to acknowledge, admire, thank, and live Christ. Without this awareness, even Jesus Christ becomes just a name."[7]

The Desire That Constitutes Our Heart

Saint Augustine admirably identified the ineradicable human needs in his famous statement about restlessness. "Thou hast made us for Thyself, and our hearts are restless till they rest in Thee."[8] The perception of this desire that constitutes the heart, which always drives people to seek the fullness of their being, has suffered the influence of historical events. Today we see that our ability to adhere to ourselves and to reality is drastically reduced. The more we look at the events of our day, the more we are struck by the effectiveness of an image with which Fr. Giussani, in the '80s, used to prophetically describe the situation in which human beings find themselves today. "It is as if today's youth were all penetrated by . . . the radiation from Chernobyl: structurally, the organism is as it was before, but dynamically it is no longer the same. . . . People are . . . abstracted from the relationship with themselves, as if emptied of affection [without the energy of affection to adhere to reality], like batteries that last for six minutes instead of six hours."[9] Since then, various authors from all over the ideological spectrum, with varying degrees of insight, have described this human drama that is particularly evident in young people.

In an article dedicated to the younger generations that appeared in the Italian newspaper *La Repubblica*, the writer Pietro Citati declared,

> At one time, adulthood came early. . . . [Today there is a continuous race to immaturity. Once,] a boy grew up at all costs. . . . Achieving maturity was a renunciation, it meant renouncing. Suddenly, with an ascetic gesture, a boy left behind all his dreams. . . . [Today, young people] do not know who they are. Maybe they do not want to know. They are always wondering who they are, . . . they love . . . indecision! They never say "yes" and never say "no." They are always in front of a doorway that, perhaps, will never open. . . . They have no will, no desire to act. . . . They prefer to remain passive. . . . They live wrapped in a mysterious inertia. They do not love time. Their time is a series of moments that are not linked together in a chain or organized into a story.[10]

This article provoked a response from Eugenio Scalfari, founder of *La Repubblica* and among the most authoritative members of what we might call the progressive left. He wrote:

> The wound was the boredom, the unconquerable, existential boredom that killed time and history, passions and hope. I see no sweetness in their eyes. I do not see that deep melancholy that we see in the young Renaissance faces painted by Lotto and Titian. . . . I see eyes that are bewildered, ecstatic, stunned, furtive, greedy without desire, lustful without lust, lonely in the crowd that contains them. I see desperate eyes . . . eternal children, . . . a desperate generation . . . advancing. . . . They are trying to escape from the plastic void that surrounds and suffocates them. Their salvation lies only in their hearts. We can only look at them with love and trepidation.[11]

Who could have imagined that the long arc from humanism and the Renaissance—begun with the intention of affirming the human—that led us to this point would have resulted in this lethargy and existential boredom?

Augusto Del Noce evocatively identified the type of nihilism that characterizes our time in relation to Augustine's restlessness. "Today's nihilism is jovial, [in that] it lacks restlessness. Perhaps you could call it the suppression of Augustine's *inquietum cor meum*."[12] This intertwines with what Benedict XVI has identified with the word "relativism," the human and cultural position in which everything is a matter of opinion and there is no truth; everything is relative, questionable, and nothing can be considered more or less true than anything else; all the options are the same. This all-encompassing indifference does not, of course, even spare the Christian faith. The more the goad of desire and restlessness is choked off, the more the ability to recognize the truth, that is, the answer to our deepest aspirations, becomes confused. But if we do not find or recognize what is able to attract our entire self, how will we overcome the aforementioned lethargy and boredom?

All this helps to explain the nature of the crisis in which we find ourselves. It is not just a religious or ethical problem. We are facing a crisis of the human as such. This reduction can even live alongside a flourishing, but reduced religious experience, as noted by an acute American commentator, Ernest Fortin. "Nietzsche had already warned us that the death of God is perfectly consistent with a burgeoning religiosity. . . . He did not think even for a moment that 'religion' was finished. What he questioned was its ability to move people and elevate their minds. . . . 'Religion' [has become] a product to be consumed, a form of entertainment among others, a source of comfort for the weak . . . or an emotional service station, destined to fulfill certain irrational needs that it satisfies better than anything else. As one-sided as it may sound, Nietzsche's diagnosis is very much to the point."[13]

In this situation Christianity must show its anthropological relevance, its human advantage, precisely because of its ability to "move people and elevate their minds," to wake them from the lethargy and passivity Citati spoke of. People of today will take the Christian proposal seriously if they perceive it as a significant response to their basic needs. In this, Christianity can count on a great ally: all the difficulties that contemporary people experience fail to eradicate the hope from their hearts that their full humanity will be fulfilled. It is the very nature of the heart that leads it to hope. But at the same time, often the difficulty of finding an answer causes the heart to doubt the possibility of a good outcome, to the point that such an outcome appears to be a dream.

Antonio Machado expressed it with a unique genius. "Has my heart gone to sleep? / Have the beehives of my dreams / stopped working, the waterwheel / of the mind run dry, / scoops turning empty, / only shadow inside? / No, my heart is not asleep. / It is awake, wide awake / Not asleep, not dreaming— / its eyes are opened wide / watching distant signals, listening / on the rim of the vast silence."[14]

This is the highest point—as an opening of the heart—which a person can reach in his quest to find that answer he cannot stop himself from seeking. Sometimes, when the answer does not come, or does not correspond to some preconceived image, he may think that it is a dream, an illusion. But immediately he recovers and cries with certainty: "No, my heart is not asleep. / It is awake, wide awake / Not asleep, not dreaming— / its eyes are opened wide / watching distant signals, listening / on the rim of the vast silence." Man, as Machado wrote, observes with focused eyes and listens to see if, from out of the great silence of the mystery, a sign manifests itself. It may come or it may not, but each of us, like each of our contemporaries, cannot stop desiring it, although sometimes we cannot even admit it to ourselves. From Plato to Kafka, history is full of examples of this secret longing. This is all the more evident the more the human situation becomes complicated. Instead of stifling the cry, it intensifies it, as Machado himself confesses before the dry elm: "My heart is waiting / also, / — before the light and before life, / another miracle of spring."[15] Man can only await this miracle, because we are not able to generate it. It can come only from the "great silence." So Montale is right when he says, "Something unexpected is the only hope."[16]

An Unforeseeable Event

This "something unexpected" happened in Jesus Christ, the Incarnate Word. With him, the Mystery entered history, becoming humanity's companion, offering himself as an answer to the human need for happiness: whoever follows him will receive a hundredfold and will inherit eternal life.[17] People of today will take an interest in Christianity if it is able to keep this promise and thus break them free from the lethargy in which they are trapped. Christianity is called to show its truth on the terrain of reality. If those who come into contact with it do not experience the newness that it promises, they will certainly be disappointed.

The misfortune is that many of those who still approach the Church in search of an answer are often faced with reductive versions of Christianity. We can imagine what would happen if any of them met a Christian such as those described by John Paul II, who think they know Christianity but do not actually know what it is.

Let us consider some of the possible reductions that weaken the strength of the Christian proclamation.

By the mid-nineteenth century, Cardinal John Henry Newman identified one of them when he said that "religion, as being personal, should be real; but, except within a small range of subjects, it commonly is not real in England. . . . Objects are barely necessary to it. . . . It is not a religion of persons and things, of acts of faith and of direct devotion. . . . Its doctrines are not so much facts, as stereotyped aspects of facts; and it is afraid, so to say, of walking round them. It induces its followers to be content with this meager view of revealed truth. . . . I am not denying that the assent which it inculcates and elicits is genuine as regards its contracted range of doctrine, but it is at best notional."[18]

For many Christians—here is what qualifies the first reduction—Christianity is more notional than real: a set of concepts without reference to concrete life. But for a person who lives immersed in reality, who struggles within the daily drama, what interest can a Christianity reduced to a notional and doctrinal framework have?

To get sense of how widespread this type of Christianity is, think of the reaction that each of us experiences in the presence of someone living the faith as a relationship with the present reality of Christ. We are surprised, as if it were something unheard of. The lack of personal experience of the Christian event makes us unable to understand it, to grasp the meaning of the words that describe it.

"Affirming the truths of faith without having been influenced by heavenly delight," says Pierre Rousselot, "would amount to accepting these truths in a sense that is not the sense in which God utters them."[19] The great Bible scholar Heinrich Schlier spoke about "a growing estrangement, or alienation of the general understanding [common mentality] from the Christian faith. . . . For the general and public awareness, Christian terminology has become largely incomprehensible." As a result, those who want to use Christian words must undertake a hitherto unheard-of task. They must first "evoke a sense of the reality [they] wish to address."[20] The great words of tradition have now become incomprehensible. We cannot work only with formulas, as true as they might be, that are no longer understood in today's world.[21]

Christianity is a fact, an event, not a doctrine. It is enough just to read a page of the gospel in order to realize this, to recognize its vast distance from any purely notional concept of Christianity. The Gospels have left us a witness made of the wonder caused by seeing a man who spoke "as one having authority, and not as their scribes."[22] It was this wonder that led people to say, "We have never seen anything like this!"[23] The Gospels always recount real events, which everyone can recognize without any precondition or particular requirement. As Benedict XVI pointed out: "The real novelty of the New Testament lies not so much in new ideas as in the figure of Christ himself, who gives flesh and blood to those concepts—an unprecedented realism."[24] In place of abstract notions, there is the drama of a God who, in Jesus Christ, involved himself with suffering humanity to the point of giving his life for it: "For God so loved the world that he gave his only Son, so that everyone who believes in him may not perish but may have eternal life."[25]

Another, equally common error is the reduction of Christianity to ethics, to values. It is an old temptation: Saint Augustine already rebuked the Pelagians for it. "This is the hidden and horrid poison of your heresy: you want the grace of Christ to consist in his example, not in his gift."[26] This reduction has today become a widespread mentality thanks to the historical fortunes of the modern era, the complex factors of which we can only mention in passing here.

After the breakdown of European religious unity following the Protestant Reformation, the so-called wars of religion were unleashed. This fact reinforced the belief that religion could not continue to be the common heritage on which to build European unity. What was needed was a new basis that could be shared by all. With Christianity removed, the only common element was reason, as conceived by the Enlightenment. The title of Kant's famous work, *Religion within the Boundaries of Mere Reason*, perfectly expresses this project.[27] The new religion had to respect the limits imposed by Enlightenment reason understood as measure. Reason, reduced to a mere measuring tool, should have been enough to organize life in this world. So, the historical person of Jesus of Nazareth did not have any appeal other than as someone who embodied the ideal of the morally correct adult, known by reason a priori. This ideal, with its values established by reason, constitutes the content of the new religion, which has since spread incessantly, permeating Christianity and reducing it ever more to ethics released from their historical connection.

This is why Pope John Paul I said that "the real drama of the Church that likes to call itself modern is the attempt to correct the wonder of the event of Christ with rules."[28] It is a diagnosis that Benedict XVI shared, in different terms. "The widespread idea which continues to exist is that Christianity is composed of laws and bans which one has to keep and, hence, is something toilsome and burdensome—that one is freer without such a burden. I want to make clear that being carried by a great Love and a revelation is not a burden, but it is like having wings."[29]

It was certainly not these two versions, the notional and the ethical one, that aroused people's interest in Christianity two thousand years ago or reawakened it five hundred years ago at the time of the Catholic Reformation, nor will it be for our contemporaries or even for those who already identify as Christians. "When, in the view of many people, the Catholic faith is no longer the common patrimony of society and, often, is seen as seed threatened and obscured by the 'gods' and masters of this world, only with great difficulty can the faith touch the hearts of people by means of simple speeches or moral appeals, and even less by a general appeal to Christian values."[30]

So, where do we start over? Speaking at the Synod of Bishops dedicated to the laity in the Church in 1987, Fr. Giussani said: "What is missing is not so much the verbal or cultural repetition of the announcement. Today's man is awaiting, perhaps unknowingly, the experience of an encounter with people for whom the fact of Christ is such a present reality that their lives have been changed. What can shake the person of today is the impact with something human: an event that echoes the original one, when Jesus raised his eyes and said, 'Zacchaeus, come down quickly, I am coming to your house.'"[31] This is the method by which Christianity happened and still happens.

In other words, "The Christian event has the form of an encounter, a human encounter." To encounter "means to come across something different that attracts us because it corresponds to our heart. So it is subjected to the comparison and judgment of reason, and causes freedom to come forth in affection. . . . What strikes and moves us are people, faces with an identity that appears truer, that corresponds more to our heart, that is less determined by the whole web of factors that make up the social climate as it is favored by those in power and passively accepted by everyone."[32] This is the method that the encyclical *Deus Caritas Est* brought to the attention of all in its opening lines. "Being Christian is not an ethical choice or a lofty idea, but the encounter with an event, a person, which gives life a new horizon and a decisive direction."[33]

This is exactly, as we have said, what the Gospels show as the beginning Christianity: an encounter with the person of Jesus.[34] Albeit in different forms, on this point all the Gospels agree.[35] John the evangelist describes the impact that Jesus had on the first two that he met on the banks of the Jordan, in a text which, according to Pierre Grelot, gives "the impression of a story written by one of its protagonists."[36] Following John the Baptist's indication, which stirs up their curiosity, John and Andrew begin to follow Jesus, who turns to them and asks, "What are you looking for?" In its disarming simplicity, this question highlights the fact that Christianity stands in history as a response to a query, a universally human quest.[37]

The two men, Andrew and John, answer with another question, "Teacher, where are you staying?" and Jesus tells them, in a straightforward way, "Come and see." This expression will remain in history as the one and only synopsis of the Christian method: "Come and see." Christianity is something you can see. There is a place where you can go. It always struck me to see that Jesus never uttered a single word of propaganda. He merely answered the thirst of those two with an invitation, so that they themselves could draw their own conclusions. What a boundless confidence in the ability of the heart of man to recognize the truth! In order to not take what this scene describes in unparalleled simplicity for granted, just think how many times we have met someone and then returned the next day to seek them out of curiosity and the foretaste of truth that had been evoked, and then the next day again. Only those who agreed to engage in living alongside Jesus could gain certainty about who he was—who it was that by his grace led them to accept the faith. It was the time shared with him that allowed them to grasp the facts that made such an acceptance completely reasonable, without in any way requiring them to ignore reason's demands.

The nature of Christianity is to be an event. No other word defines it better. Christianity is not doctrine, ethics, habit, ritual; Christianity is an event, a fact that did not exist before and, at a precise moment, was introduced into history. Everything else is a consequence of that. "It is in the *event* that something new comes into our lives. Something not expected, not predefined . . . , just as inconceivable before it happens as it is a precise, visible, concrete, tangible, embraceable fact when it does happen. . . . God, destiny, mystery, the origin of all things, has become a human face. Something truly new, a real newness, in order to be human, in order to correspond to and fulfill the heart, must be a face, a countenance or, if you will, a word. . . . The Gospel of John says at the beginning, 'The Word became flesh.' A new human face: that his how God appeared in the world."[38]

Contemporaneity with Christ

Søren Kierkegaard precisely defined the essential identity of Christianity as an event: "In relation to the absolute, there is only one time, the present; for the person who is not contemporary with the absolute, it does not exist at all. And since Christ is the absolute it is easy to see that in relation to him there is only one situation, the situation of contemporaneity."[39]

The question, then, is: How can the event of Christ, which, by its nature as a historical event, has a location in time and space, remain contemporary, not lose its corporeality and visibility, that is, its historical face, so that it can be met now and fascinate those who meet it as it did at the beginning? The episode of the disciples of Emmaus is the answer to this question. In it we see how, when the presence of Christ disappeared from the horizon of those whom he had fascinated, the disciples returned home disillusioned. Even though they had recognized him as "a prophet mighty in deed and word," his execution had so bewildered them as to shatter their hope.[40] The expression "we had hoped" would have forever remained as the epitaph of the adventure they had experienced, had something unexpected not happened, something on which no one was counting: his living presence. In order to explain the disciples' coming together after the scandal of Jesus' death, the desire to advance his cause is not enough, nor is the goal of disseminating his teachings, nor the interest in spreading his inspiration. None of these reasons would have been sufficient to rebuild the group and infuse it with the missionary impetus that characterized it from the beginning, and which is the sole justification for such a rapid spread of Christianity. It is enough to let the facts speak for themselves: how were the disciples able to overcome the scandal of the cross? Only through the grandeur of the Risen One.[41] Similarly, without the presence of the living Christ,[42] the missionary momentum and development would not be conceivable.

We are therefore faced with a human reality whose only adequate explanation is the imposing living presence of Christ, who, by the power of his Spirit, generates the Christian communities that will make him present in history. It cannot be reduced to an organization, even if from the beginning there appears to have been one, or to a pure inner inspiration, because from the beginning it is a sociologically identifiable reality, one that would not have existed if the risen Christ had not touched each of them, one by one, with his living presence. The episode of the apostle Thomas is an effective reminder of this.

The *Catechism of the Catholic Church* explains how Christ decided to remain among us: "When his visible presence was taken from them, Jesus did not leave his disciples orphans (cf. Jn 14:18). He promised to remain with them until the end of time (cf. Mt 28:20), he sent them his Spirit (cf. Jn 20:22; Acts 2:33). As a result communion with Jesus has become, in a way, more intense: 'By communicating his Spirit, Christ mystically constitutes as his body those brothers of his who are called together from every nation (*Lumen Gentium*, 7).'"[43] This is why John Paul II could say, "Christ's relevance for people of all times is shown forth in his body, which is the Church."[44] Christ remains present in his Church, making possible the contemporaneity that allows people of every age to come into direct relationship with him, following the same sacramental method that he used historically to reveal himself. Through Baptism Christ continues to incorporate us into himself by making us his body in history. "For as many of you as were baptized into Christ have put on Christ. There is neither Jew nor Greek, there is neither slave nor free, there is neither male nor female; for you are all one in Christ Jesus."[45]

In the Church—the Second Vatican Council reminds us—"the life of Christ is poured into the believers who, through the sacraments, are united in a hidden and real way to Christ who suffered and was glorified."[46] Christ's life is communicated to us in a manner so real that we are transformed into "a new creature" (2 Cor 5:17).[47] Through this transformation, impossible through man's strength alone, Christ demonstrates his presence now. The Church has a clear awareness that she is "a transparent sign of Christ for the world," not finding her consistency in herself, but in him. "This is her mission and her path: to be among men and women an ever greater presence of Christ."[48]

"The event of Christ becomes present 'now' in a phenomenon of a different humanity: a man runs up against you and discovers in you a new presentiment of life. . . . This running into a different humanity is very simple, absolutely elementary, something that comes before everything, before any catechesis, reflection, or development.

It's something that has no need of explanation, but just needs to be seen, intercepted. It is something that evokes wonder, awakens an emotion, constitutes a call, moves a person to follow because it corresponds to the structurally expectant awaiting of the heart."[49]

It is necessary to capture this presentiment of new life on the face and in the life of a real person. Without the contemporaneity of Christ's presence in a humanity that he has changed, it would be impossible to reasonably belong to the Christian faith, because it would be impossible to verify here and now its ability to respond to the longing for fulfillment that everyone, in one way or another, secretly nourishes. The fulfillment of humanity accomplished in a person demonstrates that what we desire exists as something accessible, something that you can touch, see, and recognize. This is what makes it possible for Christianity to be transmitted, to form a tradition, which is not just the transmission of doctrines, but the original experience happening anew: the encounter with a different humanity. The relationship with this new humanity is what allows us to participate in his newness and then to discover the reasons that make it reasonable for us to belong to Christ today, the human advantage of the faith.

This verification does not require any particular talent, nor does it require us to disregard anything human in us. Indeed, it can be carried out only if we bring to the table everything that we are, without leaving anything behind. Only then can we discover just who Christ is, through the ability that he has to reveal the mystery of our "I," to respond to the demands of our being, leading it to a fullness that we cannot achieve alone. "The man who wishes to understand himself thoroughly—and not just in accordance with immediate, partial, often superficial, and even illusory standards and measures of his being—he must with his unrest, uncertainty and even his weakness and sinfulness, with his life and death, draw near to Christ. He must, so to speak, enter into him with all his own self, he must 'appropriate' and assimilate the whole of the reality of the Incarnation and Redemption in order to find himself. If this profound process takes place within him, he then bears fruit not only of adoration of God but also of deep wonder at himself. . . . The name for that deep amazement at man's worth and dignity is the Gospel."[50] Whoever lives this experience will easily identify with the expression of the Roman rhetorician, Marius Victorinus: "When I met Christ I discovered myself a man."[51]

The Christian faith, therefore, not only does not fear the full use of reason (and, with it, that of freedom and affection), but demands it. Because in order to communicate in a human way, faith needs a person who uses reason to the fullest, who involves herself totally with her freedom in order to experience the newness it brings with it, and who is so authentically critical as to be willing to submit reason to living experience. The Christian faith requires that we use our heart, with all the needs that constitute it, so that we can seize the event of Christ as it happens before our eyes. Without our humanity the Christian faith would not exist, especially today, at a time when it is so deeply challenged and under siege.

Through the different humanity that he makes possible, Christ draws us and so prepares his new witnesses in his Church, as Cardinal Newman ingeniously noted:

> These are they whom our Lord especially calls His "elect," and came to "gather together in one," for they are worthy. And these, too, are they who are ordained in God's Providence to be the salt of the earth—to continue, in their turn, the succession of His witnesses, that heirs may never be wanting to the royal line though death sweeps away each successive generation of them to their rest and their reward. These, perhaps, by chance fell in with their destined father in the Truth, not at once discerning his real greatness. At first, perhaps, they thought his teaching fanciful, and parts of his conduct extravagant or weak. Years might pass away before such prejudices were entirely removed from their minds; but by degrees they would discern more and more the traces of unearthly majesty about him; they would witness, from time to time, his trial under the various events of life, and would still find, whether they looked above or below, that he rose higher, and was based deeper, than they could ascertain by measurement.

The great convert thus concludes: "Then, at length, with astonishment and fear, they would become aware that Christ's presence was before them [that the Christ's presence was in them]; and, in the words of Scripture, would glorify God in His servant (Gal 1:24); and all this while they themselves would be changing into that glorious Image which they gazed upon, and be in training to succeed him in its propagation."[52]

This communication to others has no foundation other than the attraction to Christ that the witness experiences. "For the love of Christ controls us, because we are convinced that one has died for all; therefore all have died. And he died for all, that those who live might live no longer for themselves but for him who for their sake died and was raised."[53]

Only this experience can generate a new protagonist in history, a person who is free, stable, independent from the common mentality, capable of becoming the subject of his own liberation, that is, able to take the initiative to create works that respond to the needs of all and can generate dignified work. These initiatives arise only when one has the courage to say "I," because they are an expression of passionate self-giving, of charity, of a new creation.[54] No sociological analysis, no moralism, no ideology is able to bring about in history a similar type of person. At this time, when the human being's degradation is progressing and there are no places of true education, the Church has the opportunity to show her true face, the power and beauty of the life that flows through her veins. She needs to not betray her true nature and to testify to Christianity as an event, that is, as something happening now that is able to kindle such an interest in people as to give them an awareness of self and of reality that transforms them into true protagonists of history.

The Method of Christian Presence in a Pluralistic Society: Witness

This experience of life is precisely what we are called to witness to in a situation where so many people of various ideological positions are looking for a way out of the confusion. This is the basic task of

Christians in a pluralistic society: to be ourselves, witnessing to the new life that springs from the encounter with Christ. "What is the specific and fundamental contribution of the Church to that Europe which for half a century has been moving towards new forms and projects? Her contribution is centered on a simple and decisive reality: God exists and he has given us life. He alone is absolute, faithful and unfailing love, that infinite goal that is glimpsed behind the good, the true and the beautiful things of this world, admirable indeed, but insufficient for the human heart." He alone, therefore, is able to meet the expectations of our heart and make it happy: "We have no greater treasure to offer to our contemporaries."[55] The novelty of Christianity cannot be reduced to ethical coherence. If our presence is not a witness to the fullness of life and the change of mentality that faith brings to dealing with all circumstances, its effect will be minimal. "The contribution of Christians can be effective only if knowledge of faith becomes knowledge of reality."[56]

A protagonist such as we have described is not afraid of having to live in today's cultural pluralism. And even less does he feel oppressed by presumption or complaint. It is in this context of human crisis, of mysterious lethargy and invincible boredom, that the Christian faith can show all its benefit to humanity. That will happen if we are able to communicate through an experience that faith makes life more human, more intense, more worth living. God is not "man's antagonist and an enemy of his freedom,"[57] but is, rather, the only one able to save him, exalting his dignity and his freedom. The contemporary crossroads is a providential opportunity for us Christians to discover the true nature of Christianity and its anthropological relevance, and to communicate it to our brothers as life experience. As we have seen, after the incarnation, through which concepts (we could also say values) have become "flesh" and "blood," there is no other way to communicate the truth except as embodied in our lives. This is called "witness," the category by which we understand our presence as Christians in society.

To understand what kind of presence we need in order to witness to Christ today, it may be useful to keep one observation in mind. Often, when we have to defend something in the context of a debate, in order to make our response stronger, we almost unconsciously accept the way the other frames the issue. In doing so, we allow our position to be determined by its opposition. It is reactive instead of being original, that is, instead of being a position that comes from our experience of faith. This leads to further reducing Christianity or its testimony to the mere repetition of a doctrine, of some values or ethics. With his usual realism, Benedict XVI warns that, even if the defense of principles is "essential and indispensable," that is not enough to arouse interest in them. "Simply proclaiming the message does not penetrate to the depths of people's hearts, it does not touch their freedom, it does not change their lives. What attracts is, above all, the encounter with believing persons who, through their faith, draw others to the grace of Christ by bearing witness to him."[58] Each of us knows from experience that only the testimony of the beauty of a changed life can attract people to Christ.[59]

The encounter with people who are different from others, in whose lives you can see a new intelligence about reality, a fully awakened desire, a tireless initiative, a capacity for tenderness, an embrace full of intensity, and freedom normally impossible to find elsewhere, leaves no one indifferent. The Byzantine theologian Nicolas Kabasilas describes such people with these words: "When men have a longing so great that it surpasses human nature and eagerly desire and are able to accomplish things beyond human thought, it is the Bridegroom who has smitten them with this longing. It is he who has sent a ray of his beauty into their eyes. The greatness of the wound already shows the arrow which has struck home, the longing indicates who has inflicted the wound."[60] The intensity of longing aroused in those who let themselves be seized by Christ allows them to intuit who Christ is: one who awakens our humanity from apathy and indifference in order to bring it to its fullness. The encounter with the beauty of Christ that shines through the face of a human being can become an arrow that wounds the soul, and so opens our eyes, allowing us to recognize him. This is what each of us is longing for, and our contemporaries together with us. We will be able to communicate this only by yielding to his attraction.

CHAPTER 6

———◆◆◆◆◆———

The Religious Sense, Verification of the Faith

Is the event of Christ capable of reawakening the self from its numbness, from its invincible boredom?

"[When I] see the stars burn up in heaven, / I ask myself: / 'Why all these lights, / What does the endless air do, and that deep / eternal blue? What is the meaning of / this huge solitude? And what am I?'"[1] This poem by Giacomo Leopardi splendidly expresses the experience in which our religious sense reveals itself. The impact of the "I" with reality unleashes the human question. The impact with reality inexorably sets in motion an inborn structure within us, and it mobilizes the whole dynamism of our person.

To the extent that we live, none of us, from whatever ethnic or cultural background, can avoid certain questions. "'What is the ultimate meaning of existence? Why is there pain and death? Deep down, why is life worth living?' Or, from another point of view: 'What does reality really consist of and what is it made for?'" The religious sense is the nature of our "I" inasmuch as it expresses itself in these questions; "*it coincides with the radical engagement of the self with life, an involvement which exemplifies itself in these questions.*"[2]

But why should we read *The Religious Sense* again now, in this precise moment of history? Everything sprang from the observation of a fragility of faith as a form of knowledge, a fragility characterized by a break between knowing and believing. And not just in others, but in us, too, even though we have the grace of being immersed in a certain history. "The crisis in Christian preaching, which we have experienced in growing proportions for a century, is based, in no small part, on the fact that the Christian answers have ignored man's questions: they [the answers] were and remain right, but because they were not developed from and within the question, they remain ineffective."[3] He concluded that "to question along with man who seeks is an indispensable part of preaching itself, because only in this way can the word (in German *Wort*) become an answer (*Ant-wort*)."

We, too, participate in the reduction of faith to feelings or ethics. This happens not only when Christianity is no longer proposed according to its nature as an event, but also when something of the human is lacking within us. In fact, there is one big inconvenience to Christianity: it requires human beings in order for it to be recognized and lived.

We're accustomed to understanding "religious sense" as a simple premise to faith. Therefore, it seems almost useless to us once we have reached faith, as if it were a staircase for going up to the next floor: once we've gone up, we can do without the stairs. No! Not only is a constantly alive religious sense needed for Christianity to be acknowledged and experienced for what it is—as Fr. Giussani always reminded us, quoting Niebuhr: "Nothing is so incredible as an answer to an unasked question,"[4] or one that we don't ask any more—but also, it is precisely in the encounter with the Christian event that the religious sense is revealed in all its original importance, reaches an ultimate clarity, is educated, and is saved. Christ came to educate us to the religious sense. A lively religious sense therefore means a verification of faith.

In this sense Fr. Giussani's answer to a question posed by Angelo Scola during a long interview he gave in 1987 is very meaningful.

"The fulcrum of your pedagogical proposal," said Scola, "is the religious sense of the person, isn't that right?" Giussani replied: "The heart of our proposal is rather the announcement of an event that happened, that surprises people in the same way the angel's announcement in Bethlehem surprised the poor shepherds two thousand years ago. [It is] an event that happens, prior to any consideration whether a person is religious or nonreligious. It is the perception of this event that resurrects or empowers the elementary sense of dependence and the nucleus of original evidences that we call the 'religious sense.'"[5] Therefore, the Christian event resurrects or empowers the religious sense, that is, the sense of our original dependence and original "evidence."

In fact, the pertinence of faith to life's demands is proven by its capacity to reawaken the "I," to make it become itself, to maintain it in the right position for facing all of existence, including its trials and difficulties.

By rereading *The Religious Sense* and comparing its ideas with our experience, we can verify "how Christ is useful for the journey that people make in their relationship with things, walking toward their destiny. Otherwise, if He doesn't have this influence as a real presence, Christ is something that has nothing to do with life, that wouldn't have anything to do with life. He would have something to do with the afterlife, but He wouldn't have anything to do with this life, which is exactly the position Protestantism takes."[6] If Christ is present, then we must acknowledge him not because of our words, but because of his signs. "He is, if he changes"[7]—this is the rule we have always heard. I can discover that Christ is present by the signs of human reawakening I see happen in me or in others. His presence is as objective as the signs that document it.

We can verify whether the encounter with Christ has "resurrected or empowered" our original sense of dependence, the core of "evidence" and original needs (for truth, justice, happiness, and love) that Fr. Giussani calls "religious sense" and that are awakened in the impact of the "I" with reality. Now, if it is true that these original needs and evidence will in a certain sense emerge inevitably, it is equally true that the awareness of them is normally reduced, obfuscated, or silenced. This is what can be grasped in the weakness or absence of the sense of Mystery in our perception of our "I," which is so tragically reduced—much more often than we realize—to the sum of actions and reactions, of historical and biological antecedents, or to a product of circumstances. This is why a lively religious sense, without repression or rejections, is a sign and verification of the encounter with something else, greater than oneself.

The same can be said of reason, which experience reveals as the "operative need to explain reality in all of its factors so that the human being is introduced to the truth about things."[8] Challenged by the impact with reality to be truly itself (according to its nature, "unexhausted openness") and to set itself into motion in search for the exhaustive explanation of what exists, reason reaches its authentic apex when it intuits the existence of a beyond from which everything flows and to which everything points. "The summit of reason's conquest is the perception of an unknown unreachable presence, to which all human movement is destined, because it depends upon it. It is the idea of mystery."[9] A person who does not block the rational dynamism set in motion by the impact with reality will come to live an awareness of Mystery. The more intensely she lives reality, the more the dimension of mystery will become familiar to her.

But, here too, we are almost irresistibly tempted to reduce, to use reason as a measure, instead of as a window thrown open "before the unexhausted call of the real."[10] The inevitable consequence is the reduction of the perception of reality. We can observe this in the "destitution of the visible," in the way we normally flatten or empty the circumstances and the things that happen. Reality, which presents itself originally to our reason as sign, is reduced to its immediately perceivable aspect, deprived of its meaning and depth. For this reason—as each of us can confirm from our own experience—we often suffocate within circumstances. When reality is reduced to appearance, it becomes a cage.

As then-Cardinal Ratzinger observed years ago, "By no means the least important practical function of faith is to offer healing for the reason as reason, not to overpower it or to remain outside it, but in fact to bring it to itself again."[11] The exaltation of reason, freedom from its reductions, is again the verification of a real faith.

Now, why is the reawakening of the religious sense so decisive today? Why do we feel its urgency? It is decisive because the religious sense is the ultimate criterion of every judgment, of a judgment that is true and authentically "mine." If we do not want to be "cheated, alienated, enslaved by others, or exploited,"[12] we must become accustomed to comparing everything with that immanent and objective criterion that is the religious sense. After the Christian encounter, we continue to live in the world and are called, just like everyone else, to face the challenges of life. We must face them in this particular moment in history, dominated by confusion and the "decline of desire," characterized by a suffocating rationalism on the one hand (the reduction of reality to appearance), and by spreading sentimentalism on the other (the reduction of the heart to feelings). If Christ is not incisive in our life, reawakening our humanity, broadening our reason and impeding the flattening of reality, we find ourselves thinking the same way as everyone else, with the same mentality as everyone, because the criterion of judgment we originally possess, the "heart," which is reason and affection together, is wrapped in this confusion. This means that we can continue to affirm the "truths" of the faith without being protagonists in history, because there is no appreciable difference in us.

In addition to rendering us useless for history (increasingly dominated by a power that aims to throw people into confusion, to reduce their desire and promote a reduced use of reason), this provokes the question of the reasonableness of the faith. Why is it reasonable to be Christians? Why is faith to our advantage, humanly speaking? The reason many abandon the faith is that they discover no trace of this advantage. Thus, power can continually expand its influence, finding people increasingly disarmed. "It is as if power, that is, the dominant mentality, forced our educators, parents included, to alter the simplicity of our nature [the 'original' evidence, we said in chap. 1] ever since we were children. Therefore, we need to recover the simplicity of our nature. *The Religious Sense* is nothing more than an invitation and prompt to recover the simplicity, the authenticity of our nature (not by coincidence, the third premise of *The Religious Sense* refers to the morality necessary for gaining knowledge as 'poverty of spirit')."[13]

We may become accomplices in the influence of power if we presumptuously think we can make it on our own, without an intelligent and affective following of the one thing the Mystery gave us to tear us away from nothingness: the encounter and the living experience of Church, through which Christ has touched our lives so persuasively. Even among us, the confusion can be so deep that when we try to point to a solution for the situation we live in, we find ourselves repeating the same answers as everyone else: some think the solution is to come to an agreement ("to be together"), others think it is found in politics, in greater participation in the distribution of power, or in a career, or in a new love affair, and so on. After two thousand years of Christian history, we could find ourselves in the same situation humankind was in before Christ: an unbounded variety of ultimately futile efforts, in which people emphasize their prejudices or the aspects most consonant with their personality.

"Who will deliver me from this mortal condition?" (see Rom. 7:24), we would ask along with Saint Paul. What is necessary for us? What experience? Christ saves us from this variety of ultimately futile efforts. Let us try to return to the origin.

Christ Clarifies the Religious Sense

Inviting us to put ourselves inside the events of Saint John's Gospel, Fr. Giussani magnificently describes how it happened.

> At last came this John, called the Baptist, living in such a way that all the people were struck by him, and, from the Pharisees to the humblest peasant, they left their homes to go hear him speak, at least once. That day, we don't know whether there were many or a few, but two of them were there for the first time, and they were entirely eager, open-mouthed, like people who had come from far away, and look at what they came to see with boundless curiosity, with a poverty of spirit, with childishness and simplicity of heart. . . . At a certain point, a person breaks off from the group and goes off along the path by the river. As the person moves away, the prophet John the

Baptist, suddenly inspired, starts shouting: "That is the Lamb of God who takes away the sins of the world." The people don't take much notice. . . . But those two, open-mouthed, with eyes wide open like children, they see where the Baptist's eyes are looking: at that man who is walking away. So, instinctively, they set off after him, they follow him, timid and a little embarrassed. He notices that someone is following him. He turns around: "What do you want?" "Master," they reply, "where do you live?" "Come and see," he says kindly. They went "and saw where He lived, and stayed the whole of that day with Him." We can easily identify with those two sitting there, watching that man speak, saying things they had never heard before, but that were so close, so fitting, so resounding. . . . They did not understand; they were simply captivated, drawn, overwhelmed by him speaking. They watched him speak. Because it is by "watching" . . . that some people realized that amongst them there was something indescribable: a Presence not only unmistakable but incomprehensible, and yet so penetrating. Penetrating because it corresponded to what their heart was waiting for, in a way beyond all compare. When they were little, their fathers and mothers had never told them with such evidence and effectiveness what it was that would make the years of their lives worth living. They hadn't been able to, couldn't have known how; they had said many other right and good things, but like fragments of something they had to try to grasp in the air to see if one matched with the other. A profound correspondence. . . . Little by little, as the words came to them and their eyes, full of wonder and admiration, penetrated that man, they felt themselves changing, felt that things were changing: the meaning of things changed, the echo of things changed, the journey of things changed.[14]

The account does not end here, because Giussani imagines John and Andrew going home after meeting Christ.

And when they went home that evening, as the day came to an end—most likely walking along in silence, because they had never spoken to each other as they did in that great silence in which an Other was speaking, in which He went on speaking and echoing within them—and they reached home, Andrew's wife saw him and said, "What's happened to you, Andrew? What is it?" And his children, too, looked at their father astonished: he was himself, it's true; he was himself, but he was "more" himself; he was different. He was himself, but different. And when . . . she asked him, "What happened?" he embraced her. Andrew held his wife and kissed his children: it was him, but he had never held her like that! It was like the dawning or the daybreak of a different humanity, of a new humanity, of a truer humanity. It was as if he were saying, "At last!" without believing his own eyes. But it was too obvious for him not to believe his own eyes![15]

This scene describes, far better than a lecture ever could, how the religious sense was clarified, because it had found its true object. By meeting Jesus, Andrew was himself, but "more himself." He was different. For "the object of the religious sense is ultimately the unfathomable mystery. So it is understandable that man should think of it in such a way as to have a thousand thoughts about it. But the truth is one. However, since it is impossible for man to reach it, the Mystery became a human fact, became a man, a man who moved with his legs, who ate with his mouth, who wept with his eyes, and who died. This is the true object of the religious sense. So, in discovering this fact of Christ, the religious sense is also marvelously revealed, clarified for me."[16]

This is nothing more than the application of a universal law, a law in effect since the time human beings were human beings: "A person rediscovers himself in a living encounter."[17] But here, in the encounter with the presence of the Mystery become a human fact, this law is fulfilled, becomes definitively true, because "it is in an encounter that I become aware of myself. . . . The 'I' awakens from its imprisonment in its original womb, awakens from its tomb, from its sepulcher, from its closed situation of origin and—as it were—'resurrects,' becomes aware of itself, precisely in an encounter. The result of an encounter is that the sense of the person is kindled. It is as if the person were being born: he is not born in the encounter, but there he becomes aware of himself, so he is born as personality."[18]

This encounter enables us to discover the mystery of our "I." "He was himself, but even more himself"; he had never been so much himself. Thus, during a conversation, referring to the text of *The Religious Sense*, Fr. Giussani wondered,

> Why were we the ones to write a book about the religious sense . . . ? Because we encountered Jesus, and, looking at him and listening to him, we have understood what was inside us: "Whoever knows you knows himself," Saint Augustine said. . . . Because in order to know the religious sense and develop the religious sense we had to encounter someone; without this "master" we would not have understood ourselves. Thus I can say to Christ, "You really are me." I can say "You are me" to him because, in listening to him, I have understood myself. Whereas those who try to understand themselves by reflecting on themselves get lost in a thousand paths, a thousand ideas, a thousand images.[19]

Christ Educates the Religious Sense

Precisely because Christ reveals and clarifies man's religious sense, he can also educate it. Someone might think—even someone who has already encountered Christ or lives in a Christian context—that since the religious sense is an original endowment, there is no need for it to be educated or that, once it has been awakened, it works on its own, spontaneously becoming the dimension of every instant. But it is important to understand how abstract that notion is:

> During a conversation I had with a leading university professor, he let slip this remark: "If I didn't have chemistry, I would kill myself." In the very way we take things in something like this is always at play, even if we are not aware of it. There is always

something which makes our lives worth living in our own eyes, and while we might not reach the point of wishing to die, without it everything would be colorless and disappointing. Man offers all his devotion to that "something", whatever it may be. No one can avoid being ultimately implicated in all one's actions and, whatever it may be, the moment the human conscience corresponds to it in life, a religiosity is expressed; a level of religiosity is attained. The characteristic proper to the religious sense is that of being the ultimate, inevitable dimension of every gesture, of every action, of every type of relationship.[20]

But we would be mistaken if we thought this was something that did not need to be constantly evoked. In the absence of proper education, its prodding becomes weakened and its scope of action progressively reduces. "The proof that the religious sense is not adequately educated . . . can be found in this precise point: there exists a repugnance in us, a repugnance that has become instinctive, towards the idea that the religious sense might dominate, might consciously determine our every action. This is none other than a symptom of atrophy and merely the partial development of the religious sense in us. It is that widespread burdensome difficulty, that sense of extraneousness we feel when we hear it said that "god" is all determining, the factor we cannot escape, the criterion by which we make choices, study, produce in our working lives, join a political party, carry out scientific research, look for a wife, or a husband, or govern a nation."[21]

Each person can evaluate for herself the extent of her repugnance towards letting one's whole life be determined by God. In this way, we will understand how much we need to let ourselves be educated to the religious sense. In fact, "Education of the religious sense, on the one hand, should foster the awareness of the fact that an inevitable and total dependence exists between man and what gives meaning to man's life. On the other hand, it would help man, through time, to expunge that unrealistic sense of extraneousness he feels towards his original situation."[22]

The reason for the incarnation, then, can be understood. "God's aim in becoming man was to educate people to the religious sense, because the religious sense is the exact point of departure that people have for traveling towards all of reality and towards the very Mystery that makes reality. Therefore, following Christ means being in the best condition for facing reality and walking toward destiny in the best of ways: it is called salvation, as we have called it here, not in the definitive sense of the word, but in the operative sense of the term. Those who follow Christ are in the best condition for facing reality and facing the problem of destiny."[23]

How are we educated to the religious sense today? By participating in the life of that reality where Christ remains contemporary: the Church. "The Church's function on the world scene is already implicit in its awareness that it is the protraction of Christ: this means that it has the same function as Jesus in history, which is to educate all men and women to the religious sense, precisely in order to be able to 'save' them. In this context, the religious sense or religiosity means . . . man's exact position towards his own destiny in terms of consciousness and his attempt to live it in practical terms."[24]

Therefore, it is necessary that the Mystery be a permanent presence in history. If Christ does not remain contemporary and does not go on challenging man, man returns to being irremediably alone, and each of us knows how far we can fall if we are alone.

How can we free ourselves from this inexorable decay? None of us, by our own efforts, can keep ourselves in the right position, even though the encounter with Christ has opened us up to it. The only answer to our fragility is the real permanence of his presence.

Christ Saves the Religious Sense

The historical situation in which we find ourselves today in the West, characterized by the weakening of what is human, is a true challenge for Christianity as well, as Christianity is forced to show the truth of its claim of answering the human being's needs. Not just any version of Christianity will be capable of reawakening humanity (we know this well). Neither a Christianity reduced to ideas ("notional" Christianity, as Newman called it) nor a Christianity reduced to ethics will be able to bring people out of their listlessness (in his address to the Roman Curia on December 20, 2010, Pope Benedict XVI spoke of the "sleep of a faith grown tired"),[25] out of the ever-more-egregious flattening-out of their desire, of their original impetus, of their zest for living. It is in Christianity's capacity to continually reawaken what is human that its authenticity will be shown.

Only a Christianity that preserves its original nature, its unmistakable traits of contemporary historical presence—the contemporaneousness of Christ—can be equal to the real need of men and women, and will therefore be able to save the religious sense. It is not a matter of accepting a postulate but of discovering a human newness in action. The Christian announcement submits itself to this test, submits itself to the tribunal of human experience. If something happens in people who accept belonging to Christ through the reality of the Church, something that has concretely and persuasively emerged in their own experience (thanks to their encounter with a charism), something that they could not achieve by their own powers—an inconceivable reawakening and fulfillment of humanity in all its fundamental dimensions—then Christianity will reveal itself to be credible, and its claim becomes verifiable. "For every tree is known by its own fruit."[26] This is the formidable epistemological criterion that Jesus himself offers us.

The change generated by the relationship with Christ present is such that Saint Paul did not hesitate to exclaim, "Whoever is in Christ is a new creation: the old things have passed away; behold, new things have come."[27] The new creature is the person in whom the religious sense is realized in its (otherwise impossible) fullness: reason, freedom, affection, and desire. "Christ is so beautiful that he draws me totally!"[28] exclaimed Jacopone da Todi. This beauty, as the splendor of truth, is the only thing able to reawaken people's desire and move their affection so powerfully as to make the openness of their reason to the reality before them continually possible. "The condition for reason to be reason is that affection impact it and so move the whole person."[29] The attraction of Christ facilitates an openness that would be impossible without him (it doesn't bring it about automatically).

Christ's contemporaneous presence allows reason to be used in all its openness, enabling it to reach an intelligence of reality unknown before. Every thing, every circumstance, even the most banal, is exalted, becomes a sign, "speaks," becomes interesting to experience. The person awakened and sustained by the presence of Christ can finally live as a religious person, can endure the vertigo of life, circumstance after circumstance, because he or she is able to "enter any situation whatsoever with profound tranquility, with the possibility of joy."[30] Thus, Christ's contemporaneousness is indispensable for fully living the religious sense, that is to say, for having the right attitude before reality.

If, on the contrary, Christ is not encountered and lived with as contemporary, the consequences are not long in coming. The lack of experience of Christ's ongoing presence makes us return to the situation before the Christian encounter, and even if we keep talking about Christ (as often happens), we reduce him de facto to one of the many variants of the religious sense. "To the modern man [this is a truly keen observation, which makes us aware of the situation we are experiencing], 'faith' would generically be nothing more than an aspect of religious experience, a kind of feeling with which he could live out the restless search for his origin and his destiny, which is precisely the most appealing element of every 'religion.' All modern consciousness is bent on tearing the hypothesis of Christian faith away from man, and on reducing faith to the dynamic of the religious sense and to the concept of religious experience. Unfortunately this confusion also penetrates the mentality of Christian people."[31]

There is an essential and irreducible difference between the dynamics of faith and those of the religious sense. "While religiosity is born of the need for meaning awakened by the impact with reality, faith is the acknowledgment of an exceptional Presence that corresponds totally to our destiny, and adherence to this Presence. Faith is acknowledging as true what a historical Presence says of itself."[32] This difference can be seen above all in the way reason acts. In Christian faith, there is no longer a reason that explains, but a reason that opens itself up to the very self-revelation of God, perceiving that in this way it is at last fulfilled in its dynamics.

Thus, it is clear why Fr. Giussani said that "the whole problem of intelligence [not of feelings or moods] is there"[33] in the episode of John and Andrew, in the encounter between the two men and that man who was beyond compare. Faith is an act of reason moved by the exceptional nature of a Presence.

> Christian faith is the memory of a historical fact: a Man said of Himself something that others accepted as true and that now I, too, accept because of the exceptional way in which that fact still reaches me. Jesus is a man who said, "I am the way, the truth, and the life." He is a Fact that happened in history: a child, born of woman, registered in the Bethlehem birth registry, who, once He had grown up, announced He was God: "The Father and I are one." Paying attention to what that Man did and said, so as to come to say, "I believe in this Man," adhering to His Presence and affirming what He said as the truth: this is faith.[34]

So,

> just think what a challenge the claim of faith represents for the modern mentality: that a man should exist—to whom I can say "You"—who says, "Without Me, you can do nothing," that a man should exist who is Man-God. We can never measure ourselves completely against this claim; today, neither the people nor the greatest philosophers tackle this problem any longer, and if they do so at all, it is in order to consolidate the negative preconception inherited from the dominant mentality. In other words, the answer to the Christian problem "Who is Jesus?" is deduced from pre-constituted conceptions about the human person and the world. Yet Jesus' answer is, "Look at My works"; in other words, "Look at Me," which is the same. Instead, people don't look Him in the face; they eliminate Him before taking Him into consideration. Unbelief is therefore a corollary deriving from a preconception; it is an applied preconception, not the conclusion of a rational inquiry.[35]

But what interests us above all now is to focus on the consequence of refusing the way God chose to respond to the person's need for total meaning, a need inherent in the religious sense. "Without acknowledgment of the present Mystery, night advances, confusion advances, and—as such, at the level of freedom—rebellion advances, or disappointment so fills up the measure that it is as if we hope for nothing more, and we live without desiring anything, apart from the furtive satisfaction or the furtive answer to a brief request."[36] If we do not acknowledge Christ's contemporaneousness, then true humanity, the drive of the religious sense, fades. On the contrary, those who acknowledge it see their humanity brought beyond their wildest imagination. "Saying that our consciousness, our way of thinking, and our affection, our way of loving, are converted to Christ means that this consciousness and this affection are constantly brought, transported where they would not have imagined. They are constantly asked to come out of themselves, they go beyond themselves. They are constantly brought within a terrain, within a territory beyond anything they ever conceived or felt before. They are always being introduced into the unknown; it is a measure that broadens: consciousness and affectivity are constantly introduced into an unforeseen horizon, beyond their own measure."[37] And life acquires a breathing room, importance, and intensity that it has never known before.

These passages represent both a description and a promise. Each of us has the criterion for verifying our journey of faith, our education to the religious sense: the exaltation of our original humanity. "Amen, I say to you, unless you turn and become like children, you will not enter the kingdom of heaven."[38] This could be the formula that summarizes a true education of the religious sense. And this is why Christ calls those who live with that original openness blessed: "Blessed are the poor in spirit, for theirs is the kingdom of heaven."[39] These lines show us the true purpose of educating the religious sense: to open our self completely so that we can be filled with a reality we ourselves cannot produce, but that we must accept, welcome, and embrace as a gift. Only those with this simplicity of a child, this poverty of spirit, have the disposition to welcome it. Our fulfillment as persons and whatever contribution we can make to our human brothers and sisters will depend on this.

CHAPTER 7

———◆•◆•◆———

The "Eternal Mystery of Our Being"

The Confusion of the "I"

"Behind the word 'I' today there is a great confusion, and yet it is of prime interest to understand what *my subject* is. In fact, my subject is at the center, at the root of every action of mine (thought is an action, too). Action is the dynamic with which I enter into relationship with any person or thing. If I neglect my own 'I,' it is impossible for relationships with life to be mine, for life itself (the sky, my spouse, my friend, music) to be mine . . . : by now the very word 'I' evokes for the great majority of people something confused and drifting, a term used for convenience with a purely indicative value (like 'bottle' or 'glass'). But behind the little word there no longer vibrates anything that powerfully and clearly indicates what type of concept and sentiment a person has of the value of his or her own self. For this reason it can be said that we live in times in which a civilization seems to be ending: in fact, a civilization is evolved in the degree to which it promotes the emergence and clarification of the value of the individual self. We are in an age that promotes, instead, a great confusion about the contents of the word 'I.'"[1]

This confusion is described—to give an example among many—in the following passage from Philip Roth's novel, *The Counterlife*:

> All I can tell you with certainty is that I, for one, have no self, and that I am unwilling or unable to perpetrate upon myself the joke of a self. It certainly does strike me as a joke about my self. What I have instead is a variety of impersonations I can do, and not only of myself—a troupe of players that I have internalized, a permanent company of actors that I can call upon when a self is required, an ever-evolving stock of pieces and parts that forms my repertoire. But I certainly have no self independent of my imposturing, artistic efforts to have one. Nor would I want one. I am a theatre and nothing more than a theatre.[2]

An experience that does not respond to this widespread mentality, even if we attend a great number of meetings and take part in many initiatives, is defeated! Today we are witnessing the eclipse of humanity, as Abraham Heschel says: "The inability to sense our spiritual relevance . . . is itself a dreadful punishment,"[3] one that we suffer every day.

Why has this happened?

The first observation at the beginning of every serious inquiry about the makeup of one's own subject is that the confusion that dominates today behind the fragile mask (almost a *flatus vocis*) of our "I" comes in part from an influence external to our person. It is important to keep clearly in mind the decisive influence on us of what the Gospel calls 'the world,' and that shows itself to be the enemy of the stable, dignified, and consistent formation of a human personality. There is a very strong pressure by the world that surrounds us (through the mass media, or school and politics) that influences and ends up hampering—as a prejudice—any attempt to become aware of one's own "I."[4]

What is this external influence, this "world"? It is what Pasolini called power, which does not remain outside us (as Bernanos said of the dominant opinion: "Before power, energies wear down, characters become impoverished, sincerities lose their clarity"),[5] but on the contrary, penetrates us so deeply that we become strangers to ourselves. Would that it were only an external persecution, and that our self-awareness remained intact!

This is how power goes to work on the self: "The common mentality, created by the mass media and the whole network of instruments held by power—which it strengthens constantly, so much so that John Paul II had cause to say that the danger of our era is the abolition of man by power—alters the sense of self, the sentiment of self, or, more precisely, atrophies the religious sense, atrophies the heart, or, better, totally anesthetizes it (an anesthesia that can become a coma, but is anesthesia)."[6]

The sign of this alteration of the sense of self, of this extraneousness from ourselves, is the consequent reading we do of our needs. In deciphering our needs, "all too easily we do not start from our true experience; that is, from our experience in its entirety and authenticity. We often identify our experience with partial impressions, truncating it, as often happens with affective matters, when we fall in love or dream about the future. Even more often we confuse our experience with the prejudices or schemes that we absorb from our environment perhaps unawares." These prejudices and schemes "coincide" so much with ourselves that we think they are ours; this is how far the influence of power reaches in us! The result is that, "instead of opening up to that attitude of expectation, sincere attention, and dependence that our experience suggests and fervently demands, we impose categories and explanations that constrict and distress our experience, while presuming to resolve it." We impose our schemas on experience: we cover the facts with our comments, rather than trying to understand their meaning; which means, to put it more radically, that there is no experience at all. "The myth that 'scientific progress one day will solve all our needs' is the modern formula of this presumption, a wild and repugnant presumption, because it does not consider or even know our real needs. It refuses to observe our experience clearly and to accept what it means to be human, with all the needs that this implies. For this reason modern civilization causes us to move blindly between this desperate presumption and darkest despair."[7]

The French scholar Olivier Rey says, "We are so used to this misery that most of the time we no longer even feel it."[8] We settle.

Power's influence on us is in direct proportion to our complicit powerlessness. Indeed, "no human achievement can be attributed to mere outside circumstances alone, since man's freedom, albeit made fragile, remains as the indelible mark of God's creature."[9] Original sin weakened my "I," but I remain a creature of God; I do not view myself as a piece of the mechanism of circumstances and power. This means that power has such a strong influence on us in part because of our complicity. But what could seem like harsh criticism is actually a resource for us. The human person is not ultimately defeated.

> We don't talk about power because we are afraid; we talk about power because we have to wake up from our slumber. Power's strength is our impotence. . . . We do not fear power; we fear people who sleep and, therefore, allow power to do what it pleases with them. Power puts everyone to sleep, as much as possible. Its great system, the great method is that of putting to sleep, anesthetizing, or, better yet, atrophying. Atrophying what? Atrophying the heart of the human person, our needs and desires, imposing an image of desire and need that is different from the boundless urge we have in our heart. And so people grow up limited, pre-concluded, imprisoned, half-corpses from the start—that is, impotent.[10]

This impotence is like the "drowsiness of the disciples" described by Pope Benedict XVI, which "across the centuries . . . opens up possibilities for the power of the Evil One."[11]

How can we know that power is wrong? "You know what is in the human heart, because it is in you. What is the criterion for understanding the truth about the human person[?] . . . It is reflection upon yourself in action [not a correct, clean discourse!]. There is no other!"[12] There is no other! But as Hannah Arendt reminds us, "Unfortunately, it seems to be much easier to condition human behavior and to make people conduct themselves in the most unexpected and outrageous manner, than it is to persuade anybody to learn from experience, as the saying goes; that is, to start thinking and judging instead of applying categories and formulas which are deeply ingrained in our mind."[13] What help we could be to each other if we could truly accompany each other in learning from experience! Only by discovering ourselves in action can we grasp all that we are.

The "Eternal Mystery of Our Being"

In the fifth chapter of *The Religious Sense* Fr. Giussani describes that true nature of the self, of an "I" that is not reduced.[14] As we read it, each of us can make a comparison between the human vibration of an indomitable human being searching for answers and the flattening of desire that we so often find in ourselves, which is the origin of "the bewilderment in the young and cynicism in the adult."[15]

"Nothing is as fascinating as the discovery of the real dimensions of one's own 'I,' nothing so rich in surprises as the discovery of one's own human face."[16] This is a thrilling adventure, but to set out on this adventure and vanquish our extraneousness from ourselves, we need someone to look at our humanity with us, someone who does not balk before it. As one young woman wrote a friend:

> At the moment, I really feel the need to talk with you, now that those questions I kept hidden inside me for so long, closed in and chained, have finally exploded. Finally . . . everything conspired and conspires against me, everything; even my mother told me, "Don't worry, this sadness will pass," or, "Don't think about it." But it never has passed, and I have never stopped thinking about it because it's a gripping need for meaning that never leaves me, and torments me without letting go, every moment of every day, without respite. Everyone has tried to

tame me, tranquilize me, keep me from suffering, and make everything more bearable, to sedate a restless heart that never had any intention of stopping its desiring and asking for more. Then you arrived. I've never had a friend like you. You're the only one who wasn't scared of or scandalized by my pain and my desire for the infinite. Nobody has ever looked at me this way. My heart trembled, vibrated like never before. I was suddenly invaded by the bitter awareness that till now nobody has ever looked at me the way I truly desired; everyone has set aside my uncomfortable need, sharing everything with me except what was indispensable. But a life that doesn't consider my humanity, my most visceral and profound requests, isn't life, nor is it even death; it's only a desperate cry. I can't push aside my search for meaning; otherwise, I'll suffocate. I just can't go on; everything is equal, flat, useless, boring, and terribly unbearable. The encounter with you created in me a demand for my whole life, every second, and I don't want to live for anything less. You ignited a passion in me, a passion never before experienced. I need to have people alongside me who are equal to the thought that dominates my life, people I can talk to about what is truly worthwhile. I want to be with you because you don't reduce me, or deny me, or mortify me; you don't console me and don't try to give me an answer. You don't try to distract me or cheer me up, but you share with me the expectation, the entreaty, the nobility of our pain, the greatness of this unbounded desire and the disproportion it creates. I need you because you make me look in the face, and stay in front of this terrible but dear pain that makes me so human.

Think of the Samaritan woman: the gaze of that Man revealed the true nature of her "thirst"[17] —as this girl's friend did for her.

This example helps us understand that "the starting point for the kind of inquiry which interests us here is one's own experience, oneself-in-action." Starting here, the religious element reveals itself as "the nature of our 'I' in as much as it expresses itself in certain questions: 'What is the ultimate meaning of existence?' or 'Why is there pain and death, and why, in the end, is life worth living?'"[18]

The first characteristic of these questions is that they cannot be uprooted: "These questions attach themselves to the very core of our being. They *cannot be rooted out*, because they constitute the stuff of which we are made." [19] Heschel states, "In spite of failures and frustrations, we continue to be haunted by that irrepressible quest. We can never accept the idea that life is hollow and devoid of meaning."[20] And, as Leopardi says, notwithstanding the universal shipwreck, the question endures, like a "dominant thought": "Like a tower in an empty field, / you stand alone, gigantic, in my thinking." [21] That dominant thought, "terrible but precious," [22] is the clue to something that does not drown in the conflict, that reemerges from the universal shipwreck, something that "the boundless vanity of all" [23] cannot remove. Think of the prodigal son: when he realized the boundless vanity of things, his urgent human need became even stronger than before.

The second characteristic of these questions, then, is that they are *inexhaustible*: they have within them a need for totality. "In these questions, the adjectives and the adverbs are the decisive words: *at its core*, what is the *ultimate* sense of life, *at its core*, what is reality made of? Why is it *really* worthwhile to exist, for reality itself to exist? These types of questions exhaust the energy, all of reason's searching energy. They require a total answer, an answer which covers the entire horizon of reason, exhausting completely the whole 'category of possibility.' And reason, being coherent, will not give in until it has found an exhaustive answer, 'beneath the dense blue / sky, seabirds flash by, never / pausing, driven by images below: / Farther, farther!'"[24] Beginning to recognize this "farther!" sheds new light on the road of life. Fr. Giussani said, commenting on a quote from Montale:

> The problem, in fact, is not to live relationships as if they were "gods," as if they were relationships with the divine; they are relationships with the sign, therefore they cannot fulfill, they can become road, landscape, sign, can point beyond, as Clemente Rebora said in the poem I quoted in *The Religious Sense*: "That is not why, that is not why!" All the things you take tell you "that is not why, that is not why!" And Montale, from a pagan, atheist, point of view, says: All things strangely cry, bear the writing, "Further on." And so they are treated not

as if they say, "I am everything," and this makes one enjoy things more, people, because, for example, it is much more fascinating to be companions on a journey than accomplices in a provisional enjoyment.[25]

Each of us can choose what position to take when facing life. But someone who is truly attentive to experience cannot help but recognize the structural disproportion that constitutes our "I," and which Leopardi incomparably described in these words: "the inability to be satisfied by any worldly thing or, so to speak, by the entire world. To consider the inestimable amplitude of space, the number of worlds, and their astonishing size, then to discover that all this is small and insignificant compared to the capacity of one's own mind; to imagine the infinite number of worlds, the infinite universe; to accuse things always of being inadequate and meaningless; to suffer want, emptiness, and hence *noia*—this seems to me the chief sign of the grandeur and nobility of human nature."[26]

What a sentiment of greatness! "The inexhaustibility of the questions heightens the *contradiction* between the urgent need for an answer and our human limitations in searching for it. And still we willingly read a text inasmuch as those questions vibrate and the drama of our disproportion underlies its theme."[27] This irresolvable contradiction is the "eternal mystery of our being,"[28] the thing that is most lacking today for the reasons above: power's influence on us, with our complicity. God is not missing; the "I" is missing, the sense of the mystery of our "I," the eternal mystery of our being! As a result we have no need of him, and, therefore, we look for answers where everyone else looks for them.

But when you begin to reflectively experience this eternal mystery of your own being, then the confusion that ruins life begins to be defeated and you discover a unique clarity of judgment. Here is a dramatic example from a letter someone wrote me:

[I am] married, with children, and I've fallen in love with a girl. It took me a while to understand it, because deep down I didn't want to admit it, but it's true. I tried to push away this evidence, sticking the label "Christ" on our friendship, but it was clear that it was only a psychological consolation in order not to look at how far my "I" had gone astray. Every fiber of my being vibrates for the face of that person. I started looking at my situation squarely, through and through, to discover the factors that make up my self in action, and I found that I truly am a bottomless need. Not even the face of that girl, so beautiful and pure, can satisfy it. After acknowledging this, the confusion fed by this situation dissolved in an instant, without removing the enormous sacrifice of separating from her and the pain I feel when I think of my wife, whom I love dearly, my sweet children, my friends, and the witnesses to our wedding. For the first time, I perceive deep down the mystery of my being, its infinite vastness and at the same time its nothingness and smallness. The surprise is that, in the midst of all this pain, I see before me the beauty and benefit of the truly human journey you constantly propose to us with a decisiveness and frankness that for me are the greatest sign of God's tenderness for my nothingness. If Christ weren't a real presence for me, I wouldn't be able to look at myself this way, and I am very grateful for this because I don't have to throw out anything of my humanity; on the contrary, everything that is happening to me is a provocation to ask myself to Whom I belong, to Whom I want to give my whole life. I don't want to live anymore like my brainwaves are flatlining.

Having this awareness is the only way that one can address the question of life without falling into sterile moralism. If we are able to look at the mystery of our being through to its depths, then we realize that everything is tiny compared to the capacity of our soul. So many complications come from our failure to understand this! Because chasing after the first thing that passes does not resolve anything; it complicates everything even more, and then we find ourselves right back where we started, grappling with our dissatisfaction all over again. We cannot, then, respond to the situation described in the letter in a merely moralistic way, saying, "This is the wrong choice because it's prohibited," but then thinking to ourselves, "but really we missed out on something great." If we thought this, it would mean that we had not understood anything about ourselves, about our own humanity! We have to see ourselves for the mystery we are: every thing, considered from the religious point of view, acquires lucidity and clarity.

Acknowledging the mystery that we are leads us to understand what we find inside ourselves, which oftentimes bothers us, like sadness: "great *sadness*, that fundamental characteristic of a life lived with awareness. St. Thomas defined this sadness as 'the desire for an absent good.'"[29] When I feel sadness, it is because I desire a good that is still absent. Then, "to be aware of the value of such sadness is to be conscious of the greatness of life and to intuit life's destiny."[30] In this way we can feel the truth of this sadness as Dostoyevsky describes it: "that eternal and sacred longing which many a chosen spirit, having once tasted and experienced it, will never afterwards exchange for some cheap feeling of satisfaction."[31] Anything but a misfortune! Referring again to Dostoyevsky, Fr. Giussani delves further into the meaning of that great sadness and that of its opposite, desperation, turning our common assumptions on their head:

> If sadness is a spark which is generated by the lived "potential difference" (to use an electrical term) between the ideal destination and its historical unfulfillment, if this is what sadness is, then the concealment of that "difference"—however it is done—creates the logical opposite of sadness, which is *despair*: "The mere presence of the everlasting idea of the existence of something infinitely more just and happy than I, already fills me with abiding tenderness and—glory—oh, whoever I may be and whatever I may have done! To know every moment, and to believe that somewhere there exists perfect peace and happiness for everyone and for everything, is much more important to a man than his own happiness. The whole law of human existence consists merely of making it possible for every man to bow down before what is infinitely great. If man were to be deprived of the infinitely great, he would refuse to go on living, and die of despair."[32]

A line from Cesare Pavese, which we refer to frequently, ingeniously expresses awareness of the human being's stature and a perception of the hope which pervades and unsettles all our actions: "What a man seeks in his pleasures is that they should be infinite, and no one would ever give up hope of attaining that infinity."[33] Pavese keenly perceived the meaning of the structural disproportion between the ultimate object of our desires and what we are able to attain, denouncing, at the same time, the eradicable permanence of our tendency toward the latter: "Has anyone ever promised us anything? Then why should we expect anything?"[34] Fr. Giussani pointed out that perhaps he had never thought that "expectation is the very structure of our nature"; that is, "structurally life is promise."[35] We do not decide this ourselves; this is the way it is. If we catch it in action, if we observe our experience, the self is revealed to be a promise.

The more you enter into the mystery of your own being and engage with it, the more you realize what true solitude is—not the passing feeling of loneliness, which would be nothing: "We can well say that the sense of solitude is borne in the very heart of every serious commitment to our own humanity." The more a person takes their own humanity seriously, the more they will realize the nature of their own needs and feel all the incapacity—their own and everyone else's—to answer them. "Those who believe they have found the solution to a great need of theirs in something or someone, only to have this something or someone disappear or prove incapable of resolving this need, can understand this. We are alone in our needs, in our need to be and to live intensely, like one alone in the desert. All he or she can do is wait until someone appears. And human persons will certainly not provide the solution because it is precisely their needs that must be resolved."[36]

So then it is precisely at this point that we can begin to glimpse what true companionship is. Indeed, the ultimate question that expresses the religious sense brings to light the authentic meaning of human solitude. This question "is indeed constitutive of the individual. And in that sense, the individual is totally alone. He himself is that question, and nothing else." On the other hand, and in a more profound sense, the question, "in the very same instant that it defines my solitude, also establishes the root of my companionship, because this question means that I myself am constituted by something else mysterious." "'Religion is what the individual does with his own solitariness,' as Alfred N. Whitehead wrote, [37] but it is also "where the human person discovers his essential companionship. Such companionship is, then, more original to us than our solitude. This is true inasmuch as my structure as question is not generated by my own will; it is given to me. Therefore, before solitude there is companionship, which embraces my solitude. Because of this, solitude is no longer true solitude, but a crying out to that hidden companionship."[38] For this reason, those who live in this solitude, this powerlessness, this lack, cannot help but cry, as in the poem by Luzi: "What is this lack a lack of, / O heart, / of which all of a sudden you are full? / Of what?"[39]

Nostalgia for a You

This is the culmination of the search, the culmination that we discover in ourselves, where the "I" expresses what it is if it is not reduced. As a poem by Pär Lagerkvist marvelously describes: "My friend is a stranger, / someone I do not know. / A stranger far, far away. / For his sake my heart is full of disquiet / because he is not with me. / Because, perhaps, after all he does not exist? / Who are you who so fill my heart with your absence? / Who fill the entire world with your absence?"[40]

Denoting nostalgia with his word "disquiet," Lagerkvist poetically describes what Giussani captured in this simple formula: "The very existence of the question implies the existence of an answer." [41] Nostalgia is a very human and common experience, and through it everyone can understand that the very fact of feeling nostalgia implies the existence of some other person whom I miss. Otherwise, we would not miss them; nostalgia would not exist as an experience. No one can feel nostalgia for something or someone unless that something or someone existed or exists.

An "I" that is not reduced has this nostalgia within, a nostalgia for a real and mysterious You, a nostalgia that is within the very impulse with which it enters into relationships with everything. As the Psalms uniquely put it:

> O God, you are my God—for you I long! For you my body yearns; for you my soul thirsts, like a land parched, lifeless, and without water. So I look to you in the sanctuary to see your power and glory. For your love is better than life; my lips offer you worship! I will bless you as long as I live; I will lift up my hands, calling on your name. My soul shall savor the rich banquet of praise, with joyous lips my mouth shall honor you! When I think of you upon my bed, through the night watches I will recall that you indeed are my help, and in the shadow of your wings I shout for joy. My soul clings fast to you; your right hand upholds me.[42]

Or again: "As the deer longs for streams of water, so my soul longs for you, O God. My being thirsts for God, the living God. When can I go and see the face of God?"[43]

God is not missing; the "I" is missing, a self like the one found in the Psalms, which has within it all the nostalgia and thirst for an all-encompassing answer. This is why Jesus says: "Blessed are they who hunger and thirst."[44] Blessed! Because only a reawakened, thirsting self can acknowledge him, moved. And when a reawakened self emerges, it confirms the reasonableness of the journey Fr. Giussani proposed. The struggle against power takes place on these grounds: an "I" that is present to itself is the victory over power, over the attempt to reduce the drive of its desire, to flatten it. For a self that hungers and thirsts, what power has to offer are mere crumbs, because it knows that no handout is enough to satisfy its needs. Such a self knows where it can find rest, a rest that is equal to the needs that constitute it.

The more human beings are conscious that God alone can be their true rest, the more they are moved by the very fact that the Lord exists; they cannot avoid being flooded with emotion at the fact that God exists, as Fr. Giussani so often repeated: "My heart is glad because Christ lives."[45] We are flooded with emotion and silence; his presence fills us with silence. "For your way and your judgments, O Lord, we look to you; Your name and your title are the desire of our souls."[46] But this desire cannot survive even a few minutes if it does not become an entreaty, because the true form of desire is entreaty: it is called *prayer*.

—◆·◆·◆—

CHAPTER 8

Broadening Reason

In his historic lecture at the University of Regensburg, Pope Benedict XVI challenged all of us to a "broadening of our concept of reason and its application."[1] Is this broadening of reason possible? On what conditions?

The Scope of the Question

A sincere and honest approach to this challenge thrown down by the pope must, first of all, not make us ignore the objective difficulties in which we find ourselves immersed historically. Each person, whose reason originally takes the form of "unexhausted openness" before the "unexhausted call of the real,"[2] as the boundless curiosity of children testifies, comes into the world within the historical context of a people.[3] And every people possesses a culture, that is, a way of looking at and conceiving reality, of relating to it. As Romano Guardini acutely observed, culture is "all that man creates and is in his living encounter with the reality that surrounds him."[4] So, every new member of a people is introduced into reality by means of the culture of her people, her tradition, and she is historically defined by it.

Is it possible for a person necessarily marked by her own culture to broaden reason so as to enter into relationship with other people who are likewise marked by their cultures? No one can fail to see the importance of this question for our present-day situation.

The context in which we find ourselves is clearly marked by the possibility of large-scale migrations and encounters between different peoples, in an undoubtedly new situation for the history of humankind. The difficulty in answering this challenge is visible in the fact that it seems that there are no solutions other than, on one hand, the clash between cultures and civilizations, with the risk of exploding into violence, and, on the other hand, the indifference expressed in multiculturalism. But there is a fact that sets another possibility before our eyes.

The Cultural Value of a Friendship

Two people, a professor and a student, Wael Farouq and Paolo, meet because Paolo wants to study Arabic. They belong to two different worlds—one is a Muslim, the other a Catholic. They are both inevitably conditioned by their respective settings. But something unexpected happens: they become friends. This event forces each of them to try to understand the other, to open up his reason beyond the extent to which he had formerly looked at the other until that moment. It is friendship as a real fact that forces the two of them to broaden their reason, because each one wants to identify with his friend, to learn the other's way of perceiving, to discover the other beyond all stereotypes. It seems a tiny, a minute experience compared with all the problems of today's world, but the fact that two people belonging to such foreign worlds meet and become friends, and that this is the beginning of a journey that leads to mutual knowledge thanks to their readiness to broaden their reason, is not simply a private issue, however edifying. It has an importance much wider than the perimeter of the relationship between the two. Their experience constitutes something truly new in a cultural context that hovers between clash and indifference. But before deepening the cultural importance of their personal relationship, let's stop a moment to take the fact in.

What enables us to be friends even though we are historically determined by different traditions and cultures? It is a presence in each of us—whatever latitude of the planet we are born at—of the same elementary experience, a "complex of original needs and 'evidences.' So original are these needs or these 'evidences' that everything that man does or says depends upon them."[5] We can identify this structural human identity with the biblical term "heart." "The need for truth, for love, for justice, for happiness—these questions make up the human heart, make up the essence of reason, that is, of the awareness a person has of reality in *the whole of its factors*."[6]

Then-Cardinal Joseph Ratzinger indicated this essence common to all human beings as the radical condition necessary to make encounter and friendship possible between persons, cultures, and traditions. He stated in 2003: "A meeting of cultures is possible because man, in all the variety of his history and of his social structures and customs, is a single being, one and the same. This one being, man, is however touched and affected in the very depth of his existence by truth itself."[7] *The Religious Sense*, by Luigi Giussani, deals exactly with this depth, with this heart that is yearning for the true meaning of things. The book presents itself as an opportunity to rediscover human experience in all its breadth and the depth of its needs, for people of cultures and traditions different from ours. This is the challenge we have taken on in publishing the Arabic edition of the book, at this moment of history,[8] explicitly for an audience that largely professes the Islamic faith.

The Primacy of Facts

The French philosopher Alain Finkielkraut grasped very well the cultural importance of a particular event. In his book *Nous Autres, Modernes* (We Moderns), he reflects on the value of facts for the growth of our understanding and for overcoming preconceived measures and frameworks. Even to understand metaphysical issues, he says, one has to follow the "lesson of the facts." The book begins with a long digression in which he sets himself to listen to a fact:

On August 13, 1977, Roland Barthes wrote in his diary, "All of a sudden, not being modern left me indifferent." An astounding phrase, if you think about it. For, in those years, to be modern was much recommended, if not actually vital, and in the aesthetic field it was Barthes himself who awarded the precious label. For at that time the author of *Writing Degree Zero* was among those rare, chosen few who laid down the rules on modernity. He was one of those who picked the team. Between the new and the old, Barthes was categorical. He separated continually the new from the short-lived, the contemporary from the defunct. And now, all of a sudden, alone with himself, he realized that the dividing line passed through his own heart. He was the judge and the accused at the same time. He was exercising at his own cost a right of life and death over the things of the spirit. He excluded what he himself loved; *the values he proclaimed condemned some of his deep inclinations.* His taste suffered because of his verdicts, but he dared not confess it for fear of not being modern. A strange, tenacious fear transformed him into a clandestine dissident to his own doctrine. All of a sudden, the intimidation ceased. Barthes stopped being afraid. His other "I" came out of hiding and he began at last to breathe in the open air.[9]

This episode is interesting. Not even a modern man like Barthes, in the habit of using reason as measure and of granting the precious label of modernity, can avoid, at a certain moment, coming to terms with his own humanity, to the point that the judge becomes the accused before his heart. Here begins the interior fight between his proclaimed values and his deep inclinations. There is something in us that resists every interpretation and at the same time unmasks it, when it reveals itself unjust and violent. Something in us survives the storm of interpretations: our deep inclinations. Barthes experienced this violence: his taste suffered from his verdicts. He found himself faced with the true choice: to follow the deep inclinations that had emerged from experience and were revealed in his taste, or to remain stuck to his prejudices, which expressed themselves in his verdicts.

It is here that freedom is at risk and fear can dominate it. It is a temptation that Franz Kafka spoke against when he affirmed that, at times, in order to flee from freedom and responsibility, people prefer to suffocate their own being.[10] Barthes wins this battle in the only way possible: he yields before the evidence of experience. And he stops being afraid. When this happens, Finkielkraut observes, his "I" emerges from its hiding place and begins at last to breathe in the open air.

What can provoke such a radical change? Finkielkraut goes on,

> Some weeks before firing his modern Super-Ego without notice, Barthes noted in his diary, "I see the death of the dear being, I am desperate . . . [etc.]" The dear being is his dying mother. And there is a link between this despair and that firing. Barthes stopped proclaiming himself modern and stopped alternating between his criteria and his tastes *when he saw his mother die.* "*All of a sudden*, not being modern left me indifferent." His new attitude is not the outcome of a doctrinal reflection, but of a simple event. An intimate and base event compared not only to the artistic but also the political values at stake in his adhesion to modernity. It was private grief that drove Barthes to denounce his public image.[11]

So it was a "simple event"—his mother's death—not a doctrinal reflection, that drove Barthes to broaden his reason; an event as "intimate and base" as you please compared with the values at stake in his adhesion to modernity, but crucial for uncovering the truth. It is truth's nature as event that requires it to be revealed in an event. This is why Finkielkraut maintains that the event is the supreme method of cognition. "An event is something that breaks in from outside. Something unforeseen. This is the *supreme method of knowledge.* We have to give back to the event its ontological dimension as a *new beginning*. It is something new breaking in that stops the gears turning, and sets a process in motion."[12] This means that without an event there is no knowledge; we remain stuck in the mechanisms of what we already know. It is the event that breaks out of the mold, that forces reason to broaden itself and sets it in motion.

The importance of an event can be seen by the kind of change it brings about. If to be modern means—as Barthes says—"to separate" oneself, that is, to use reason separated (*ab-soluta*) from its relationship with reality, then the change consists in the victory over this separation. Finkielkraut goes on: "In a conference in 1978 at the Collège de France, Barthes confessed his desire to break 'with the uniformly intellectual nature' of his previous writings, and to begin a *new life*, that is, a practice of writing that would allow him to go out of himself, taking himself no longer to the 'arrogance of generalization,' but to sympathy with the Other."[13]

This is the change that begins to bring out a new "I": coming out of oneself to open up to an other. It is the victory of sympathy over separation. Barthes, therefore, had the audacity to be truly reasonable, according to the basic maxim of Jean Guitton: "'Reasonable' describes someone who submits his own reason to experience."[14]

The Nature of Reason

We can grasp the epochal relevance of the victory over the separation revealed by Barthes if we understand the authentic nature of the crisis in which we are immersed. María Zambrano identified well the core of the issue when she stated that what is in crisis is precisely the mysterious link that joins our being with reality, which is so deep and fundamental as to be our most intimate foundation.[15] This break in the link with reality is not insignificant for understanding the nature of reason and its use. As we have seen in the episode of the friendship between Wael and Paolo, and in that of Barthes, when you allow yourself to be truly struck by reality, the energy of reason is freed and reveals.

But daily life witnesses that reason, though it necessarily starts off from things that happen, tends to detach itself from experience in order to interpret it and manipulate it according to prejudices and principles—often subconscious ones—which reason is unwilling to call into question. Thus, we end up accepting only a part of reality, the part that fits in with our own explanation, the interpretation we are able to give. It is, in the end, the limitation of every ideology, in the accusation that Hannah Arendt effectively throws out: "Ideologies always assume that one idea is sufficient to explain everything in the development of the premise, and that no experience can teach anything because everything is comprehended in this consistent process of logical deduction."[16]

The great rule of knowledge, on the contrary, might be summarized in Fr. Giussani's meaningful formula: "Reality becomes transparent in experience."[17] Martin Heidegger used a similar formula to express his point of view: "Experience is the proper mode of presence, i.e., of being-present."[18] Something is present to me to the extent it enters into my horizons and interacts with me. Otherwise, it is extraneous to me, it remains unknown, and it is as though it did not exist. And note this well: even the reality of reason itself can become extraneous to us.

So we had better go back to experience. In the experience of the encounter with reality, reason reveals itself as the need for overall meaning, sustained by the indomitable question: "Why?" It is not satisfied with partial or secondary solutions; it wants to attain ultimate meaning, and is, therefore, forever thrust open to reality, constantly at work. Here, in this seeking and openness to reality, are explained both the definition of reason as "awareness of reality according to all of its factors"[19] and the whole concept of rationality that lies at the basis of *The Religious Sense*.

So reason is not a tool of intellectual embroidery that we can easily do without. It is an existential necessity. As Agostino Gemelli points out: "Man does not live passive . . . he lives *wanting*,"[20] that is, desiring, hoping, loving. There is nothing more inhuman, therefore, than an idea that claims to separate cognitive and intellective activity from the desirous and loving "I," as if the need for universality inherent to reason necessarily required elimination of the concrete, living subject. "There is a *profound unity*, an organic relationship between the instrument of reason and the rest of the person. Man is one, and reason is not a machine that can be disconnected from the rest of the personality and then left to operate alone like some spring mechanism in a toy. Reason is inherent in the entire unity of our self."[21] This unity is the condition for reason to act in a healthy way: "The condition required for reason to be reason is that the affectivity take told of it and so move the whole person."[22] It is this very affection, friendship (as we have seen), and a certain sympathy with and towards the other person, that enable reason to keep its openness without succumbing to the temptation to become a measure, thus making true knowledge possible. This is why reason does not exist without affection.

The reduction of relationship with reality caused by reason understood as a measure leads to nihilism. What form does nihilism take today? It takes the form of an emptying, an impoverishment of reality. Reality is emptied, it contains nothing but what can be counted or calculated, and is reduced to simply something to use. Reality is denied as a sign, that is, as being something full of being and promise. Heidegger affirms, "The essence of nihilism is the history in which there is nothing to *Being* itself [and its mystery]."[23] This is the outcome of reason understood rationalistically, which, since it cannot dominate the dimension of depth and meaning, has closed its doors on it (admitting only what is calculable and measurable). It has done more: it has done away with the question about the ultimate meaning of things (reason that measures is interested only in "how" things are, and it never asks "why"; the question is only relative, and never intended in its ultimate sense).

This elimination has today become a common heritage; it is lived without pathos and, apparently, without drama. Today, nihilism is no longer a theory, but the practice of a life lived in apathy and dispersion. The nihilism in fashion today is a cheerful nihilism, in the sense that is without restlessness, it has suppressed the *inquietum cor meum* (my restless heart) of Augustine. This does not happen without a price: as Benedict XVI masterfully explained in Verona, the primary result is "a radical reduction of man, considered a simple product of nature and as such not really free, and in himself susceptible to being treated like any other animal."[24]

When, on the contrary, nihilism's strong theoretical position comes into play, and asserts that only nothingness underlies all things as well as the self, and, therefore, everything is an illusion and the present world makes no sense, our experience rebels against this claim, because every one of us has experienced that things *are* as the prime and immovable fact, that is, as a gift that precedes every thought and every reflection, one in which we are already immersed and always have been. "If things *are*, they cannot be explained saying *they are not*."[25] The Spanish philosopher Xavier Zubiri writes, drawing out the consequences of this for the cognitive sphere: "What is proper to reason are not its presumed evidences, not its empirical or logical rigor, but above all the force of the impression of reality, according to which profound reality imposes itself coercively on the sentient intellect. The rigor of reasoning never ceases being the poetic expression of the force of reality, of the force with which the reality in which we are already impressively immersed imposes itself on us. Therefore, the problem of reason does not consist in verifying if it is possible for reason to reach reality, but precisely the opposite. The real question is: how should we keep ourselves within the reality in which we are already? It is not a matter of coming to be in reality, but of not going out of it."[26]

This is freedom's task. The first condition for understanding is to accept the datum just as it presents itself. The first thing we need in order to know is to let what shows itself *be*: not to take possession of the matter ready to be perceived through our own categories, but to put ourselves at the service of the object, to adore.[27] "It is a passivity which makes up my original activity of receiving, taking note, recognizing."[28]

The impressiveness of reality does not leave reason indifferent. Reality acts on reason as an unavoidable invitation to discover the meaning of the friend or of the fact. To block this dynamic is to block knowledge. "Reality presents itself to me in a way that solicits me to pursue something else. . . . Reality solicits me . . . to engage in a search for some other thing, something beyond immediate appearances. It latches on to my consciousness, enabling it to pre-sense and perceive something else. Faced with the sea, the earth, the sky, and all things moving within them, I am not impassive—I am animated, moved, and touched by what I see. And this motion is towards a search for something else."[29]

Reality presents itself to reason as sign. It is what Montale expressed so splendidly in these lines: "Beneath the dense blue sky, seabirds flash by, never pausing, driven by images below: Farther, farther."[30] And Shakespeare, too, when he wrote: "Show me a mistress that is passing fair, / What doth her beauty serve, but as a note / Where I may read who pass'd that passing fair?"[31]

This dynamic of sign is not complete if it does not reach its culmination: the acknowledgment, full of astonishment, of the existence of the Mystery that makes all things. "The summit of reason's conquest is the perception of an unknown unreachable presence, to which all human movement is destined, because it depends upon it. It . . . is the idea of *mystery*."[32] And, again: "The world is a sign. Reality calls us on to another reality. Reason, in order to be faithful to its nature and to the nature of such a calling, is forced to admit the existence of something else underpinning, explaining everything."[33]

It is by no means obvious how one is to follow the dynamic of reason, thrown open and set in motion by the imposition of reality pressing down on it, without impediments or restrictions. On the contrary, it involves tireless and loyal commitment.

Educating to the Use of Reason as the Task of the University

The challenge of broadening reason indicates a first, great need, which is always crucial and today more urgent than ever: that of education. And if any place is eminently called to educate people in the use of reason, that place is the university. It is a matter of the university's authentic reason for being. If it does not foster a true use of reason, it fails in its task; if it educates reason then it fulfills a mission in the true sense of the word. But how can universities fulfill this vocation?

Remembering his days at university, Benedict XVI recalled the feeling of *universitas*, that is, the fact that, "despite our specializations which at times make it difficult to communicate with each other, we made up a whole, working in everything on the basis of a single rationality with its various aspects and sharing responsibility for the right use of reason—this reality became a lived experience."[34]

The first element of educating to the use of reason that I wish to highlight—which is also the most delicate and critical—is this tension between the specialized areas of study and the idea of "everything on the basis of a single rationality." Universities, because of how they are structured today, contribute to educating reason through the study of the various branches of knowledge, the various specializations. A person is captivated by a preference, which leads them to foster a passion and to engage with one particular aspect. The task falls to the educator not to close all the person's energy on this one aspect alone, squandering it, but to relaunch the cognitive prospect as openness to the whole, starting with that particular factor: "Modern scientific reason . . . bears within itself a question which points beyond itself and beyond the possibilities of its methodology."[35]

The single rationality has today turned into scientific reason, and its range of action falls exclusively within the reality that can be described in mathematical terms and subjected to experimental protocols. Anything that cannot be translated into mathematical terms or cannot be demonstrated experimentally is considered unknowable, the realm of sheer subjectivity, where anyone can say whatever they want: *tot capita tot sententiae* (As many heads, so many opinions). This is the dogma of scientific rationalism: "[A certain view would hold that o]nly in the field of science and mathematics can the truth about an object be perceived and affirmed. With any other type of knowledge—concerning destiny, the affective and political problems—one can never reach objective certainty, a true knowledge of the object."[36] Giussani, too, spoke out against it: "Only in the field of science and mathematics can the truth about an object be perceived and affirmed. With any other type of knowledge—the proponents of such a hypothesis argue—concerning destiny, the affective and political problems, one can never reach objective certainty, a true knowledge of the object."[37]

We speak about knowledge, then, according to the fashionable preconception, and of certain knowledge only when we can follow the scientific method, that is, when the subject of our inquiry can be "mathematicalized," and calculational reason can be applied (the ideal of modern science is the Cartesian *mathesis universalis* [all-encompassing mathematics]).[38] The mathematicalization (quantification) of reality lies at the root of "scientificity": everything that is not quantifiable/calculable or reducible to mathematical terms cannot, therefore, be known with certainty, does not belong to the realm of things that can be addressed reasonably. The mathematical/experimental use of reason is the only one that is culturally permissible and recognized. In conclusion, for us, "certain" ("reasonably certain") is the same as "demonstrated by calculation and confirmed by experimentation."

Thus the ambit of "authentic" knowing is reduced to a small field of abstract and formal truths, together with their resulting technical and scientific applications. What happens as a result of this unprecedented restriction, this domination by scientific rationalism? That reason and knowledge no longer have any relationship with life, with life's issues, with the experiences and questions that are most properly human. Reason becomes detached from existence. Benedict XVI perfectly captured this devastating outcome: "If science as a whole is this and this alone, then it is man himself who ends up being reduced, for the specifically human questions about our origin and destiny, the questions raised by religion and ethics, then have no place within the purview of collective reason as defined by "science," so understood, and must thus be relegated to the realm of the subjective."[39] Nevertheless, "the scientific attitude—in the proper sense of the term— cannot, we already know, be the exhaustive approach to experience. Indeed, it is precisely 'through experience' that we know that there are dimensions and phenomena which do not reduce themselves to either the physical-chemical or biological spheres."[40]

But who ever said that reason is exclusively associated with one single motion and one single phenomenon? "Reason is much larger than this; it is life, a life faced with the complexity and the multiplicity of reality, the richness of the real." Reason "implies many methods, procedures, or processes depending upon the type of object in question ."[41] It would be irrational to insist on applying one and the same method for realities that are irreducibly different.

The great physicist Erwin Schrödinger put it this way: "I consider science an integrating part of our endeavor to answer the one great philosophical question which embraces all others . . . : who are we? And more than that: I consider this not only one of the tasks, but the task, of science, the only one that really counts."[42] Only in the pull toward totality inherent in every branch of human knowledge, this pull toward the union of all the various branches, can the various specializations save reason in its nature. Edmund Husserl explained this well: "The mere sciences of facts create mere men of facts. . . . In the misery of our life—one hears said—this science has nothing to say to us. On principle it ignores those very problems that are the most fundamental for man, who, in our troubled time, feels he is at the mercy of destiny: the problems of the meaning or meaninglessness of human existence in its entirety. Do not these problems, in their generality and their necessity, perhaps require, for all men, . . . a rationally based solution?"[43] A bit further on, Husserl continues: "Considered closely, these problems, like all those that have been ignored, are inseparably united in this: explicitly or implicitly, in their meaning, they contain the problems of reason—of reason in all its specific forms."[44]

And the scientist John Barrow writes: "Out of all the possible universes, ours is exceptional because it is suitable for life. . . . This is a truly extraordinary fact, which must be interpreted in order to scientifically explain our own existence in the universe. . . . When science reaches the point of asking fundamental questions like how the universe came to be, it has profound resonances with religious thought."[45] It is critical to point out that it is not when science backs away from reality or surrenders its role, but rather when it is most truly itself, that it creates profound congruence between itself and the religious sense. It seems this point has registered with the Harvard University commission charged with revising the curriculum after thirty years; the commission is proposing new courses of study in "Faith and Reason," as part of the curriculum students would take prior to choosing a specialization. The declared purpose of this change? To help gain an understanding of the complexity of the world.[46]

Fifty years ago the great mathematician Francesco Severi pointed out the same connection after his scientific and theoretical studies led him to conclusions that instigated a religious conversion: "[Everything I study is] in the light of an absolute that, like a flexible barrier, opposes . . . our surpassing it by cognitive means."[47]

Universities fulfill their original vocation when they contribute to developing reason that is open to the truth in all its forms, engaged with the wide range of realities through a correlated range of paths, not silent in the face of the ultimate depth of questions. With a great deal of realism, Professor Augusto Marinelli[48] acknowledges: "I do not think universities today consider themselves [to be the place for educating people in the search for truth]. I do not believe there is any passion for knowing or seeking the truth as a cornerstone of academic life. By that I mean that I see universities being more oriented toward technical objectives and toward formation in a specialized field: in short, the underlying questions are taken for granted. The risk, however, is that of reducing the *universitas* of knowing to the *universitas* of notions: in essence there is a challenge to re-launch, especially at the present moment, to recover the meaning of the university, viewed in the totality of its dimensions. Our perception of the educational task of universities may have extremely important consequences not only for the choices of an individual professor, but also for those of the individuals who lead the institutions.[49]

The second aspect of educating reason that I would like to linger on is the statement that the right use of reason is, as Benedict XVI said, a shared responsibility. We are all aware—I say this as a professor to my fellow professors—of an authentic need to help one another. Only a true academic community can redeem each of us from our inevitable partiality. When one lives with a genuine pull toward the enlargement of reason, other people are no longer an obstacle that places limitations on my research; they become a good, because they prevent me from isolating myself, constantly calling me back to an open gaze toward totality. Only a communal generation of one's own endeavors can save the nature of reason and the truth of one's quest.

"The communital dimension does not replace freedom, personal energy, and decision. Rather, it is the condition for their affirmation. If, for example, I place the seed of a beech tree on a table, it will not develop into anything, even after a thousand years (assuming that everything remains the same). If, on the other hand, I take this seed and plant it in the ground, then it eventually becomes a tree. Now the humus does not replace the irreducible energy, the incommunicable "personality" of the seed. Rather, the humus is the condition needed for the seed to grow. The community is the dimension and condition necessary for the human seed to grow."[50]

The third and critical point—related in some ways to the second—is the need for witnesses. The broadening of reason cannot be brought about by merely defending a correct view of reason, however rightly. It happens first of all and above all when people see in action a humanity that already lives by a "broadened" reason, and they experience it as a good for themselves. There is an essential need for witnesses to the true and vast use of reason, who can reawaken others to the same usage and stand up to the challenges that the "globalized" present poses. Indeed, in the words of Luisa Muraro, "The modern notion of reason, which has confined itself within limits that leave out the essential questions of man and the very name of God, is rendered insufficient for a true dialogue with whole humanity."[51] What we need is an experience of reason that can bring us out of "the little patch of earth that makes us here so fierce,"[52] as Dante said, an experience that reopens us to the constituent questions of our lives.

This is where the true alternative to nihilism begins, which universities can contribute to and make possible: the emergence of reason that is open, thirsty, eager to answer the fundamental questions raised by the real, by life.[53] By promoting the formation of this alternative, universities can make a crucial contribution to the most pressing issues of our time, starting with dialogue between different cultures and traditions.

CHAPTER 9

———◆·◆·◆———

Freedom Is the Most Precious Gift
Heaven Gave to Humanity

"Freedom, Sancho, is one of the most precious gifts heaven gave to men; the treasures under the earth and beneath the sea cannot compare to it; for freedom, as well as for honor, one can and should risk one's life."[1]

Joseph Ratzinger has highlighted the fact that freedom is as valued today as it was when Cervantes wrote these words. "In the consciousness of mankind today, freedom is largely regarded as the greatest good there is, after which all other good things have to take their place."[2]

The similarity between the two statements, however, should not cause us to miss the differences between then and now, which concern the way we think about and live freedom. If for Cervantes freedom was so precious that "one can and should risk one's life," today it is difficult to find people who venture down the path of freedom. It is a value that is just as scarce as it is popular. How many truly free people do we know? We are faced with an enormous desire for freedom, but also the inability to be truly free, that is, be ourselves, within reality. It is as if, in fact, everyone is constantly conforming to what is expected of them. You put on one face at work, another with friends, yet another at home, and so on. Where are we truly ourselves? How many times do we feel stifled in everyday life, without the slightest idea of how to break free, just waiting to change the circumstances or for them to change on their own! In the end, you find yourself stuck, longing for a freedom that never comes.

At a time when people are talking a lot about freedom, we witness the paradox of its absence. And what is even worse, we have settled for living without it. Kafka pointed out, "Men are afraid of freedom and responsibility. So they prefer to hide behind the prison bars they build around themselves."[3]

"The history of recent centuries could be summarized as a progressive reduction of the person to a depersonalized individual or to a formal freedom, pushing real freedom to the margins."[4] Let us try to understand why.

The Modern Reduction: Freedom as Absence of Bonds

Jesus' genius has given us a memorable lesson in the well-known parable of the prodigal son, one that is helpful for understanding the journey of modernity that led freedom to this level of formalism.[5] We all know the story well (Lk 15:11–32): "There was a man who had two sons; and the younger of them said to his father, 'Father, give me the share of property that falls to me.' And he divided his living between them. Not many days later, the younger son gathered all he had and took his journey into a far country."

The parable describes a normal home in Palestine during Jesus' time: a father with two sons. There is no indication of any conflict in the family relationships. The fact that they have wealth to divide amongst themselves means that it is a family with a certain level of prosperity. The text gives further confirmation through other details:

they have servants, the father wears a ring, they have access to beautiful clothes and sandals and a fattened calf. All signs of the kind of family the prodigal son belonged to. That was his home, the place where he was a son and, therefore, where he was loved. Home is the place where one is truly oneself, because one does not need to prove anything to anyone. The prodigal son was loved for the very fact of being a son. Home was the place where everything was his, and reality was friendly, where he could hear his father say, "All that is mine is yours." Everything was ordered to the satisfaction of his needs in the familiarity with his father.

Despite all this, he does not seem satisfied and asks his father for the share of property that belongs to him in order to leave home. The lure of autonomy overcomes his heart. His desire for freedom pushes him to break his most meaningful bonds. He does not seem to care much about having to leave his father and his home, his place of belonging. Perhaps everything seemed an obstacle to his yearning for freedom; perhaps he felt stifled at home. He wanted to break the ties that kept him bound to it, bound to a tradition, and go far away.[6] Nothing could get in the way of the fulfillment of his desires. The road would be completely open. He thought in this way to be able to reach a level of freedom he had never before experienced.

What could push the son to such a radical choice? Perhaps he had been attracted by the fame of cities like Alexandria, Antioch, Ephesus, and Corinth, which appeared full of promises of freedom for a young man of means like him. But, in reality, this view had taken root in him before, when he succumbed to the allure of autonomy that had crept into his heart. He was not able to resist the seduction of making it on his own, without father, or home, or real belonging.

Reality soon wakes him from his dream. The boy finds nothing that lives up to his desires; nothing satisfies him enough to captivate him. Everything passes over him without leaving a trace. No bonds, no history with anyone. The absence of constraints begins to show its true face: loneliness. "He squandered his property in loose living. And when he had spent everything, a great famine arose in that country, and he began to be in want" (Lk 11:14). He began to realize that autonomy was only an illusion.

But the worst was yet to come. "So he went and joined himself to one of the citizens of that country, who sent him into his fields to feed swine. And he would gladly have fed on the pods that the swine ate; and no one gave him anything" (Lk 11:15–16). So ended the adventure of autonomy[7]—instead of a father, a master; instead of a home, swine. Where was the promise of freedom? He was starving and could not be filled even with husks that the pigs ate, because no one gave him anything. Boredom became his companion.[8] Nobody cared about his fate.[9] It was the culmination of the breaking of all bonds, including the bond with reality, which was now inhospitable and alien.

On the other hand, the eldest son proves that the experience of freedom is never automatic, never assured externally. He remains at home, with his father, where everything is his. But, since he does not realize what is given to him, even he does not experience freedom. This is demonstrated by his reaction to the mercy of his father at his brother's return. He gets angry. He does not want to join the party and confronts his father. "'Lo, these many years I have served you, and I never disobeyed your command; yet you never gave me a kid, that I might make merry with my friends. But when this son of yours came, who has devoured your living with harlots, you killed for him the fatted calf!'" (Lk 11:29–30). You can, therefore, live in your own home as a servant, without the joyful knowledge that you are a son. "And [his father] said to him, 'Son, you are always with me, and all that is mine is yours'" (v. 31). The eldest son is free in name only. This is the definition of formalism.

Beneath the rubble, within the young son something remains alive—his heart. Not even all the disasters he has caused can remove the yearning for freedom from his heart: "But when he came to himself [that is, he came to his heart] he said, 'How many of my father's hired servants have bread enough and to spare, but I perish here with hunger!'" (Lk 11:17). Worn out, he cannot help but wish for freedom and, with it, the one who made it possible: his father. He quickly decides. "'I will arise and go to my father, and I will say to him, "Father,

I have sinned against heaven and before you; I am no longer worthy to be called your son; treat me as one of your hired servants."' And he arose and came to his father" (vv. 18–20). It is the memory of his father that keeps his nostalgia for freedom alive. With the decision to return, he recognizes that the only real freedom is filial: not to live as an orphan even though he is a son, but to live consciously embracing his sonship, his relationship with his father.

This is always possible, even for us now, because there is always a father who awaits our return: "But while he was yet at a distance, his father saw him and had compassion, and ran and embraced him and kissed him" (v. 20).

Whatever the condition in which we find ourselves, each of us is called to freedom, to recognize it as the most precious gift that heaven has ever given to man. The path may be arduous, but it is always possible. How?

What Is Freedom?

Feeling That We Are Free: A Phenomenon of Satisfaction

"How do we come to know what freedom is? Words are signs with which a person identifies a specific experience: the word 'love' singles out a certain experience, as does the word 'freedom.'"[10] The starting point for understanding the meaning of life's most important words is to look at experience, as Fr. Giussani always taught.

If we sincerely observe ourselves, when do we feel *free*? Imagine that a girl learns that her friends are having a party and there arises in her the uncontrollable desire to go. She goes to her dad and he, surprisingly and contrary to habit, says no. The girl's discouragement and anger are the unmistakable signs that she does not feel free. Only when, after a fairly heated dialogue, her dad finally agrees to let her go does she feel free.

We feel free *when we see a desire fulfilled*. Freedom becomes experience in the satisfaction of a desire. This is the truth that is hidden within the immediate, instinctive impression we all have of freedom and which is expressed in the simple phrase, "To be free is to do what you please."

Freedom as Capacity for Complete Satisfaction

But it is also true that we do not settle for a moment of satisfaction, a moment of freedom. We want to be free forever, not only on a few occasions. We want to be completely free. Therefore, "experience indicates that freedom presents itself to us as a total satisfaction, complete fulfillment of the self, as perfection. Or we can say that freedom is the capacity for the end, totality, for *happiness*."[11] Freedom is for man the opportunity and the responsibility to be fulfilled. Starting from certain and particular experiences of satisfaction, freedom is revealed as "capacity" for total, complete satisfaction, that is, for perfection, for self-realization, realization of our human desire.

Desire Is Infinite

Now, the more we achieve our immediate and partial desires, the more the original depth of our desire comes to light. When we were children we were happy with candy. Not anymore. Our experience— if we pay attention to what it tells us, if we are sincere about what comes out of it—makes us discover the true nature of our desire. It is inexhaustible.

We all know that life does not always punish us, preventing us from satisfying our desire. On many occasions we can achieve what we desire, but this does not definitively satisfy us. After a while we are back to square one. This is why I have often thought that we begin to realize the drama of life not when life says "no" to desire, but when it replies "yes." When it says "no," in fact, we can still wait for it to say "yes." The drama begins when life says "yes" but it is not enough. When a person has this experience in relation to their work, to their spouse, to life events, they eventually ask: so what is enough to satisfy me? "*Quid animo satis?*"[12]

I have a friend in Barcelona who is a painter. Her dream was to organize a large gallery showing of her work. A few years ago she finally achieved her goal. The outcome, as she told me, went beyond all her expectations. So I could not believe it when she told me that on the day of her great success she spent the whole afternoon crying. Why would one cry after a success? Was my friend abnormal? Did she have a problem? No, she had the same experience Cesare Pavese had when he was awarded the Strega Prize. "In Rome, apotheosis. And so?"[13] Why is the big gallery show or the Strega Prize not enough? Why are you not fully satisfied after a success? What will satisfy us, then?

What does the dissatisfaction that comes after success teach us about the nature of desire, the nature of man? As Pavese had deeply understood, it puts before our eyes the "infinity" of our desire. This is the unique feature of human beings: their desire is greater than the "infinite universe," to use Leopardi's words. It is precisely because of this breadth of our desire that we can "accuse things of inadequacy and nothingness, and suffer lack and emptiness, and yet, still boredom."[14] But what is for many the misfortune of life—to feel the inadequacy of everything, to suffer lack and emptiness—for Leopardi is the utmost sign of the greatness of human nature. We can feel the inadequacy precisely because, structurally, we have within us the criterion for judgment: our infinite desire, what the Bible calls "heart." If this criterion were not within us, if we did not have the ability to judge by virtue of it what corresponds to us, or not, the affirmation of man's dignity would be just empty words, and man, when all was said and done, would be dependent on power.

How is this original desire of ours awakened? It is a decisive question for today, in an age when desire itself cannot be taken for granted, because it is constantly threatened by the nihilistic pressure of our context.

The Journey of Freedom

Whatever the situation in which we find ourselves, reality continues inexorably to encounter us, stirring up in us wonder, that is, curiosity and desire. It is always the impact with reality that activates our humanity, in all its dimensions and capacity. "The capabilities within us are not self-made, but they also do not translate into action by themselves. They are like a machine that, besides being built by others, needs someone else to start it up. Each and every human capacity, in a word, must be stirred up, must be roused to action."[15] What sets the human self or "I"—desire, reason, and freedom—in motion is the impact with reality.

It is, therefore, what happens to us that awakens desire, insofar as it is full of attractiveness. Far from remaining indifferent, we are primarily attracted by the beauty—by the goodness—of reality. In the encounter with reality that attracts, freedom is set in motion. In this impact, which occurs relentlessly (because no one can consider himself to be outside of reality) and that attracts us, freedom is brought to bear from the start. How? In *responding*. Freedom is invited to take the first step of its journey: to decide whether or not to give in to the attraction of reality in front of it. This nonneutrality of freedom plays a crucial role in the choice about the ultimate meaning of reality, because freedom's position affects the discovery of meaning that reason is called to carry out. Indeed, whoever rejects the attraction exerted by reality is already censoring data, and is therefore less reasonable than those who take it into account.[16]

This highlights a primary aspect of self-possession that characterizes freedom.[17] As powerfully attractive as reality may be, it does not eliminate freedom's *capacity to choose*. Rather, it sets that capacity in motion. All the impressive attraction of being does not spare us the responsibility to decide. On the contrary, it provokes it.

On what do we base our decision whether or not to follow the urging of reality? On the correspondence to the needs of the heart that that urging demonstrates. The reaction to being that occurs in me is already the first judgment by which I move. When I am in awe of the mountains and I say, "How beautiful!," I express a judgment on those mountains, just as when I cry out in pain at suffering unjustly inflicted on me or others. The judgment, in which I recognize whether something corresponds to me or not, is what prepares and directs the move, the choice of freedom.[18]

Now let us ask ourselves: What is at stake in choice, in each choice? Adherence to what appears to us and what we recognize as a good. That is, choice is aimed at achieving an end. Why do I want the ability to choose? To adhere to what strikes me and attracts me. My freedom, writes Juan Ramón Jiménez, is to take from life that which seems best for me and for everyone.[19] The girl wants to be able to choose to go to the party, to freely participate in the good she glimpses. It is precisely in this participation that she finds her desire satisfied and, therefore, feels free.

The power of choice is a feature of a person's freedom still journeying towards its full realization, which consists in adherence to what corresponds to the heart, that is, the good, destiny. To limit ourselves only to the first aspect—the possibility of choice—means, in fact, to give up the fulfillment of freedom, because the reason I exercise my ability is in order to choose to adhere to what I desire, to bind myself to what fulfills me, to the infinity I look for in pleasure, the You that calls to me in the attractiveness of things, to the You who makes me be, to Him to whom I can say: "You are my truth, You are my self, I am You who are making me." It is in this participation in what corresponds to me that my freedom is realized, that desire finds satisfaction.

The Relationship with the Mystery, the Foundation of Human Freedom

How is it possible to speak of freedom? Man—every human being— at one time did not exist and at a certain point begins to exist. He seems to emerge from the womb of the universe and of history and then return and be reabsorbed. But if human beings sprang *entirely* from the biology of father and mother, if they could be entirely attributed to the developing reality that houses them, it would be impossible to give full meaning to the word "freedom," that is, make sense of that freedom that imposes itself on us as a fact. "In only one case is this point in the circle, this single human being, free from the entire world, free, so that the world together and even the total universe cannot force him into anything. In only one instance can this image of a free man be explained. This is when we assume that this point is not totally the fruit of the biology of the mother and father, not strictly derived from the biological tradition of mechanical antecedents, but rather when it possesses *a direct relationship with the infinite*, the *origin* of all of the flux of the world . . . : God."[20]

This is the meaning of the *Catechism of the Catholic Church*'s affirmation that God directly infuses the soul into the body. "There is a 'something' in me which is not derived from any empirical phenomenon. . . . It directly depends on the infinite, which makes the whole world."[21] This is the greatest truth of the Christian doctrine of creation. The fact that we are created in the image and likeness of God means that we are called to a unique and direct relationship with him. The vocation of life is this relationship. Called, not just to anything, but to God, to full happiness. Man is *capax Dei*: capable of God.

That there is in me this direct relationship with the infinite is what prevents human beings from being reduced to their biological, psychological, sociological antecedents, and so on. The attempt to reduce the self to one or other of these factors will always fail. Sure, they have an impact on me, but they do not determine me, they do not decide who I am. A person can never be reduced to a cog in the workings of internal or external circumstances. The self can always emerge above and beyond the circumstances or its own feelings or moods.

To paraphrase Hannah Arendt's thought, only because I have not created myself am I free. If I had created myself, I could calculate myself and thus lose my freedom.[22] We are a direct, irreducible relationship with the Infinite. This is the ultimate reason for man's greatness. It is such a greatness that it sometimes frightens us. Therefore, it requires a sincere openness and a courageous honesty to recognize and accept the relationship with the Infinite, which is expressed in our desire and which underpins our freedom.

Freedom is at risk today. Few take it seriously and love it. "The worst threat to freedom is not the fact that people allow it to be taken away—for someone who lets it be taken away can always win it back—it is that people forget how to love it, or no longer understand it."[23] Because, as the Spanish poet Rafael Alberti says, "Freedom is not possessed by those who do not thirst for it." It is exactly what María Zambrano decries: "Man once again is chained to necessity, but now by his own choice and in the name of freedom. He renounced love for the sake of the exercise of biological functions; he has exchanged his passions for complexes; and thus he does not wish to accept his divine inheritance, thinking that he will thereby free himself from suffering, from the passion that the divine suffers among us and within us."[24] Freedom instead consists precisely in accepting this "divine inheritance." First, because only the divine mystery can underpin that ultimate irreducibility-to-all-conditioning without which there is no freedom. Second, because only the infinite Mystery can be the proper subject of my freedom, can completely satisfy my desire. Finite freedom, since it is the capacity for total satisfaction, can be fulfilled only in infinite freedom.

Therefore, freedom means adhering to Being, the Mystery that makes us, the real and mysterious You that is making me at this very moment. It is in accepting the Father, like the prodigal son, that I become free. Perhaps we, like that son, needed to leave home and then feel nostalgia when we lost everything. And so we discovered the good of having a Father, and that acknowledging him does not jeopardize our freedom, but on the contrary, makes it possible.[25]

The Mystery that made us knows of our resistance to this abandonment in his Father's arms, as Péguy writes, imagining God reflecting on his creation: "I know man well. It is I who made him. He is a strange creature. / For in him operates that liberty which is the mystery of mysteries. / Still one can ask a great deal from him. He is not too bad / . . . But what one can't ask from him, damn it, is a little hope. / A little confidence, a little relaxation. / A little delay, a little abandonment. / A little pause. He is always resisting."[26]

But the *rejection* of the Infinite is not without consequences for freedom. This refusal leaves freedom without its proper object. By not adhering to the infinite Mystery human beings remain at the mercy of all the forces of power at play in every circumstance. Without the recognition of the Mystery as root and complete fulfillment of every desire and partial attraction, freedom is nothing more than an illusion. If freedom is the experience of a satisfaction, we can verify the status of the journey of our freedom by the degree of genuine satisfaction that we experience in relationship with people and things. We can do what we like, but we cannot escape this verification. How many times a day do we have a real experience of freedom, that is, fullness, satisfaction, in the minutiae, in the contingency of everyday choices, in choosing goods and partial attractions? What usually prevails is a feeling of being stifled; you feel trapped everywhere, just waiting to escape. How many people escape into the imagination in order to bear "lack and emptiness"? "Without acknowledgment of the present Mystery, night advances, confusion advances, and therefore, at the level of freedom, rebellion advances; or disappointment so fills up the measure that it is as if we hope for nothing more, and we live without desiring anything, apart from furtive satisfaction or the furtive answer to a small request."[27]

Instead, by adhering to the Mystery in everything, man becomes free. It is there where he can find the satisfaction of his desire for totality. Our greatness, as Leopardi reminded us, is to feel the desire for the infinite vibrate within us. But to be aware of the nature of our desire is to understand that we are not able to answer it. Just as people receive the desire for totality, so they must receive the fulfillment of this desire. The fulfillment exists, and it is God himself who awakens in us the original depth of our desire. We should not resist, we should surrender. Without such surrender to the only One able to fulfill our desire and to bring about freedom, desire becomes corrupted and freedom loses its way, without an ultimate object.

Only a relationship recognized and lived with What satisfies us frees us from whims, from the dictatorship of desires—which is the reduction of desire to anything within reach—and makes us consistent in all circumstances and irreducible to any power. Therefore, writes Fr. Giussani, "Christian religiosity arises as *the one and only condition for being human.* This is man's choice: either he conceives of himself as free from the whole universe and dependent only on God or free from God and therefore the slave of every circumstance."[28]

But how can a man have the clear awareness and affective energy to adhere to the Mystery while it remains a mystery? How can the yet unknown and mysterious object stir up freedom's energy in order to fulfill it? As long as the object is obscure, one can imagine what one wants and decide the relationship with that object as one pleases. This is what happens in the experience of falling in love. Until the person who takes hold of my entire self appears on the horizon of my life, I continue to do what I please. The knowledge that such a person exists somewhere does not free me from being at the mercy of everything that appears in front of me.

I know that I want the Infinite, that this Infinite exists because I always yearn for him, as Lagerkvist said, but every day I seize a particular, I pursue this or that object, which then leaves me unsatisfied. This is man's fate, unless God deigns to visit him, as Wittgenstein wrote in his *Diaries*: "You need redemption, or you will lose yourself. . . . *For that, as it were, a light must shimmer through the ceiling under which I work and above which I do not want to rise.* This striving for the absolute which makes all worldly happiness appear too petty . . . appears to me as something glorious, sublime to me; but I myself turn my gaze toward worldly things; unless 'God visits me.'"[29]

The Companion That Makes Freedom Historically Possible

Only when the Mystery, like the beloved, shows his face can a person have the clarity and the affective energy to adhere, that is, to engage all his freedom. With Jesus the Mystery became "a presence that attracts affection," to the point of igniting people's desire and challenging like nothing else their freedom, that is, their ability to adhere. For human beings it is enough that they give in to the overwhelming attractiveness of Jesus' person. As happens to someone in love, it is the fascinating presence of the beloved who awakens in them all the energy of their affection. They only have to surrender to the appeal of the one in front of them. "What we need is a man, / not wisdom, / what we need is a man / in spirit and truth; / not a country, not things, / what we need is a man, / a sure-footed, and a hand held out / strong enough for all / to take it, and walk / free, and be saved."[30]

And like the beloved, the Mystery present is also discovered in an encounter. Unexpected. Like a surprise! As happened to John and Andrew, the first who encountered Jesus and stayed attached to him throughout their lives. Their freedom was so challenged by his exceptionality that they could not go on living without having to reckon with that Person. In the encounter with Jesus such an unthinkable correspondence happened, something impossible elsewhere, that they never again left him. "Therefore [their] genuine freedom is the fruit of a personal encounter with Jesus."[31] The freedom of those who have met him has found a fulfillment beyond compare: the "hundredfold here on earth," as Jesus called it, that is a satisfaction a hundred times greater, a foretaste of the full and final satisfaction.[32] The apostles were not visionaries, and if they had not experienced a better life for themselves, sooner or later they would have left him.

It is this relationship that clarifies man's otherwise confused desire. As William of Saint-Thierry says, Christ is the only one who "can teach me how to see the things that I desire."[33] It is he, Christ, who fully reveals man to himself, as *Gaudium et Spes* says.[34]

In order to attract man without him resisting, as Péguy said, the Mystery uses the method of preference. Just as it introduces us to love not through words, but by making us fall in love, in the same way, in order to reveal what freedom is, the Mystery stirs up all our desire for totality by putting before us a presence so attractive and correspondent that we may have, "contemporaneously," the experience of the fulfillment of this desire.

Caro cardo salutis: Flesh is the pivot of salvation.[35] Flesh, the Word made flesh, is the pivot of salvation. Only an affectively attractive presence in the flesh is able to overcome our resistance. An overwhelming attraction is the only hope for us, always so tempted by the lure of autonomy, by that almost homicidal affirmation of ourselves that plunges us into nothingness. Only the attraction of Being that shines in the face of Christ, present here and now in the flesh of the Church, can defeat the allure of nothingness.

Why is that man so appealing? Who is he? He is Christ, a man full of God or God made man. A man who accepts belonging totally to the Mystery, to the Father. He accepts that it is an Other who fills his heart. In him is the fulfillment of the human vocation. Therefore he is the only one to introduce us into the Mystery of the Father, in whom our freedom is fulfilled. Sons and daughters in the Son.[36]

But in order for Christ to be revealed as the fulfillment of my freedom I must let him enter the depths of my being. In fact, we discover that we have found the One who fulfills our desire for freedom at the very moment in which we become free, that is, become his. In order to fully reveal himself, he waits for my freedom to take a position, for me to freely decide for him.

Indeed, Christ did not come to spare us the exercise of freedom, as sometimes we wish had happened. But what would a salvation be that was not free? This is God's drama, once again expressed by the genius of Péguy: "I long, I am tempted to put a hand under their belly / To support them with my broad hand / Like a father teaching his son to swim / In the current of the river / And who is divided between two feelings. / For on the one side if he supports him for ever and if he supports him too much / The boy will rely on him and never learn to swim, / But on the other if he does not support him just at the right moment / The boy will swallow a nasty mouthful. . . . This is the mystery of the liberty of man, God says, / And of my management of him and of his liberty. / If I support him too much, he is not free. / And if I do not support him enough, he will fall. / If I support him too much, I endanger his liberty / If I do not support him enough, I endanger his salvation: / Two goods, in a sense, almost equally precious. / For this salvation has an infinite price. / But what would salvation be if it were not free."[37]

The Need of His Presence Now

We cannot avoid lapses, failures. But, then, how can we ever be put back on our feet? The only possibility is that Christianity continue to happen as an event. Without the Christian event constantly happening again there is no possibility of real freedom. And its continuation is a sign of its truth: as truth, it lasts. Only in this way can our freedom experience a constant reawakening and be constantly set in motion, so as to be able to realize itself.

Where does the Christian event continue? In the Church: "The freedom of God becomes present through the people that his presence has changed, people changed by his presence. His presence, the presence of God made man, is revealed through these changed people. The proper sign of this change is this capacity for unity—impossible for human beings—which is called by its full name, the Church."[38] The Mystery endures in history and continues to make real freedom possible through the change of these people, whose apex is the communion among them. Communion is the victory over the absence of bonds, which is the fruit of sin.

The Church thus becomes a place of freedom, a freedom possible to anyone who approaches her. Only if she is a community that makes the real freedom of those who belong to her possible in history can the Church respond to the objection that freedom is not possible in belonging. She will therefore prove that, instead of the absence of bonds, freedom is lived belonging.

But this real freedom in the community of the Church is possible only if she educates me so that I recognize the Mystery, the only reality that can make me free within the circumstances. This is the profound meaning of Saint Ambrose's statement, "*Ubi fides ibi libertas.*"[39] Only such a community can make real the aspiration for a home where freedom is lived: "The eagerness to liberate *and* to build a new house where freedom can dwell," to use Hannah Arendt's words, "is unprecedented and unequaled in all prior history."[40] The bond with Christ in the Church rebuilds the bond with everything and everyone.

Today, too, Christianity meets man's desire for freedom. However, if it wants to have any chance, it cannot present itself in any of the reduced versions that have marked recent history (moralism, spiritualism, abstract jargon). It must be offered in its original nature as event, therefore, through the testimony of an experience. Christianity must present on the world's stage people who are free, the spectacle of "free people" in reality (at work, in personal and social matters, in circumstances of every kind). It is this free person who will bear witness to Christ.

The person of today does not need a religious message, but the experience of an encounter. "One meets the Christian Fact by meeting people who have already had this encounter and whose life, in some way, has already been changed by it. . . . Hearing the Gospel quoted or even listening for hours to the thoughts that the Gospel evokes in a certain person is not an encounter. That is watching a performance—when it is one—of the sentimental reactions or arguments that take their cues from a religious inspiration. Instead the encounter is with an event, which can also be a person speaking, but what is striking is not so much the words themselves as the change, however it may have happened, in the one who speaks."[41] We can see this in the following letter I recently received:

> I was hospitalized for a week to perform tests as a result of the disease that I have had for thirteen years: Parkinson's (it began when I was thirty-eight years old). They put me in a room where an elderly lady was already being treated. She was experiencing serious problems related to my same disease: she could not be still because of the involuntary movements by day or night and had contractions in her throat and her tongue, so they could not even feed her. Exhausted from dystonia and the dyskinesia, in the end, she would scream hysterically. She could not find other means to make herself heard than yelling. For me it meant no sleep and no rest either by day or by night. I immediately realized that I had to be patient because when you are hospitalized you know you can run into situations like this. I tried to calm her down as best I could, calling her name, reassuring her, trying to let her feel my presence, because she did not have the opportunity to be assisted daily by relatives. After two days of this situation I found myself truly worn out. So I went to look for the head nurse and I told her that I could not handle it anymore because I could never rest, and I asked her if she could do something. Then I went back in the room in tears. As I entered, though, I remembered what Fr. Giussani

taught us, "Live your circumstances in the way the Mystery comes to meet you." And then, as I looked at that older woman writhing and screaming, who was crying out a need, a dramatic plea for help, remembering the words of Fr. Giussani changed the position of my heart and my mind. Crying had surely done me good, but that was not what relaxed me. What gave me the strength to continue with her was this awareness that the Mystery became a Presence for me within that situation, in that room. And then I said: "Either I suffer through this circumstance, or I live it, embrace it." So I began, in addition to reassuring her, to pay more attention to her reactions to the dosages of the medication that they administered to her. After a couple of hours her primary care physician came with other doctors and they were wondering what to do to help this lady, because they could not manage to get the therapy right. Then I found the courage to report what I had observed about her reactions to the medications and dosages. I added that when she felt reassured and around others (even if they were there to visit me), she quieted down, a sign that she needed medication, but also companionship. From then on, every two or three hours, when they came to check on her, they asked me how she had spent the time after the last dose, to the point that one evening a doctor asked the lead physician if I had been placed in charge of this patient. The lead jokingly replied, "Oh yes! We cannot discharge her. She is becoming useful for understanding how to manage this therapy!" At that point, I pointed out that they also had to ask me how I was doing, because the situation had been truly unbearable for so long. The lead doctor then assured me that they were working on hurrying my tests in order to discharge me. And so it was. That evening, a nurse came into the room to tell me that, if only for one night, I could sleep in a single room in order to rest. I then apologized for the reaction I had in the morning, due to the terrible fatigue, but he replied, "Ma'am, you don't need to apologize for anything, and you should also know that you are the only one who was able to last." When I was discharged a nurse thanked me for the help that I had also given them by not constantly ringing the bell, but trying to look after the patient the best I could. He told me, "Do whatever you can, never change the way you are. Always stay the same." I wanted to tell this story because in my own experience one fact was clear: not that I'm good—that I was able to live this circumstance differently from other people who wound up in that room before me—but that because of the presence of Another, suffering can be borne and become livable. It is the recognition that the Mystery lives within the circumstances that changes them, that changes you, first of all. You live the circumstance better and you make life better for those who are called to live it with you.

This is freedom in action: not the self wedged into the mechanism of the circumstances, but a self that finds in recognizing the Mystery within the circumstances the possibility of real freedom. "If [man] wants to be free from all that surrounds him, if he wants to be free of all that exists around him . . . , he must be dependent on God. Dependence on God is the freedom of man."[42]

Like that woman, we can experience freedom in each and every circumstance because we have met a free man who taught us to live all the circumstances in the only way by which we can avoid having them crush us: in recognition of the Mystery, that is, as sons and daughters.[43] Fr. Giussani, as we saw it ourselves, lived his life and his illness in this way, and he taught us to recognize the positivity of reality in any circumstances. It is to him that we will always be grateful. The most beautiful way we can honor him is to be witnesses to the fact that the only possibility of real freedom is the recognition of the Mystery present. Thank you, Fr. Giussani.

PART 3

AN EDUCATIONAL EMERGENCY

---◆•◆•◆---

CHAPTER 10

Introduction to Total Reality

Education is the great challenge that we all have to face. It is not by chance that we speak of an "educational emergency." Education has always been crucial in introducing younger generations to life. What is different today than in the past? Why do we speak today in such dramatic terms of educational emergency? It is only in answering these questions that we can understand the significance of the contribution Pope Francis has made to this issue ever since he served as archbishop of Buenos Aires.

What is the challenge we are facing? In an article published in [the Italian national paper] *La Repubblica* a few years ago entitled "The Eternal Adolescents," on today's younger generation, Pietro Citati wrote: "Young people today do not know who they are. They prefer to stay passive. . . . They live wrapped in a mysterious inertia."[1] An educator with extensive experience relating to young people, Luigi Giussani used an image to describe this "mysterious inertia": "It is as though the young people of today have all been affected . . . by radiation from Chernobyl."[2] It is as though the body no longer has any energy, because of the radiation.

The consequence of the weakness described above is that "what one listens to and sees is not really assimilated. What one is surrounded by, the dominant mentality . . . , power, creates [in us] a sense of estrangement from ourselves." It is as though we have been torn away from our selves. "One remains . . . abstracted in the relationship with oneself, as though drained in terms of affection."[3]

We are therefore "abstracted," estranged, not only from others, but from ourselves. Just think how long people are able to remain by themselves for a moment of silence. We have to escape right away, distract ourselves. It is as if there were an inability to be with ourselves, as if we never felt at home. The detachment from ourselves becomes a detachment from everything: nothing can truly interest us, and, therefore, indifference prevails.

Responding to this situation with rules or ethical appeals is unthinkable, since these have already proven themselves to be ineffective. They are incapable of making the person who needs to be educated spring into action; they are incapable of awakening the desire of the "I." Without the "I" in action there can be no education.

Where Is the Starting Point?

Where, then, does one start up again in this situation? Despite everything, that "hot point" of the soul, which Cesare Pavese spoke of, lingers on within man.[4] It is precisely around this hot point that a proposal that truly corresponds to one's humanity can turn. Pope Francis pointed this out quite clearly: "Man is not at peace within his own limits; rather he is a being 'on a journey' . . . and when he does not enter into this dynamic, his person disappears or he becomes corrupt. What moves man to begin this journey is an inner restlessness that pushes man to 'step out of himself.' . . . There is something, outside and within us, that calls us to undertake this journey."[5] That restlessness, of which Augustine spoke, lingers on in the depths of man's being. It indicates the depth and breadth of desire, the hot point of the heart.

But the attempt to put desire to sleep is always at work:

Worldly systems seek to quell man, to anesthetize his desire to embark on this journey, with promises of possession and consumption. . . . In this way man is alienated from the possibility of recognizing and listening to the most profound desire of his heart. Our attention is drawn to the numerous "alibi" that manipulate our desire . . . and offer, in exchange, an apparent peace. . . . Greed, lust, avarice, anger, envy, sadness, sloth, boastfulness, pride. . . . [These] are certainly pretexts, cop-outs that hide something else: fear of freedom. . . . They act as a refuge. Fundamentalism is based on the rigidity of a uniform thought, within which the person seeks protection from destabilizing instances (and crises) in exchange for a sort of existential quietism.[6]

In this context, then-Archbishop Bergoglio advised educators to be careful not to use educational tools in any way to reduce desire: "Discipline is a means, a necessary remedy at the service of the overall education [of the person], but it should not be transformed into a mutilation of desire. . . . Desire is opposed to necessity. The latter is satisfied as soon as the want is filled. Desire, instead, is the presence of a positive good; it constantly increases, grows in structure and draws us towards something 'greater.' The desire for truth proceeds 'from one encounter to the next.'"[7]

In this regard, the well-known psychoanalyst Massimo Recalcati observes that "desire cannot be quashed by a mere satisfaction of needs; rather it shows itself to be different from beastly cravings precisely because it is animated by a transcendence that opens it to the new, to that which is not yet known, not yet thought, not yet seen."[8] Therefore, the great challenge for an educator is how to reawaken desire: "How can we teach our students not to be afraid to seek the truth? How can we educate them to be free? . . . What do we have to do to ensure that our young people . . . become 'restless' in their search?"[9]

We should answer: educating, that is, introducing young people to the relationship with reality. And yet, some would say, young people do not appear to be interested in this relationship, because of that mysterious inertia that turns into an unassailable boredom. So let us ask ourselves: Why is authentic interest absent, why is it so difficult for young people to truly engage with something, and why is it so difficult to find adults who at forty or fifty years have not become skeptical?

A Spanish philosopher, María Zambrano, captured the extent of the problem: "What is in crisis is the mysterious nexus connecting our existence with reality, something that is so profound and fundamental that it is our most intimate sustenance."[10] What is in crisis is the nexus with reality. We can see this from the fact that reality is not capable of drawing the self; there is nothing that truly conquers us: boredom prevails and the person seems emptied, because it is deprived of its nourishment, its "sustenance."

Nevertheless, there seems to be something paradoxical in this diagnosis. Indeed, today no one would say that young people are not interested in anything. Rather, they appear to be interested in everything; never before have they had so many opportunities. Why, then, after rapidly consuming every kind of stimulation, do they fall so easily into a state of passivity and boredom? Because without meaning reality loses its attraction. This, then, is the goal of an education that addresses adequately the seriousness of the problem: to educate is to introduce the young person to reality in all its dimensions, including its meaning. This is what Pope Francis said in his message to Italian schools: "I love school because it is synonymous with openness to reality. . . . Going to school means opening one's mind and heart to reality, in all of its aspects and dimensions. We do not have the right to be afraid of reality!"[11]

Reestablishing the Nexus with Reality

As we can well understand, this is a problem that affects everyone: associations, schools, the Church, and political parties. We are not dealing with a particular problem but with the problem of all problems: how to reestablish a sufficient nexus with reality. What is capable of awakening the interest of our person? To get a handle on this situation we need a kind of education that rises to the level of the emergency. Josef Andreas Jungmann defined education as an "introduction to the total reality."[12] Because without recognizing and affirming its meaning, a person will not be truly interested in reality. For example, if we adults give a child a toy that he has never seen before, and we leave him alone with it, he may be in awe of it, but how can he understand what that toy is? You would need a user's manual, which in the example would mean telling the child: "If you do this and that, you will get to enjoy how it works." It would be inhuman to give a child a toy and not show him how it works. Without offering him an hypothesis on how to use it, we would abandon him to his reactions: tears and boredom.

So, again speaking to teachers and students, Pope Francis said that "school educates us to the true, the good and the beautiful. All three go together. Education cannot be neutral. It is either positive or negative; it either enriches or impoverishes; it either makes a person grow or it oppresses him, it may even corrupt him. . . . A school's mission is to develop the sense of the true, the good and the beautiful. And this happens through a rich journey."[13]

Being introduced to the totality of reality is not without consequences for one's relationship with it. If we do not perceive its meaning, reality does not move us to the point of becoming interesting to us. This is the origin of nihilism, of that position that ends in boredom, because nothing arouses my interest. We thought that reality could go on being attractive even without a meaning, reduced to mere appearances, and that young people could be interested in transmitting mere notions and data, without communicating a theory about meaning. But this did not happen. With the reduction of reality to its immediate aspect, to appearances, a new form of nihilism has appeared, a weak, jovial, cheerful one, in which desire is not awakened, curiosity is not awakened. Now, only he who manages to arouse the self from this feebleness will be able to make a contribution to the dramatic situation in which we find ourselves.

From where can we start again, then? From reality. But not a reality reduced to appearance, because otherwise we grow tired of it, it leaves us dry, it cannot capture us or interest us for an extended time. From reality in its entirety and strength of provocation. Reality arouses an interest by attracting us; it proposes itself above all through its beauty, as Jorge Mario Bergoglio said: "How many abstract rationalisms and 'extrinsicist' moralisms would be cured . . . if we began to think of reality first as beautiful, and only later as good and true!"[14]

Reality, which comes to meet us in its beauty, sparks questions. I still remember, after many years, what happened when I brought my high school students to the planetarium in Madrid. After the visit we went back to school and I started to ask them questions about what, of all the things they had seen, struck them most—the stars, the galaxies, and so on. But no one was curious about the number of stars or interested in how many galaxies there may be. Instead, struck by what they had seen, they filled the board with questions such as: Who made all of this? Whom does it belong to? What is the meaning of all of this? What is its purpose?

This is the problem: we have been given the gift of the most beautiful toy, that is, life, all of the cosmos, but we did not come into this world with the user's manual under our arm. This is why we ask ourselves the meaning of what we see and what has been given to us, we ask ourselves how to live, how to learn to enjoy what we have, how to learn to face reality in an adequate way, so that life can truly be life, intensely lived and fascinating to live.

There must be a working hypothesis: "To educate people in such a way that they seek the truth, then, requires an effort to harmonize contents, routines, and assessment methods. . . . It is not enough to provide explanations and information to attain this harmony. . . . It is necessary to provide, to show, a living synthesis of them."[15]

A Witness Is Required

It is at this point that a witness is required. Indeed, Pope Francis says:

> This can only be done by a witness. In this way we enter into one of the most profound and beautiful aspects of being an

educator: witnessing. This is what consecrates the educator as a "*master*" and makes him a companion on the path to seek the truth. By his example, the witness challenges us, revives us, accompanies us, and lets us walk, make mistakes, and even repeat our mistakes, so that we can grow. Educating . . . requires you, dear teachers, . . . to "know how to give reasons"; not just through conceptual explanations and isolated contents, but by your conduct and embodied judgments. . . . Everything becomes interesting and attractive, and at last the bells will ring to reawaken a healthy "restlessness" in the hearts of young people. The paradigmatic example of the master–witness is Jesus himself.[16]

Recalcati, from his own standpoint, adds, "To become human, life requires the living presence of an Other. . . . If this encounter does not occur, life is exposed to disassociation from its meaning; it appears to be without meaning." Indeed, "how is this desire passed from one generation to the next? Through a living testimony to how life can be lived with desire."[17]

But witnessing is not possible unless educators take their own restlessness seriously, first of all: "To educate is of itself an act of hope. . . . Dear educators, . . . I pray that restlessness, the image of the desire that moves all of man's existence, opens your heart and points you in the direction of that hope that does not disappoint. That, as educators, you become authentic witnesses in close proximity to everyone."[18] This is critical because, the Pope adds, "young people understand that, they have a 'nose' for it, and they are attracted by professors whose thoughts are open, 'unfinished,' who are seeking something 'more,' and thus they infect students with this attitude."[19]

Our responsibility begins here. In order to take on this responsibility, one must not succumb to the temptation to despair, as Pope Francis reminds us once again: "Temptation is an invitation to stop along the way, to despair. How can one not fall, when many, many utopias have already fallen? . . . This temptation is a serious one and the extent of its power is known by anyone who has courageously followed his heart. . . . He alone knows the difficulty and the depth of

the problematic nature of his desire. . . . In this context . . . every educator is tempted by despair."[20]

We adults have to recognize that we have not always lived up to
that need.

> Let us look at young people. . . . Do we prepare them for
> sweeping horizons or for those just around the corner? . . . We
> want to ask forgiveness from young people because we have not
> always taken them seriously. Because we do not always give
> them the tools to ensure that their horizons do not end just
> around the corner; because often we are not able to excite en-
> thusiasm in them by showing them those broader horizons that
> enable them to appreciate what they have received and must
> share with others. Because many times we did not know how
> to make them dream! . . . And when young people see a testi-
> mony to shallowness in us, their leaders, then they do not have
> the courage to grow. . . . If we do not prove capable of testify-
> ing to the existence of such an outlook and work, then our life
> will end up in a corner of existence, crying bitter tears because
> of our failure as educators and as men and women.[21]

I will conclude with words of Pope Francis that sound as an
urgent call to take responsibility: " [May young people] gain from our
testimony—since one teaches more by example than with words—
the fertile culture of life. . . . It is not just drugs that kill, it is not just
drugs that generate the culture of death; the same happens as a consequence of the selfishness of heart in us who have the responsibility
to educate, as a consequence of our closed-mindedness, of the indifference with which we pass by someone who is stuck on the sidelines
of life, without teaching them to overcome their immobility and draw
closer to life."[22]

CHAPTER 11

———•◦•———

The "Hot Point"

The book *Contro i papà: Come noi italiani abbiamo rovinato i nostri figli* [*Against Fathers: How We Italians Have Ruined Our Children*] by Antonio Polito is a cry, a provocation, a question: Where are we leading our children? Many parents will identify with this interrogative. It is a question that often becomes worry, and sometimes anguish, because many parents do not know where to turn, where to look, in order to emerge from the impasse in which they find themselves. This is an evident sign of the confusion that dominates our time. We have seen the birth and development of many beautiful things, many scientific achievements. But we do not know how to offer something truly meaningful to those dearest to us, to our children, so that they can make their way amidst the confusion that surrounds them.

Polito, an astute observer, grasps the greatest challenge that society is facing, which is the challenge of education, with respect to which the other challenges—economic, social, and political—are but consequences. And he identifies not only the challenge, but also its origin: fathers. Or, more generally, adults, be they parents, educators, teachers, or clergy—that is to say, everyone who has proven to be, with some exceptions, incapable of offering a hypothesis of a response at the level of their children's needs. From the very first pages of the book the author is trenchant in addressing the issue: "Who among us fathers . . . can deny to himself the truth that everything around us tells us that education (understood in a much broader sense than mere instruction) is the crucial factor for the success of a community and, within it, of our children? So why have we completely abdicated our educative role, to instead become our children's awkward defense attorneys?"[1] This is the challenge.

How can we see that parents have abdicated their educative role? In two basic ways.

A Misguided Sense of Protection

Parents have wanted to spare their children the struggle of living at all costs. "Instead of being parents, we have gradually become our children's defense attorneys, always ready to fight so that the road to nothingness is paved for them [strong words], because there is no ambitious goal without an arduous journey. This is a widespread cultural phenomenon, and it is becoming a trait of our national character. . . . And it is acting as a brake not only on the economic growth of our nation, but on its psychological growth, as well."[2]

In other words, instead of launching our children toward an ambitious goal that corresponds to their needs, to their hope, to their heart, the path toward which is necessarily arduous, we have preferred to smooth the way for them, so that they don't have to work too hard, so that they can avoid the uphill struggle. Instead of Steve Jobs's "Stay hungry, stay foolish," from his famous speech at Stanford University, we have preferred "stay satisfied, stay conformist." "The fault is ours. We are the real 'big babies,'" writes Polito. We have pursued a social model that is aimed at making life easy for our children, without realizing that by doing this in the name of our children, we are ruining them. "We don't want them to be hungry even for an instant. Rather, we have built our lives and our society around their nourishment. . . . Around protecting them from need, with social consequences that are significant and not always positive."[3]

We have lived "a misguided sense of protection toward our children. Misguided because it actually betrays a collective distrust of their means, the fear of letting them swim with their own strength as soon as possible. And they feel this distrust, and it depresses their self-confidence."[4] In my opinion, these are extremely astute affirmations of how we, by protecting them, give a judgment about their abilities, their possibilities to be themselves, to grow, to develop. We do not say it explicitly, but they grasp this judgment anyway. In short, we have practiced a harmful paternalism. Polito calls it the "slipper society,"[5] directed at preserving our young people from any sort of effort.

I am struck by the parallel with what Fr. Giussani said in 1992, in an interview for the Italian newspaper *Corriere della Sera*:

> Italy . . . frightens me. . . . It is a societal situation where there is no adequate ideal, where there is nothing that goes beyond the utilitarian aspect. It is a utilitarianism pursued without any ideal horizon. This cannot last. My fear is that endless conflicts will be unleashed. . . . *Why did all of this happen? You have seen many generations grow up. What was the triggering factor of a fall, a worsening, like this?* No one proposed anything to all of these generations of people. Except one thing: the utilitarian anxieties of their fathers. *Are you talking about the 'god' of money?* The 'god' of money or the security of an easy life, a life without risks. And one made up entirely of things. . . . Who knows, maybe this desire to make our children's lives, or the lives of a given group of people, less difficult will someday break through the boundaries. That is, if those who have this desire understand that, in order to accomplish it, they need an ideal, a hope.[6]

Fathers thought that, by sparing them the effort and protecting them from need, they were doing what was good for their children. In reality, what they were doing for them was paving the road to nothingness. Eugenio Scalfari maintained that "the wound [in these young people] was the loss of their identity and memory," perhaps—

at least this is my opinion—because someone took this identity away from them. It is peculiar. First, the adults do all that they can to make them lose their identity, and then they complain about the fact that they've lost it. "The wound was the silence of fathers who were too busy achieving success and power."[7]

Today, we are facing a profound human crisis, which we can sum up in this mysterious torpor, this insurmountable boredom, this lack of humanity in which we often find ourselves when the mentality the book denounces is victorious. This profound human crisis is seen in the passivity of many young people, who seem almost incapable of getting interested in something truly meaningful, or in the skepticism of many adults, who do not show them anything for which it would be worthwhile to work in order to get out of this situation. It's as if young people did not find interests that were worth fully involving their humanity. It seems like nothing is able to interest them to the point of setting them in motion, and thus, as often happens in the classrooms of our schools, boredom is what dominates.

Parents, we could say, have committed an enormous error. Where was, and is, this error? In the confusion about the nature of the human heart. We think that we will solve our children's problems by minimizing their needs, putting them to sleep by providing everything and removing obstacles, instead of reawakening them, challenging them in their nature. We have ignored their humanity just as we ignored our own, that original nature, which Leopardi describes in an unparalleled way: "Human Nature, / if you are merely weak and worthless, / dust and shadow, why aspire so high?"[8]

To this human nature—which is the nature of our young people, and our own—we cannot just respond with a utilitarian minimalism, with a sentimental do-good philosophy that neither respects nor challenges the depths of the human question.

The Reduction of the Self to Antecedent Factors

This brings us to the second error denounced by Antonio Polito—the other root of the unsuccessful educational strategy he criticizes in his book. On this point I am very much in agreement. The origin of the problem is, above all, cultural. What is the error? The error that

made us terrible parents is twentieth-century thought, whose great discovery was the identification of superhuman forces—be they psychological, social, or biological—capable of removing from man's shoulders the burden of responsibility for his actions. Great consolatory philosophies, like the system of thought originated by Freud, in which the rational and conscious ego, the seat of individual responsibility, becomes a poor wretch at the mercy of forces greater than he is, [laying] "the foundations for a reduction of ethics to psychology" (Valeria Egidi Morpurgo). . . . Or philosophies like Marxism, which transport the same mechanism for zero responsibility onto the social plane. Do you remember one of its most famous assumptions? That it is the social being who determines conscience, not the other way around. Therefore, our conscience is just a servant who goes where class conflict takes him. And the liberation of man cannot be anything but the result of a collective process that unfolds over us. . . . All individual responsibility is finished, everything is transferred onto collective processes and movements. As the anthropologist Robert Ardrey wrote in *The Social Contract*, this is "a philosophy which for decades has induced us to believe that human faults must always rest on somebody else's shoulders; that responsibility for behavior damaging to society must invariably be attributed to society itself; that human beings are born not only perfectible but identical, so that any unpleasant divergences must be the product of unpleasant environments." . . . And finally Darwinism, . . . which explains all human behaviors as inevitable consequences of the evolutionary history of the species, and not as conscious (to varying degrees) choices made by individuals. Fear and courage, selfishness and altruism, laziness and industriousness: nothing that we are can be attributed to the education that we have received, to the example that was offered to us, to the culture in which we have lived. No, everything is Nature, everything descends to us from our ancestors and from the instincts that developed in the struggle for the survival of the fittest.[9]

I'm not sure that we understand the significance of this error: the human being, reduced to his biological and sociological antecedents, becomes a puppet, a marionette in the hands of "superhuman forces." And thus there is no more "I." The "I" is like a stone that is swept away by the current of these forces. The "I" as a personal, autonomous reality, with a capacity for freedom, able to act as a subject in history and circumstances, is no more, because everything is unloaded on antecedents of every type: psychological, social, or biological. Polito calls it the "opiate of de-responsibilization."[10] Without the "I," without freedom—because everything is determined by these factors—what responsibility is possible in the face of reality's provocations?

The consequence of this mentality is a particular conception of the human being.

> Rousseau defined the child as "a perfect idiot." And in 1890, William James described the mental life of a newborn as "one great blooming, buzzing confusion." It is because of this presumption that, convinced of being in the presence of likable "idiots," we speak and act in front of them as if we were not listened to, understood, and judged. I don't know about you, but I was never able to be in a room with one of my children after the age of seven or eight months without noticing that his five senses were thrown wide open in my direction, without feeling the unsettling sensation that inside those bodies, not yet capable of moving on their own or feeding themselves with their own strength, hummed perfectly oiled brains, already working.[11]

This touches on a point that we cannot allow ourselves to ignore. As Polito's admission shows us, despite all of the reductions carried out by twentieth-century thought, the elementary experience of the relationship with our children still impedes this reduction. It is as if we perceive, even tangibly speaking, that we cannot reduce them to what we usually reduce them to—our thoughts.

Polito continues: "You understand well that if it were like this [i.e., if children were listening intelligently], our behavior as parents would be radically mistaken, and we would have to radically change [because if the kids have functioning brains, something has to change]. No more 'poor baby, he's too young to understand.' . . . The child understands, he comprehends that something is right and something else is wrong."[12] Try to commit an injustice toward him, and you will see that he understands! Children are anything but reduced to antecedent factors of the biological, psychological, or any other type!

Polito labels as "bad teachers" those who, rather than recognize children's originality and the fact that their children have functioning brains, "culturally" promote the reductive mentality previously described, whose result is the annihilation of the self:

> There are adults around who do more than minor damage as fathers, in the sense that they inflict it on an entire generation of children. They are the bad teachers, understood in the literal, not the metaphorical, sense of the term: people who teach badly, erroneous things, sloppy methods, and pernicious ideas. It is the dense group of those veterans of the turmoil of the '60s and '70s who, instead of going into politics or business, obtained their success in academia or communications, and who today, from TV screens, newsstands, or bookstores, sketch the world as it is and as it will be before the eyes of our young people. It is through their words and their images that our children learn to hope or to despair. Thus the role of these father-gurus could be even more important than that of biological fathers.[13]

Here, then, Polito reaches a bitter conclusion: "We are the first generation of fathers in history to have elaborated a complex and highly selfish strategy of survival through the *captatio benevolentiae* [trying to get on the good side] of our children. We pretend to do it for their good, but in reality we do it for our own." And, he adds, "Our society has therefore grown old before its time in its hopes and expectations."[14] By reducing human beings to their biological, psychological, or sociological antecedents, we have taken away their dignity—both that of adults and that of our children—and we express this in the way that we look at them. They read this judgment in the way in which we treat them, much more so than we realize.

But it only takes a minimal relationship with them to discover that the self is there, and that there is something in the self that is irreducible to these "antecedent" factors. Fr. Giussani called it "elementary experience," a complex of needs—for truth, for beauty, for justice, for happiness, for fullness—which is the core of the human self. And because of this, young people understand, they understand very well! They don't have to take a course to see when a way of treating them is unjust or when we don't love them or when we don't give them time. To take away from them the criterion of judgment is to take away their dignity, because it is like saying: "You are stupid. I will explain to you how things are." But they understand very well how things are, precisely because they have within them the criteria for judgment, they have within them an elementary experience, expressed in those fundamental needs: they don't have to go to Harvard and take a course in justice to understand when they are treated unjustly. Just try to treat them unjustly, and you will not have to wait for their judgment! Our children are far clearer and more ruthless than we are when it comes to justice and injustice, truth and falsehood. We are amateurs with respect to the clarity of judgment that they have about things. And yet we think they are inept, incapable of judgment.

Instead, what a change, what a difference when we treat them as they are! Yet, as Pope Benedict XVI said, "an odd darkening of the mind"[15] has happened [in many very able people], and we no longer see what is elementary. And with this obscuring of thought we reduce our young people's dignity, their capacity for being, their self with all of its possibility to evolve, and, at the same time, we restrict our concept of love to courtesy and kindness, while it ought to be love in truth.

A Living Proposal

If this is the situation, it calls for the awareness that the launchpad for starting over is those very "functioning brains," as Polito put it. That is, it is that heart that cannot be reduced to its antecedent factors, the human being with her needs and expectations. These very expectations must be reawakened and find a sufficient answer. An answer that fits our human proportions must take a shape that corresponds to what Pavese called the "hot point." Now, as we hinted earlier, the hot point is ordinarily blanketed with slumber, submerged in boredom: when young people do not find relationships that meet the level of their need (which often they try to drown out with a slew of distractions), the hot point often stays buried within them.

The question, then, is who is able to reawaken the "hot point," the "I" of young people—and of adults, as well. This is the challenge that we all have before us, our generation and our institutions: schools, the family, the Church, political parties, entrepreneurs, everyone.

In order to reawaken the "I" from its slumber, from this seemingly insurmountable boredom, a lesson, an ethical reminder (although perhaps helpful), or a homily will not suffice. What is needed is adults who, with their lives, are able to provoke in young people an interest in their own existence, their own destiny. But it is difficult to find adults who are not skeptical. How often, instead, have I found myself talking to university students whose parents respond to their enthusiasm for an ideal by saying, "No, life will slowly straighten you out."

Only a witness, one who incarnates a way of living that is capable of attracting the heart, challenging reason, setting freedom in motion, can reawaken this "hot point," this hidden need. Whoever meets such a person cannot be immune to their appeal, to the challenge their presence brings to life. Pope Paul VI said that today we need witnesses more than we need teachers.[16]

What is needed is a living proposal, a witness. Or, to use a word that today is not politically correct—but which, when emptied of the connotations we attach to it and used in its original sense, proves crucial—an authority. In other words, someone who makes me grow, who generates me with his presence. What is needed is an authority, a presence that challenges the "hot point" in order to launch me toward that "ambitious goal" to which I am called by my structure as a human being. "We experience authority when we meet someone who possesses a full awareness of reality, who imposes on us a recognition and arouses surprise, novelty, and respect. There is an inevitable attraction within authority and an inexorable suggestion within us, since the experience of authority reminds one more or less clearly of one's poverty and limitations. For this reason, we tend to follow a person with authority and become his 'disciples.'"[17]

But we must clarify a further factor. "Even a clear presentation of the meaning of things and the real, intense authority of the educator is insufficient to meet the needs [which today we must face] of the adolescent. He must instead [at the same time] be stimulated to *personally confront his own origin* [without this young people will not be themselves, and so we cannot spare them this effort]. This means that the student must verify the traditional contents being offered to him, which can be done only if *he himself takes the initiative*: no one else can do it for him." The hypothesis of meaning we propose must be submitted to verification by our children, so that they can verify its pertinence to life, its capacity to respond to the challenges of life. Without verification, the hypothesis will never become theirs, and they will therefore run the risk of getting lost. So "true education must be an *education in criticism*." Criticism means comparing what is proposed to us with the desires of our heart. "The final standard of judgment must be found inside of us, for otherwise we are alienated. The ultimate, inner standard of judgment is identical for all of us: it is a need for the true, the beautiful, and the good. . . . In the past, people have been too afraid of criticism,"[18] of this verification and this risk, Giussani always said, which are indispensible for generating an autonomous subject.

Fr. Giussani continued,

The purpose of education is to fashion a new human being; for this reason, the active factors of the educational process must guide the pupil to act with increasing independence and to face the world around him [circumstances] on his own. To do this, we must increasingly expose him to all the elements of his environment, while also gradually allowing him more responsibility for his choices. This is in agreement with the outlines of an evolutionary path according to which the pupil must, at some point, be able to "do it himself" in every circumstance. The teenager must be guided gradually as he matures toward a personal and independent encounter with the reality that surrounds him [otherwise, the result will be that he does not grow].[19]

The pivotal nature of the educator's position, of his or her human solidity, comes to the fore here.

It is here that the educator's stability becomes important, for the increasing autonomy of the student is a "risk" for the teacher's intelligence and heart, and even for his pride. Then again, it is precisely the risk of confrontation that helps create the pupil's personality in his relationship to all things; it is here that he develops his *freedom*. . . . It is the student who must undertake the task, because only thus can his freedom truly develop. This love of freedom that leads us to accept the risk inherent in the process must be a constant guideline for educators. . . . An educational method that watchfully accepts the risk of the teenager's freedom is really a source of deliberate faithfulness and devotion to the worldview that is being offered and to those who offer it. Precisely because of his discretion and respect for the student, in a certain sense the role of the educator is to step back behind the overshadowing figure of the one Truth by which he is inspired. The teacher has become a living witness, and his teaching and leadership elicit a deep, sincere fondness in the student and become engraved in his memory. Even more, this fondness does not depend on the qualities of the teacher. The outcome is a lasting sense of gratitude and a bond with the teacher, and a conviction which is independent of him.[20]

An Invitation to Freedom

The goal of the educative process is not to "convince" the other of what we believe. That would be coercion. Because at the center of this process are two freedoms in relationship with each other.

Freedom is always put into motion by an attraction, because the human heart is thirsty for truth. Each person seeks what corresponds to her original needs for goodness, beauty, truth, justice, and happiness, which are awakened by everything that happens. Education is, therefore, an invitation to humanity's freedom, to begin a journey to discover the truth of things. If this does not happen, then any curiosity and fondness that may even have been awakened sooner or later fade away, and boredom wins. Only the truth has the strength to endure in time. The dynamic of freedom is not arbitrary, it is not doing whatever you want, because a person is truly free when he recognizes and adheres to the meaning of reality. Indeed, without a meaning there would be no adequate reason to live.

Education is a great challenge for the human heart. Without it, the development of the person as reason and freedom is impossible. The more young people are challenged in their reason and freedom, the more they prove to be enthusiastic participants in this adventure. The problem is that, unfortunately, they do not find many adults who challenge them, and thus they degenerate.

I would like to conclude with a quote from Rabindranath Tagore, which speaks of all the love that a father or other adult should have towards those they wish to see grow. When this love is there, the young person recognizes it because it leaves him the room to grow. "By all means they try to hold me secure who love me in this world. But it is otherwise with thy love which is greater than theirs, and thou keepest me free."[21] Love makes us free and gives space to the freedom of others, so it may grow. This is the challenge young people pose to us, which we adults have the task of accepting.

———◆·◉·◆———

CHAPTER 12

A Communication of Yourself

Education is something that I have very much at heart, especially since I was a teacher for so many years.

The Current Challenge

If there is a watchword for all of us today, we can express it succinctly with the expression "educational emergency," because we see the difficulty of our society (our society means us, we teachers, we parents) in transmitting a reason for living, that is, in truly introducing to reality all the new members of our people.

To put it very concisely, what are the unequivocal signs of this emergency?

In terms of the students, I would describe today's situation with one word: disinterest. Teachers don't find themselves in front of classrooms of young people who are all eager and willing to study, interested in what they have to learn. The first question for any teacher, therefore, is how to stimulate interest in the subject matter. Today, we can't take for granted that the student wants to learn; there may be thousands of excellent teachers, willing to teach all their knowledge, but the problem is that there are not students who have the desire to learn.

So, how can we reawaken their interest? How can we generate the human subject? How should we put ourselves in front of the students and in front of what we have to teach, in order to begin that process that enables our students or our children to introduce themselves to reality? The consequence of their indifference, which prevents all their capacities from being set into motion, is passivity. We see so many young people "parked" in the schools or other settings. But often we adults are no different. Many teachers clearly feel sad or alone in the face of all the challenges before them. I still remember one of my fellow professors, whom I met once at the entrance of the seminary where I lived. He was returning a bit upset from class, and I asked him, "What happened?" He answered, "Look, I just told my students that I have less satisfaction than a mechanic, because if a mechanic tries hard, he can fix a car, but I've devoted endless effort, and half of them have to repeat the year." So, to provoke him, I said, "Is this normal? How do your other colleagues fare?" He said, "They change their methods once, twice, three times . . . until they give up."

This situation applies to us teachers no less than to the students—after you stop trying, seeking, what do you do? You behave like the students: you endure the class hours, with heaviness in your heart. What interest can a teacher like this ever create in the students? This indifference towards reality, which leads inevitably to passivity, shows us clearly the nature of the crisis in which we are involved. It is not just a problem of the schools; it is a problem of the human, it shows up in the passivity of many young people, who are almost incapable of becoming interested in something for the long term, and it can be seen in the weariness, loneliness, and skepticism of so many adults, who fail to find an interest that makes it truly worthwhile to fully engage their own humanity. And thus they do not even have the capacity for involving the young people, engaging their interest in what they have before them. As Charles Péguy said: "The crisis of teaching isn't a crisis of teaching: it's the crisis of life."[1]

The situation in which we find ourselves is a challenge above all for us. Many attempts at facing this challenge have already failed, for example, saying, "Since we can't interest them, we can at least give them rules so that the river won't overflow; let's appeal to the people's, the students' moral strength." We all know that this does not help to arouse interest. The fact that we constantly have to appeal to this kind of extrinsic moralism means that we have already acknowledged defeat.

The first question is whether we are willing to look this challenge full in the face, to take it on, to deal with reality exactly as it is, or whether we prefer to look for a way to manage without focusing on the true struggle before us. Saint Augustine wondered, "What moves man in the depths of his being?"[2] This is so apt! In this situation we are living in, what is able to move man at the center of his very self?

In order to respond, think of what happens to a toddler when you put a toy in front of him. It begins to arouse all his interest. I've often given this example: imagine you're in a class and you've brought a device that's new to the kids. You've forgotten the cord and you say, "Wait a second. I'll go look for the cord." How much time do you think will pass before the kids get up and crowd around the table to see what it is?

Reality is what arouses our interest. For the child, it's not enough to have the toy in front of him to continue to be interested. It's not enough for us to explain the chemistry of the toy, the physics of the toy, the writing in Chinese, the size. If the child doesn't understand the point of that toy, we'll eventually see it forgotten in a corner of his room. Because partial explanations, partial data aren't enough for the child. Reason is the urgent demand for totality, for total meaning. You cannot introduce the toy without this total introduction. This is why we have always repeated that education is the "introduction to the total reality." What happens with the toy happens with everything: with the job that keeps you busy for hours and hours every day, or with the person you love, or a beautiful sunset, at a certain point it is impossible not to ask: "Well, what's the point?"

If it is so easy for reality to arouse interest, then why is there this indifference? Because what is in crisis is the nexus with reality. It does not mean that this nexus does not exist. We cannot avoid the relationship with reality. We are always in relationship with it. There is not an adult or a young person on the world's stage who is not immersed in reality and for whom reality does not arouse questions.

In his autobiography, the French Orthodox theologian Olivier Clément described how his father, a nonbeliever, had "educated" him to cut off his questioning, but he had not stopped him, as a young man, from being struck and interrogated by reality. When Olivier was eight years old, his friend Antoine died. Standing before the coffin, he looked at his father and asked, "Papa, where is Antoine?" His father, consistently with his atheism, answered, "Antoine's nowhere. He's dead." You would think that this would have cut short Olivier's inquiry, but when he was twelve, walking with his father one night under a starry sky, he asked again, "Papa, what is beyond the stars?" "Beyond the stars there's nothing."

Nobody, no power in this world can stop this dynamic, this impact of the self with reality that continually arouses questions, inquiry about meaning. No power can prevent a starry sky from reawakening the question of meaning. And what happens with the stars also happens with work, affection, time, everything that happens to us; reality continues to arouse questions, even in this situation of ours. Is it reasonable to keep working, after ten or twenty years, with all the chaos now in the schools? It is as if the Mystery, through reality, does not allow us to stop, and continues knocking on our door, reawakening the urgent demand for meaning. No power, no situation can stop the Mystery from knocking!

For this reason, saying that the nexus with reality is in crisis doesn't mean that this urgent knocking doesn't continue to happen; it is impossible for it not to happen. The desire to find an answer that makes the instant we are living in reasonable is continually reawakened in us in any circumstance—not only the beautiful ones, but also the ugly ones; in fact, more so: what meaning is there in working as a teacher in this situation? This desire is the principal resource for any educative effort, because it stimulates curiosity and questions about all the concerns of life. For this reason, in response to the question of whether it is possible to educate in this situation, we have to say *yes* right away, because this desire is continually reawakened.

So, wherein lies the problem of our nexus with reality? Fr. Giussani identified it in this way: in the face of this desire and these questions awakened in us by reality, we succumb to "an option permanently open to the human soul. It occurs when there is a sad lack of committed interest and an absence of curiosity towards all reality."[3]

Questions are inevitable; the desire to find an answer cannot be pushed aside, but we can choose not to consider the questions, not to let ourselves be drawn forward all the way to a conclusion by the questions, and thus to block this curiosity. Freedom enters into play, not pursuing the interest aroused by reality, not pursuing that curiosity that reality awakens in us. And when we succumb to the human soul's option to fail to engage with reality, what happens? We don't discover the meaning, and when we don't recognize the meaning of reality, it no longer interests us. If the child does not know how to use the toy, pretty soon he will abandon it in a corner of his room.

Therefore, the question of whether or not we are introduced to the total reality is by no means without impact for our relationship with it: if we do not perceive the meaning, sooner or later reality will not interest us, and we, too, like the young people, will become passive. We thought that reality would continue to be attractive without meaning. We thought that the meaning was an extra that we could do without: "We can explain physics or chemistry to the kids, without giving them their meaning." We thought we could reduce education to the transmission of knowledge, data, but this hasn't proven sufficient to continue to interest the kids in what they have before them. If we don't introduce the meaning, their interest, which reality goes on provoking in any case, falters and is supplanted by the nihilism that suppresses desire, not because reality does not constantly reawaken it, but because desire cannot maintain itself if it does not find an answer to this urgent demand for totality, this need for meaning. The absence of meaning depresses desire, just as it eliminates the child's interest in the toy.

But this situation is not inevitable. It depends on a decision that we have made, a lack of engagement, an ultimate immorality that opposes this need for meaning that constitutes us.

Mark my words, we find ourselves before a question that cannot be given just any answer. This is the deceit of relativism. We know that it is a lie, because not all answers correspond to the need we have. Not just any answer will give meaning to our daily work, our pain, our need to know how to live our circumstances so that they will not become a tomb for us. The problem of education is whether we have a suitable answer for this urge inherent in living, such that we can communicate it in our living. Education is not the kids' problem; it is the adults' problem, our problem. Only if we adults have this engagement with the real in its totality can we communicate a meaning. I am enthusiastic about this, because there is no hideaway, no circumstance that spares us this engagement. We cannot manage all right with a user's manual! This is the grace of working with kids: that we can't manage with a set of instructions, and that not just any old answer will do. We see it in the signs of passivity and weariness.

This is why we have to begin looking this situation full in the face. Do we want to deal with this, or do we want to do something alongside life, alongside problems? In this context, is there any hope? Is there something that can move man in his most intimate depths? This is the same as saying, how can I be there? How can I say "I'm here" with all my self, to the kids at school, to my kids, and to myself, in reality?

How Did This Happen?

In order to understand this situation, we do not have to engage in all sorts of mental machinations; once again, we have to look at our experience: has something happened that has reawakened our interest, that has set us back into motion? What has facilitated in us renewed commitment to authentic engagement? Can we identify something real? My answer is, yes. It is called "encounter." We encountered a winning attraction that carried within it a hypothesis of meaning that drew us after it; it was something so awe-inspiring that it helped us to set our whole "I" into motion. It could have happened in many ways: a preference, something that we have had to acknowledge, that established itself within us and reawakened all our needs. "Encounter . . . has an incomparable newness, freshness, and value. However, we can encounter a tradition, which has its roots in the centuries, within our present reality through a phrase, a word, or a gesture. This is to say that the encounter with that community or that friend brings us tidings that spring from a life lived through the centuries, through tradition."[4] Why does it set us in motion? Because it carries within it what corresponds to the heart: it corresponds so much that it incites all our needs, reawakens the desire to plunge into the fray, and makes us free to move within it.

"Just as we have not arranged the encounter, neither are our actions conditioned by our success."[5] Therefore, in this whole situation of tiredness and confusion, why can I start anew? Because something happened that makes my action free, and not dependent on the confusion, the troubles, the environment, my colleagues, the kids; my actions no longer depend on this, ultimately.

> The motive that moves us and justifies our diffusion is not within ourselves but is at our depths, where we find an Other [*Other* with a capital *O*], him whom we adore. We do not wish to form a party or faction or our own program. We wish to realize something that is other, pure, pristine, that does not depend on us but on the One who made us. For this reason, if the encounter is accepted simply, it gives us a great freedom of spirit that never hinders us but allows us to act independently of our cultural attainment or shrewdness and even beyond our heart. We have this faith and confidence because an Other acts within us. Our freedom is that simplicity and naivety that allows us to never tire of turning to whomever, of extending once again to whomever the invitation to that definitive encounter in the life of a human being.[6]

Nobody can prevent this event, which constantly reawakens the "I," from happening. And only if this continues to happen, if this remains as the wellspring constituting my "I," am I free to enter into any circumstance, and thus to enter into the whole of reality, liberated from my weariness and solitude. Then you understand why everything begins to become interesting. "In the experience of a great love . . . everything that happens becomes an event in its sphere."[7]

What happened and what can happen even after the encounter? "For many of us, the announcement that salvation is Jesus Christ [that is, that salvation lies in this encounter] and that the liberation of life and the human person, here and in the other world, is constantly bound to the encounter with him, has become a merely 'spiritual' call. We think of concrete things as something else: commitment to the labor union, activism to have certain rights recognized, getting organized, . . . and, therefore, [we think of] meetings, not as expressions of a life need, but rather as a mortification of life, a burden, dues to pay for a belonging that inexplicably finds us still in the ranks."[8] At a certain point—and I say this to shed light on a temptation we have fallen into before, and into which we could fall again— Christ was no longer indispensable for us in living our situation; we could do without him, because concrete life was another thing. Christ didn't seem indispensable for living the concrete—not that we denied him, but he simply became a premise, a spiritual reminder that we no longer needed for plunging into the fray. We were conceited and we dug our own graves.

But with time we see the consequences. With all our self-important efforts, we cannot cut it: many of us are in the tomb with a stupendous educative proposal! We believed we could spare ourselves the commitment to communicate the newness in the way in which we live the reality we face, through the theorization of an abstract method. Fr. Giussani warned of this danger: "We have to help each other defeat a danger . . . : [that of] reducing our commitment to a theorization of a socio-pedagogical method, to the resulting activism and its political defense, instead of reaffirming and proposing to our fellow human beings a fact of life."[9] But how could we think we can manage if we change the only method that can reawaken in people an interest in reality, that is, without making this winning attraction present—an attraction to which we must first of all surrender ourselves and which, if God wants, will communicate itself through us to others as well.

A New Beginning

For this reason, a new beginning is needed, one that does not start from "What should I do?" but from "Who am I? What am I?" It is not a rhetorical question; rather, "it is the point of departure that no evil can take away from us." If our troubles take away this point of departure, it is because it is not clear. The situation is never what defeats our person; it clarifies it, and makes our own fragility surface. It is not the environment that creates the fragility; it is not the situation in which we find ourselves that creates the fragility; instead, the situation brings to the surface our inconsistency, our lack of freedom. This "'What am I?' . . . is the constant principle of resurrection, like the reef that the storm covers but can never wash away, and that rises out of the water again the instant the wind dies down."[10]

Therefore, there has to be a renewal in us of "a different self-awareness [born of an encounter] and thus a different sense of the human, because we draw our sense of the human from ourselves. This is the new creature spoken of in the New Testament,[11] the new seed that is in the world, a new human being because he has a new sense of himself and thus of the other. . . . This new consciousness of oneself is called faith and is characterized by the fact that it is as if I were no longer myself, but something else that is in me."[12]

This is not a "spiritual" reminder that has nothing to do with the situation. This faith that is a new, different self-awareness is not something alongside human reality; it is not like a garment we put on. It is the reality of the person, it is your meaning and substance. This consciousness that is faith generates presence in the very moment you cross the threshold of school, when you're in front of the nursery school children or among the high school students. Otherwise, what in the world are we doing in the school?

Being defined by this new self-awareness means living a certainty that helps us enter in a different way into the whole reality of teaching. How can someone manage to go to school without being constantly filled with this certainty and this consciousness? "Truth must be realized in life,"[13] as Nikolai Berdjaev said. Realizing the truth in life means entering into reality (for a teacher, it means going to school) filled with this Presence. "The cultural phenomenon catches fire and spreads only if it is generated by a foundational *certainty*. . . . This certainty is the event of Christ in the adult, who in turn proposes it to the young person, who sees it present in the older person before him or her."[14] You can recognize the presence of this certainty from the fact that it creates a passion for things and feeds an interest in everything.

The symptom of this certainty is

> fondness for everything one encounters. . . . The more powerful a person, in terms of certainty of consciousness, the more his gaze, even in his habitual way of strolling along the street, embraces everything, valorizes everything, and misses nothing. He even sees the yellow leaf in the midst of a tree's green foliage. It is only our certainty of the ultimate meaning that enables us to perceive, as if we were metal detectors, the merest filings of truth in everyone else's pockets. It is not necessary, in order to be a friend to someone, for him to discover that what you say is true and come with you. It's not necessary. It is I who go with him because of that little filing of truth that he has. . . . Only the certainty of truth makes us feel immediately fraternal, maternal, and fond of every fragment of truth that exists in each person; therefore, truth is the friend of everyone.[15]

This is the test that we can all use on ourselves: if we have this certainty, we can freely enter into everything and be free from bondage to the outcome. This is the great choice each of us faces: to depend only on God and, therefore, be free from the whole universe; or to be free from God and, therefore, the slave to every circumstance, bound by every outcome.[16]

The way we engage in school, in reality, the way we face any circumstance, is the test of our dependence on the Mystery: when we live this original dependence, we experience a freedom of the other world in this world. This is because "Christianity is a new way to live in this world. It is a new life. Above all, it does not represent a few particular experiences, ways of doing things, additional gestures, or expressions or words to add to our usual vocabulary. . . . The Christian looks at all of reality in the same way as a non-Christian, but that which reality tells him or her is different and he or she reacts in a different way."[17] For this reason, the Christian can enter into reality, into all of reality, without foregone conclusions. And reality, entering into it, is the verification of the faith, of the certainty gained in life. Otherwise, faith is reduced to something parallel, alongside of life.

This is what excited me when I met the CL movement. For a long time, I had thought that my superiors in Madrid were wasting my time assigning me to teach high school, when I wanted to dedicate myself to my research. But when I met the CL movement and I realized the encounter I had had, I said to myself: "You're really an idiot, because what the Lord is making you do is verify your faith at school." I'm grateful for my ten years of teaching high school for this precise reason, because otherwise I would have been able to find the "theological" reason to justify my escape from school, as some of my colleagues did. I could have just found a sudden "vocation" for parish life. But for me this would have meant to go away defeated, with my theological justification alongside me in the casket. But thanks to God, what I encountered, the encounter I had with the movement and Fr. Giussani's proposal, permitted me to verify my faith deep down. And when I did leave the school (because they moved me to a different job), I was freer, gladder, happier, more certain than when I began. Being forced to stay in front of kids I hadn't chosen, or with colleagues I hadn't chosen, I had not the slightest temptation to run away. That's why I often told Fr. Giussani, "I'll always be grateful to you because, since I've met you, I've been able travel on a human journey," that is, to verify the importance of my faith in my life, in the way I lived at school. I was able to see that faith was not merely a spiritual call. I am very grateful that I was never spared—because I was a priest or because I taught in a certain school—the journey of entering into reality myself in front of the kids, with the subject matter I had to teach. Given what I had encountered, which enabled me to take my desire seriously, if I had not entered personally into reality, I would not have verified faith's ability to change and I would have gone away defeated, because I would not have been able to substitute faith with some beautiful educational theories.

In fact, education is not explaining reality or forming some argument about it; it is helping another person—students or friends—to enter into reality. The moment I realized this, going to school became a party for me. If we want to introduce the others to reality, we cannot do it—to use a Spanish proverb—"looking at the bull from the stands." Only if the kids see the victory in our face, in our visage, in the way we act, in the way we react, in the way we live everything, will they be interested in what we want to communicate to them; only then will they get the desire to live this way, the way they see us living. Because "education is a communication of yourself, that is, of your own way of relating with reality," Fr. Giussani said. Communication of yourself does not mean communicating your ideas, your theories; it is communicating your own way of relating with reality, because "man is . . . a living modality of the *relationship with reality*. . . . Therefore, communication of yourself means communicating a living way of relating with reality."[18]

I am grateful that the circumstances of my life forced me to realize that education means communicating yourself, that is, your particular way of relating to reality. After ten years of teaching high school, I became a professor at the university, and because I was a member of CL, I could not speak even an instant outside the hour of lesson; I wasn't permitted to do anything "extra-curricular." But I am very grateful for this, because it obliged me to communicate what I held most dear in class, in the way I taught, without needing to add anything else. Nobody could stop me from teaching in a certain way and transmitting the contents in a certain way. I did not need anything else outside the hour of lesson, and nobody could stop what I said during class from becoming the topic of dialogue in the university dining room.

We don't need anything else, anything parallel or alongside, if we accept the challenge of reality, because the way a person lives reality is what provokes us. "The beginning is a Presence that imposes itself. The beginning is a provocation, but not to the 'brain,' . . . to our life; whatever is not a provocation to our life wastes our time and energy, and blocks us from true joy,"[19] and therefore, in time, no longer interests us. "The educative presence is the presence of the adult as a unified person,"[20] and this concerns everything, from teaching methodology to the environment. Indeed, if we do not reach the point at which this newness of gaze, sparked by the encounter, opens us to discover more the way to go to deal with and communicate the subject matter in a new and more fulfilled way, if we don't reach that point, if we don't arrive at the level of teaching methodology, we succumb to dualism.

A teacher writes,

I came back to high school teaching after a five-year absence, and found again a situation that I had already experienced for some time. I can say that I work hard at preparing lessons, enriched year after year with the experience of so many gatherings, readings, exchanges of thought, and judgments made together with other teacher friends. So, I don't think that the content of my communication is lackluster; if nothing else, the students (I've always believed) have something of substance with which to compare their own thought. And yet I continue to note (yesterday as well as today) that when I examine my students (especially the better and more conscientious ones), their answers contain elements that don't come from what I told them, but from what's written in their textbooks. So when they return home after an interesting lesson of mine, they learn from their books notions that are the exact opposite of what I've proposed—the "after" cancels out the "before." This makes me understand how important it is to embrace reality in all its aspects, including teaching methodology, that is, the set of materials that are part of the learning process. I realized that if our educative concerns don't reach that point, it's as if we surrender from the outset to a cultural challenge that should be our responsibility, only ours and not delegated to others.

This is the challenge. The number does not matter: if there are ten people who accept this challenge, count me in. If someone wants to do something "alongside," I am not interested.

From teaching methodology to the environment, as I was saying. The second factor of presence is being inside the environment. "Christianity is the announcement of God incarnate, and this means not only that God took on flesh, but also that he has remained immanent in, organic to time, space, and history. Thus we need to be inside the normal fabric of life and the modality with which society, with a power that penetrates everywhere . . . , involves individuals and conditions them, manipulating them for its purposes; we need to be inside, in the environment. We need to be organic to the world in its intricate concreteness. . . . Presence means being with all your humanity inside the environment."[21] This is the verification of the faith: each of us is called to verify whether the certainty of faith allows them to be in any situation in a more human way. Otherwise, why should I be interested? Why does Christ interest me, if not because he enables me to stay in reality in any situation, before any circumstance?

Faith "is either within the environment, or it's not true"; it cannot prove itself true. If faith is unable to make me live any circumstance better, if it does not introduce me to the totality of the real, it is useless to me. And sooner or later there will happen to me what has happened to so many Christians for whom faith was no longer pertinent—it didn't have anything to do with life. It is not that they denied it, but they just stopped being interested in the life of faith. We are trying to verify our faith within all of reality, because "the environment is whatever aspect of the normal fabric of life and the practical modality with which the world involves and conditions us; therefore, it is the family, the apartment house, friends, the labor union, the work environment, politics, everything."[22]

If we don't enter into reality with the desire to personally verify the faith, we teachers, instead of expressing a call to students, become mere transmitters of propaganda: "Propaganda is to spread something simply because it is one's own idea or because it is of personal interest. The calling, instead . . . is to awaken something that is already in the other."[23] But how do I awaken it? Only if I become a presence through the way I live reality do I awaken the interest of others. I cannot manage just by communicating a discourse since in this way, I'm just a propagandist, and I don't awaken anything in the other. "I appeal to my companions to help them find their truth, their true names (in the biblical sense), to find themselves. My Christian appeal is thus the strongest contribution to one's freedom, because freedom means to be oneself. For that reason, our calling is the supreme gesture of friendship." Awakening others, not making them become "ours," means that whatever road they must take to reach their destiny is up to the Mystery, not to me. What interests us is testifying to Christ, testifying to the power of Christ, who awakens the "I" of the other. Then whatever they do is their own business; the goal is not to bring them to "our" group. For this reason "above all, we are never called to determined forms, criteria, or schemes, or to particular organizations, but rather to that promise that constitutes the human heart. We repeat what God placed in others' hearts as He created them, placing them in a given setting, shaping them. For this very reason, we do not know where God will lead them."[24] But we often think we already know what the Mystery has decided for them!

I am so often amazed by our lack of the sense of the Mystery, because we already think we know the plan. But the plan

is His [God's]. We cannot know what their vocation will be [this sentence alone is enough to make us reconsider everything we do]. Ours, therefore, is above all a calling to that which constitutes the value of a human life, to a destiny, a vocation, its fulfillment, and nothing else. In proposing to the other, we relive the motives for which we appeal to him or her. It is exactly that splendor, the expression of this "reliving" of ours, that constitutes the calling to the other [the splendor, this "reliving" of ours, is called witness, not argument!]. Thus, the call is not something extrinsic to us, almost like a task outside ourselves. Once our adherence is no longer vital, our appeal becomes automatic, as if we were expounding a formula or ideology. Such an appeal is usually propaganda, which only generates arguments, making us feel estranged from others. We must do things in such a way that everything—the initiatives that we undertake, the invitations we extend—is pervaded and animated by a genuine concern for the ideal. We have the same concerns as others, because they are human preoccupations. But we have something else: our every gesture is underpinned by the profound desire to love the person, that is, to help him or her to be truly free, to walk toward his or her destiny. This is the law of charity: the desire that the others be themselves, that they "save" themselves. . . . We want to go to school or work, we worry about achieving a good grade or a fair wage, we have a curiosity about things and events and a desire to have relationships that fill time and avoid boredom. But, above all, we want to be people who, beyond attending school, going to work, or being friends, always strive for the ideal, the supreme ideal, Christ and the Church.[25]

If our proposal is conveyed by living before others, testifying to what was given to us through the way we face circumstances, then the recipients are everyone—everyone!—because we live before everyone and we cannot know in advance whom the Lord wants to move in their innermost depths through our testimony; we cannot know. For this reason, "it was terribly mistaken to think our educative efforts in school should become set in alternative works,"[26] thinking that what the Lord desired would ensue from these works. As the wrecking and destruction of the human person intensifies, we can find more people willing to join us, but it would be cold comfort if we were able to attract only "some": do they come because they are attracted, or because they don't have anything better to do? With our proposal, are we able to challenge and move those who have something serious in mind, and who are drawn by a winning attraction they have before them, or not?

This brings us to understand the relationship between the way in which the Mystery acts and how we should respond. It is not up to us to decide who moves someone's innermost depths; it is the Mystery who works, through the last person to arrive, or through whomever he decides. Our job is to obey the way he does things. Therefore, the first move of any authority, any person with responsibility, will be to obey that way in which the Mystery makes things emerge. And if he makes things emerge through one person or another, we should all strive to see how we can go to meet them, help, not try right away to absorb that person into the structure. The Lord isn't incompetent, and he moves things and people according to his method. He, who knows everyone, knows how to act. Either we respect this and obey this method—and thus the first authority is the one who obeys the most, not who manages the most—or we absorb people.

This is the reason we accompany each other and the others, in short, to be friends for each other, that is, witnesses. We are friends amongst ourselves and the kids if we testify to each other this modality of staying in reality, a method awakened by the faith. This enables us to embrace everything and everyone, even in the particulars of life and school.

PART 4

A NEW PROTAGONIST
ON THE WORLD SCENE

———————•◦•———————

"Lady, Your Beauty Was a Ray of Heavenly / Light to My Thinking

The family is at the center of public debate. The attempt to regulate new forms of cohabitation, different from marriage conceived of as the definitive and fertile relationship between a man and a woman, has sparked heated debate, bringing a process begun many years ago to its peak.

This debate has brought to light, on the one hand, that the dissemination of a contrary mentality through the mass media (film, television, and the press) has not prevented many people from having a positive experience of family. Although the traditional family is no longer a fashionable model for living, the inextricable experience of a good that people have had in their own family life endures. We are grateful for this good, and we want to pass it on to future generations, in order to share it with them.

On the other hand, the good we have experienced has not prevented the assertion of other forms of cohabitation, different from marriage. Here we must consider, too, another, no less important fact: this process began when the vast majority of national legislation in Europe concerning marriage still defended the traditional model derived from Christianity. All the protection the law had to offer did not prevent the spread of a mentality against marriage, and was not able to stop the shift.

Regaining the Self

How did this happen? How is it possible that all the clarity we had gained concerning the nature of marriage, confirmed over the course of centuries, could be called into question in such a short space of time, and so pervasively as to become the mainstream mentality? Pope Benedict XVI reminded us: "Good structures help, but of themselves they are not enough. Man can never be redeemed simply from outside."[1]

Trying to understand the current situation seems to me to be particularly critical in order to respond to the urgent needs that arise from it.

Sadly we realize that many people find themselves unable to stand firm before the many difficulties they go through, external and internal. And it is not enough to know the doctrine of marriage to stand up to life's blows.

Each time it becomes clearer that the maturity of the human subjects approaching marriage cannot be taken for granted. The reality is that, regardless of their goodwill, many young people reach marriage without a sufficient awareness of the nature of what they are about to undertake. Nor can this awareness be taken for granted when it comes to young Christians, who not infrequently approach marriage in the same condition as their non-Christian friends, the only difference being that they get married in church and have the desire to live more or less according to the idea of marriage defended and professed by the Church. This lack of awareness is a problem that cannot be solved simply through the premarital courses we know, which by nature cannot address the circumstances of those who attend them. The challenge is serious, indeed, and it concerns the entire Christian community, putting to the test its ability to generate adult personalities, men and women, who are capable of approaching marriage with the prospect of a positive outcome.

There is one thing that in my mind is pivotal for shedding light on the specific relationship that is established between a man and a woman. The crisis of the family is one consequence of the anthropological crisis we find ourselves in. The spouses are two human subjects, an I and a You, a man and a woman, who decide to walk together towards destiny, towards happiness. The way they approach their relationship, the way they conceive of it, depends on the image each one has of their own life, of their self-realization. This implies a conception of humanity and its mystery. "The problem of the proper relationship between man and woman," said Benedict XVI, "has its roots in the most profound essence of the human being, and can find its answer only from this. It cannot be separated from man's ancient and ever-new question about himself: 'Who am I? What is man?'"[2]

So the first help that can be offered to those who want to marry is to help them to become aware of their own human mystery. Only in this way will they be able to focus adequately on their relationship, without expecting from it something which by their very nature neither can give to the other. How much violence, how much disappointment could be avoided in marriage relationships if people were to understand their own nature!

This lack of awareness of man's destiny leads people to found their whole relationship on a deception, which can be formulated in these words: the conviction that a You can make the "I" happy. In this way their mutual relationship is transformed into a refuge, so desired, yet quite useless for solving the problem of their self-fulfillment. And when the deception is eventually discovered, because the other has not lived up to expectation, disappointment is inevitable. The marriage relationship cannot be founded on anything but the truth of each of its protagonists. It is the loving relationship itself that contributes in a particular way to discovering the truth of the "I" and of the You, and along with the truth of the "I" and the You is revealed the nature of the shared vocation.

Indeed, the "eternal mystery of our being" is revealed to us by the relationship with the person we love. Nothing reawakens us, nothing makes us so aware of the desire for happiness that constitutes us, as the person we love. The presence of the beloved is so great a good that it makes us grasp the depth and the true dimension of this desire: infinity. What the poet Cesare Pavese said of pleasure can be applied to a loving relationship: "What a man seeks in his pleasures is that they should be infinite, and no one would ever give up hope of attaining that infinity."[3] A limited I and a limited You arouse in each other an infinite desire, and they find themselves launched by their love towards an infinite destiny. In this experience each of them discovers their own vocation. They feel the need for each other so as not to be paralyzed in their own limitations, with no other prospect but the boredom of loneliness.

In the loving encounter between man and woman, at the very moment in which the boundless dimensions of our desire are revealed to us, the possibility of fulfillment appears. Or, more precisely, as we perceive in the person we love the promise of fulfillment, the whole infinite potential of our desire for happiness is enkindled. This is why nothing makes us understand the mystery of our humanity better than the man-woman relationship, as Benedict XVI reminded us in his encyclical *Deus Caritas Est*. "In love between man and woman, where body and soul are inseparably joined . . . human beings glimpse an apparently irresistible promise of happiness. . . . All other kinds of love immediately seem to fade in comparison."[4]

In this relationship, a human being seems to meet what takes them beyond their own limitation and enables them to reach an incomparable fullness.[5] This is why historically people perceived a relationship between love and the divine: "Love promises infinity, eternity—a reality far greater and totally other than our everyday existence."[6]

This is the experience that the Italian poet Giacomo Leopardi spoke of in his hymn to Aspasia: "Lady, your beauty was a ray of heavenly / light to my thinking."[7] The poet perceives the woman's beauty as a "divine light," as the presence of God. Through her beauty, it is God who is knocking at the man's door. If the man does not grasp the nature of this call, and instead of accepting it as such stops short at the beauty he sees before him, this beauty soon reveals itself as unable to fulfill its promise of happiness, of infinity.

"Yet it's not she whom he reveres and loves, / even as he holds her, but the other. / At last he sees the error of his misplaced / feelings and becomes enraged, and often / wrongly blames the woman."[8] The woman, with her limitation, awakens in the man, who is also limited, a desire for fullness out of proportion with her capacity to answer it. She awakens a thirst that she is unable to quench, a hunger she is unable to satisfy. This is what gives rise to the anger and the violence that married couples so often experience and the delusion they feel if they do not understand the true nature of their relationship.

The woman's beauty is truly a "divine light," a sign that points beyond itself, to something greater, something divine, out of all proportion with its limited nature. Her beauty is calling out before us: "It is not I. I am only a reminder. Look! Look! What do I remind you of?"[9] With these words C. S. Lewis's genius captured the dynamics of the sign, of which the man-woman relationship is a moving example. If he does not understand these dynamics, a man makes the mistake of stopping short at the reality that arouses his desire, like a woman who receives a bunch of flowers and is so taken by their beauty that she forgets the face of the one who sent them to her, of whom they are a sign, thus losing the best thing the flowers brought her. If we do not acknowledge the other's character as sign, then we are inevitably led to reduce him to what appears to our eyes, and sooner or later he will prove incapable of answering to the desire he has aroused.

Thus if husband and wife do not encounter what the sign is pointing to, the place where they can find the fulfillment of the promise that the other has aroused, then they are condemned to be consumed by a pretension from which they cannot free themselves, and their desire for the infinite, which no one like the person loved arouses, is condemned to remain unsatisfied. Faced with this dissatisfaction, many today see no way out but to change partners, giving rise to a spiral in which the problem is merely postponed until the next disappointment.

The German poet Rainer Maria Rilke identified very keenly this drama in loving relationships, sensing that ending up in this spiral cannot be the only way out: this is the paradox of love between man and woman: two infinites "meet two limitations,"[10] two infinite needs to be loved meet two fragile and limited capacities to love. Only in the ambit of a greater love do they not consume themselves in pretension and not resign themselves, but walk together, each towards a fullness of which the other is sign.

Only in the ambit of a greater love can people avoid being consumed with the claim, laden with violence, that the other, who is limited, must answer to the infinite desire he awakens, making impossible both the fulfillment of the person whose desire has been awakened and that of the person he loves. In order to discover this, one must be ready to comply with the dynamics of sign and must stay open to the surprise that this can have in store for us.

Leopardi had the courage to run this risk. With a penetrating intuition of the love relationship, the Italian poet glimpses that what he was seeking in the beauty of the women he fell in love with was Beauty with a capital B. At the summit of human intensity, the hymn "To His Lady" is a hymn to the "dearest beauty" that he seeks in everything beautiful; his whole desire is that Beauty, the eternal idea of Beauty, take up tangible form.[11] It is what happened in Christ, the Word made flesh. This is why Luigi Giussani defined this poem as a prophecy of the incarnation.[12]

And Christ, Beauty made flesh, places "himself at the core of man's affection and freedom," at the "core of these natural sentiments, the place he rightfully assumes is their true root."[13] This is Jesus' "claim," which we find expressed in certain passages of the gospel which may at first glance seem paradoxical: "Do not think that I have come to bring peace upon the earth. I have come to bring not peace but the sword. For I have come to set a man 'against his father, a daughter against her mother, and a daughter-in-law against her mother-in-law; and one's enemies will be those of his household.' Whoever loves father or mother more than me is not worthy of me, and whoever loves son or daughter more than me is not worthy of me. . . . Whoever finds his life will lose it, and whoever loses his life will find it. Whoever receives you receives me, and whoever receives me receives the one who sent me."[14]

In this way, Jesus reveals the importance of the promise his person constitutes for those who let him in. It is not an interference on Jesus' part in the most intimate level of human feelings, but rather the greatest promise ever made to man: the fulfillment of all his human desire, which is Jesus' very person. Therefore, if you do not love Christ, Beauty made flesh, more than the person you love, the latter relationship withers, because Christ is the truth of this relationship, the fullness to which both partners point, and in whom their relationship is fulfilled. Only by letting him in is it possible for the most beautiful relationship that can happen in life not to be corrupted and die in time. This is the audacity of his claim.

Marriage and Virginity: Possession with Detachment Inside

Responding to the disciples' shocked reaction when he announced the indissolubility of marriage, Jesus presented them with an answer that may well seem even more enigmatic: "He answered, 'Not all can accept [this] word, but only those to whom that is granted. Some are incapable of marriage because they were born so; some, because they were made so by others; some, because they have renounced marriage for the sake of the kingdom of heaven. Whoever can accept this ought to accept it.'"[15]

So saying, Jesus added a new category of celibate person: those who become so for the sake of the kingdom of heaven. Clearly he is describing a freely made choice. Pope John Paul II commented on this passage, saying:

> In his call to celibacy "for the Kingdom of heaven," first his own Disciples and later the entire living Tradition would soon discover the love that turns toward Christ Himself as Bridegroom of the Church and spouse of souls, to whom he has given Himself to the very last, in the Pascal mystery and the mystery of the Eucharist. In this way, celibacy "for the Kingdom of heaven," the

choice of virginity or remaining single for one's entire life, became, in the experience of the disciples and Christ's followers, a responsive action specific to the love of the Divine Bridegroom. Therefore, it has acquired the meaning of an act of spousal love, that is, of a spousal gift of self, to return in a special way the spousal love of the Redeemer: a gift of self, understood as sacrifice, but made above all for the sake of love.[16]

The pope's observation sheds light on what virginity is: the absolutely gratuitous relationship with other people (and things) that Christ introduced into history. Virginity is living things according to their truth. It came into the world as the imitation of Christ, that is, of the way a man who was God lived. The only reason that can support something as immense as virginity is identifying with the way in which Christ possessed reality: carrying out the will of the Father.

The person of Jesus is so great and precious a good because he alone fully corresponds to the human thirst for happiness. And the exceptional correspondence he brings about in those who meet him makes them capable of relating to reality in an absolutely gratuitous way.

But how do people called to virginity contribute to God's kingdom? Those called to virginity have been chosen to "cry out before everyone, at every instant (their entire life is made for this) that Christ is the only thing that makes life worth living, that Christ is the only thing that makes the existence of the world worthwhile. . . . This is the objective value of the vocation: the form their life takes plays for Christ in the world, fights for Christ in the world. The form itself, the very form of their life! . . . It is a life that, by its form alone, cries: 'Jesus is everything.' They shout this before everyone, everyone who sees them, everyone who comes across them, everyone who hears them, everyone who watches them."[17]

The vocation to virginity is closely bound to the vocation to marriage: answering the Lord's call, people who live celibacy "cry out" to married people the truth of their married love. "The realization of this call also serves in a particular way to confirm the spousal importance of the human body in its masculinity and femininity. . . . One might say that this renunciation carried out by single individuals, men and women, is indispensible in a certain way, so that this spousal meaning of the body may be more easily recognized in the entire ethos of human life and above all that of married and family life."[18] Virginity is, therefore, an authentic hope for married people; it harkens to and manifests the root of the possibility to live marriage without claims and without deceptions: "By virtue of this witness, virginity or celibacy keeps alive in the Church a consciousness of the mystery of marriage and defends it from any reduction and impoverishment."[19]

Virginity is also something everyone is called to. As Fr. Giussani pointed out, "Virginity is the ideal Christian virtue in every relationship, including the relationship between a man and a woman who are married. The culmination of their relationship, the peak moment of their relationship, is when they sacrifice themselves, not when they express their possession. This is because, on account of original sin, in seizing we slip. It is like someone who wants something, and runs toward it, and as they are about to come up on it they run so fast that they break their nose up against it: they slip, stumble. This is why we call virginity possession with detachment inside."[20] True possession—the one we can experience—is possession with detachment inside.

In the Ambit of a Greater Love

At this moment, the task of the Christian community appears in all its importance: that of favoring an experience of Christianity as fullness of life for each person. What enables a married man and woman to avoid being consumed by pretense or resignation? It is necessary for them to live in the ambit of a greater love, that is, that there be a place where they can always rediscover Christ as the fulfillment of their humanity. The ability to embrace another person in their diversity, a capacity for unlimited gratuitousness, and a capacity for forgiveness that can be constantly renewed come from the relationship with Christ in his Church.

Without Christian communities able to accompany and sustain married couples in their adventure, it will be difficult, if not impossible, for them to have a successful outcome. In their turn, the couple cannot exempt themselves from the work of education in which they are the main protagonists, thinking that belonging to a Church community will free them from hardships.

Well aware of this situation, Benedict XVI proclaimed a need "to ensure that families do not feel alone. A small family can encounter difficult obstacles when it is isolated from relatives and friends. The ecclesial community therefore has the responsibility of offering support, encouragement and spiritual nourishment which can strengthen the cohesiveness of the family, especially in times of trial or difficulty. Here parishes have an important role to play, as do the various ecclesial associations, called to cooperate as networks of support and a helping hand for the growth of families in faith."[21] This invitation, full of tenderness and realism, at the same time identifies a task to carry out.

The family as such has need of a place where it is supported, and this place can only take the form of living Christian communities, where families experience the fullness of faith.

For families, belonging to the Church—to that scrap of the Church in which each of us experiences the universal presence of Christ—is a requirement of life, of the inexpungible experience of a good. Clinging to each other in a fraternal way, creating hospitable homes, is the greatest help that Christians can offer to everyone to foster the reawakening of an interest in family. "Overcoming solitude in the experience of the Spirit of Christ not only draws us near to others but also opens us to others to the very depths of their being. . . . The community becomes essential to each of us, to our lives. . . . 'We' becomes the fullness of 'I,' the law of the I's fulfillment."[22]

Bearing witness to this possibility for relationships is the original contribution that married Christians can make in the face of the struggle many of their acquaintances suffer through. It is a gratuitous witness that challenges the reason and the freedom of those who are unable to find a sufficient answer to their need for happiness. It is testimony offered in the awareness that "we hold this treasure in earthen vessels, that the surpassing power may be of God and not from us."[23]

Here the nature of the marriage vocation is fully revealed: walking together towards the only One who can answer the thirst for happiness that the other arouses constantly in me: Christ. In this way it will be possible not to move from one husband to another, like the Samaritan woman in the gospel,[24] without finding satisfaction. The awareness that she was unable to solve her own drama by herself, despite changing husbands five times, made her perceive Jesus as a good so desirable that she could not help crying out, "Sir, give me this water, so that I may no longer be thirsty."[25]

Without an experience of Christ as human fulfillment, the Christian ideal of marriage is reduced to something impossible to realize. The indissolubility of marriage and the eternity of love seem to be dreams beyond reach. In fact they are the fruit of such an intense experience of Christ that they appear to the couple themselves as a surprise, as the witness that "nothing is impossible for God."

Only an experience of fullness of life like this can show the rationality of the Christian faith as totally corresponding to man's desire and needs, even in marriage and the family.

A true relationship between parents is also the best educative proposal for the children, who, through the beauty of their parents' relationship, are introduced, as by osmosis, into the meaning of existence. Children's reason and their freedom are constantly solicited not to detach themselves from such beauty, that beauty which shines out in the witness of Christian couples that men and women of our time need to encounter.

———•◆•———

CHAPTER 14

With the Audacity of Realism

I hear from many people that these times are characterized by great difficulty for those who do social work and have businesses. It seems like an earthquake, with everything crashing down. Today we find ourselves navigating "against the wind." In this context, can we find the reasons to be audacious and realistic?

The Crisis and the Person

It seems to me that the starting point for a recovery is to acquire an elementary awareness: that any entrepreneur or worker involved in any kind of work for a business is a *person*. It may seem like saying that water flows downhill, but it is not so obvious. Everybody takes it for granted, reducing the person to his or her abilities. But the person is not just the sum of what they know how to do. Saying that an entrepreneur is a person means saying that before anything else, she or he needs clarity concerning his or her own origin and own destiny, concerning the source of his or her own worth, without which all the rest, starting with work capabilities, proves inadequate. It is all too evident that today the earthquake hits the center of one's "I," one's substance. In this sense, the recession can be an unlooked-for but precious opportunity for discovering the truth of oneself, the grounding for one's substance, and thus for laying a foundation suitable for facing the situation, the difficult challenge we have before us, one that is never detached from the exercise of one's profession.

What are the essential characteristics of the self? The genius of Dante Alighieri comes to our aid: "Everyone can vaguely apprehend some good / in which the mind may find its peace. / With desire, each one strives to reach it."[1] Where can such an "I," with this desire for good that constitutes it, find its own substance, in order to stand firm in the midst of an earthquake? This is the truest challenge of the circumstances we find ourselves facing. What can rise to the level of the human being's thirst? To find an answer, mere opinions, interpretations, and chatter are not enough, because they have no effect.

This is the level at which we Christians can offer our simple contribution, that is, if we are the first to accept the verification of faith in our daily circumstances. Only those who undertake the path of this verification can confirm, through their testimony, that only Christ present in the Church corresponds to the constitutive needs of the human heart: "Christ, He alone satisfies the desires for truth and goodness [that Dante speaks of] that are rooted in every human being's soul."[2] Only Christ ensures the satisfaction that generates affection capable of sustaining life in any eventuality, like a secure anchor in the midst of the storm. This is where one sees whether the encounter with circumstances has matured a certainty in us that enables us to offer our fellow human beings a sure foothold.

This is what our experience makes clear. Only Christ, present here and now, can be the suitable foundation for an operative friendship like yours wants to be, one that wishes to face the world. Only in the companionship of true friends will you be able to look at the reality of your business with freedom, without being overcome by the fear that blocks you from acknowledging how things stand, and this freedom from fear is the one condition for being able to face your circumstances with some possibility of success. I am talking about a companionship of friends that pushes each one to look at all the signs of the situation in which we find ourselves without disregarding any of them, a companionship that encourages and supports willingness to acknowledge the instructions of reality and obey them, changing everything that has to be changed, a companionship that helps us to have the audacity to make decisions, even risky ones, most appropriate for facing the challenges that lie ahead, before it is too late.

Experience will make you discover the most precious value of your friendship: helping each other have a truer gaze upon reality. Compared to this, any other self-interest or advantage of any kind is too little for times of earthquake such as ours.

Saint Thomas Aquinas understood well the nature of the challenge: "From nature springs the fear of death; from grace springs audacity."[3] "So then, saying 'audacity springs from grace' means it comes from a Presence different from us."[4] I can have the audacity I need only if I am willing to base everything on that presence, on that true companionship that offers me a real foothold. Therefore, Fr. Giussani said, "Emblematic of audacity is *Navigation* by Andrea Pisano (a small bas-relief . . .). There are the silhouettes of two disciples rowing, parting the waves of the lake on their way to the other shore, and they are simultaneously tense but calm and sure: behind them in the boat is Jesus. The journey, the passage, the crossing toward destiny becomes possible only when there is *a presence* (if one were rowing alone, his sight would fog, and he would stop right away). The journey becomes simple if there is a presence, that is, let's say it outright, if there is a *companionship*."[5]

The Origin and the Work

Since any works and firms associated with the Company of Works[6] were founded by people belonging to the Christian experience, an experience often lived in the movement of Communion and Liberation, it is particularly urgent these days to clarify what the relationship is between CL and these works created by people educated within it.

First, we must note that the goal of the movement of Communion and Liberation is educational: to educate people who can then shoulder their own responsibility and take the initiative to generate works; this responsibility is totally entrusted to the adult, to the person. The movement does not enter into the management of the work, because it would be like admitting that the movement is incapable of generating adults who shoulder their own responsibility; this would be the total failure of the CL experience. It is not that the movement does not care about the works. No. The movement shows that it cares and is present by carrying out its own work, which is the generation of the adult. From the very beginning, Fr. Giussani maintained that the movement's role was to generate adult subjects, capable of creativity at every level and of assuming responsibility for what they create. He did not feel the need to set a "guardian" to keep an eye on people. He betted and "risked" everything on the awareness and freedom of people educated in faith in the movement. He always stressed that the responsibility of works belonged to the people who created them and not to the movement, because otherwise, "the experience of the Church would be instrumentalized, and the communities would be transformed into pedestals and cover for decisions and risks that can only be personal ones."[7]

Second, the work is entirely of those who do it; thus there is no work "of" the movement. The movement has no works, except for the Sacred Heart Institute [a high school in Milan], which Fr. Giussani wanted as an example for everyone in the sphere of education. No other work or business (for profit or not for profit) falls under the direct responsibility of CL. The movement is not part of the board of directors of this or that work, and thus, not being part of it, does not take on responsibility for the decisions the board of directors makes.

All the people who, as adults, decide to give life to a work must be conscious of their total responsibility for the work. This is particularly important, because at times one notes a lack of precisely this awareness. And so it can happen that things are left adrift when instead there should be an intervention, a taking of responsibility as adults. If everyone were truly aware of his or her responsibility, certain things would not happen.

This is a call to personal responsibility, and it is part of the growth of mature Christians we all wish for. In other words, this is the responsibility of the layperson that the Church wants each person to shoulder, so that, in doing things, laypeople can witness to all the beauty of the Christian life, all the newness that is born of the "new creature." This is why it seems to me that we have a long road before us, not for lack of many stupendous experiences among you, but because it is necessary to learn still more from what happens, or from the possible deficiencies that can reveal themselves in the works, to avoid running risks and making mistakes.

The capacity of an adult—who participates in the experience of Communion and Liberation—to generate a work is a sign of the vivacity of the movement, of its educative energy in generating people sensitive to the needs of others and able to get together to set up initiatives, works, that constitute answers appropriate to people's needs. We will never give up on this. I cannot tell you how often I remain speechless before so much creativity, initiative, and generosity! This is the fruit of the education received in the movement of Communion and Liberation. It is a very beautiful thing that testifies to faith's capacity to generate subjects able to become protagonists through the creation of works. Such a richness of initiative is a fact, evident to all, and cannot be called into question because of our failures or the mistakes that anyone can make. Rather, acknowledging them, asking for forgiveness, and correcting ourselves offers us the chance to regain awareness of our own responsibility in the work in which we are engaged.

This responsibility involves, in addition to realism and prudence in realizing works in society, making the difference of these works shine out, for example, in the way you treat staff and the way you relate with clients and suppliers. These signs may seem simple, but we all know that they "cry out" the uniqueness of a work, which reechoes its origins.

Before concluding this point, I would like to take the opportunity to say something about the Company of Works Association (CdO), often presented by the newspapers as the "economic arm" of CL, leading some to think that CL depends economically on the CdO. Nothing is further from the reality.

Since the very beginning, the movement has been supported exclusively by the economic sacrifices of the people who belong to it. Those who belong to the movement commit to a monthly donation of a freely decided amount, the so-called Common Fund that Fr. Giussani always indicated as a gesture that educates us to adopt a communal conception of what one possesses, to the awareness of poverty as an evangelical virtue, and as a gesture of gratitude for what one experiences in the movement. Precisely for this educative reason, what is important is not the quantity one gives, but the seriousness with which one remains faithful to the commitment. To support the life of our communities in Italy and the world and its charitable, missionary, and cultural initiatives, the movement of Communion and Liberation needs nothing else, and for this reason we are free from everything and everyone in carrying out our task as a movement.

Belonging and Responsibility

We often hear it said that belonging to the Church or an ecclesial movement amounts to a limitation to one's personal responsibility. In reality such belonging promotes the assumption of responsibility. Everything depends on how one views the nexus between belonging and responsibility.

There are types of belonging that, instead of helping the member mature and grow in responsibility, step into his place, almost as if belonging to a certain group could spare the risk of personal responsibility and justify one's behavior a priori. However, there is a belonging that generates the person in her responsibility, her freedom, her initiative. It reawakens all the hidden energies of the subject.

"The communitarian dimension," as Fr. Giussani always said, "does not replace freedom, personal energy, and decision. Rather, it is the condition for their affirmation." The community is like the soil for the seed.

Now, the humus does not replace the irreducible energy, the in-communicable "personality" of the seed. Rather, the humus is the condition needed for the seed to grow. The community is the dimension and condition necessary for the human seed to bear fruit. For this reason, we can say that the true, the most intelligent persecution, . . . most ferocious persecution is the modern State's attempt to block the expression of the communal dimension of the religious phenomenon. As far as the State is concerned, a person can, in conscience, believe what he likes, as long as this faith does not imply that all believers are one and, therefore, have the right to live and express this reality. To obstruct communal expression is like cutting off the roots that nourish the plant: the plant soon dies.[8]

It seems that we have before us many examples of what happens when the opportunity for this decisive communal expression for the growth of the person is blocked.

The test of belonging is its capacity to cause the seed to germinate, that is, to generate adults with a capacity to stay in reality, to judge, to understand reality, to be willing to listen to it. At this level, affirmations of principle do not suffice. What is needed are testimonies that document how people flourish through their belonging, and how belonging generates mature persons.

The Risk of Personalism

To conclude I would like to add a parenthetical note to point out that it is also possible to have a distorted understanding of responsibility, when, for example, personal commitment turns into a form of personalism, making oneself the center of everything, relativizing objective criteria. To get straight to the point, without mincing words, I would say directly that at base personalism is a wrong way to respond to the problem of life, to chase after the self-fulfillment we all yearn for. Like individualism, it derives from a misunderstanding of the nature of the self. The "I" is a relationship with the infinite. But if we fail to realize this, then consciously or unconsciously we will try to respond to our human need by "making ourselves the center of everything," which can never satisfy the desire for the infinite of which we are made. Besides failing to produce results, personalism is also useless for satisfying the human need that gave rise to it in the first place.

It is nevertheless important to add that the personalism of any given person is made possible only by all the other people who, in a complementary way, go along with it, thinking they can solve the big questions of their lives by offloading their responsibility onto the "boss" who exercises this personalism, or on a so-called leader. So, "the relationship with the leader, when he is followed because he is the head of the organization upon which one has dumped all one's hopes and from which one expects the actualization of one's own project, tends to be absolutely closed in an individualistic dependence. The obedience that is established is obedience to the organization, of which the leader is the crucial point and the guardian, and this eliminates the creativity of our persons, because everything is established and defined by the structure to which one adheres. Everything becomes schematic."[9]

How does one get free of this personalism? The same way we overcome any type of idolatry: coming across a presence that provokes us because of the promise of fulfillment that it carries and places before us. Only those who realize the true nature of their human need can understand that only the following of that presence that provokes us, because of the promise it contains, responds to our need. But the key is the very conception of following. Following cannot be conceived of as following orders of someone upon whom we have dumped our own responsibility with the hope that this person will resolve the problem of our own life. "Following is the desire," said Fr. Giussani, "to relive the *experience* of the person who has provoked you and who provokes you with their presence in the life of the community; it is the tension to become not like that person in his concreteness, full of limits, but like that person in the value to which he gives himself and that redeems him deep down even in his human limitations. It is the desire to participate in the life of that person in which something Other is brought to you, and your devotion is to this Other; you want to adhere to this Other, within this journey."[10]

Only a person committed to reliving the experience of the person who provoked him or her can reach the Other—the One in whom one finds that to which one aspires—and can thus relive this experience. And he then becomes free, he can finally shake off all personalism and has no need to focus everything on himself. On the other hand, if he finds himself in the opposite position, he can begin to say "I" without delegating the responsibility for his own decisions to others.

The grace that we should wish upon everyone is to meet people that are a provocation, that arouse the desire to follow. With their presence, they help others to take themselves seriously, to get involved and to make their contribution to the common work. The hope is that you yourself, in your workplaces, be these presences.

————◆◆◆————

CHAPTER 15

Crisis: A Challenge to Change

"And God Saw That It Was Good"

"And God saw that it was good . . . very good."[1] This affirmation, repeated six times in the first chapter of Genesis, expresses the fundamental conviction of the people of Israel about reality—it is good, *very* good. It is not a naive affirmation, made by some inexperienced person from outside the real history of people and their afflictions. As we know, these first chapters of Genesis were not written at the beginning of the history of Israel, but many centuries later, at the end of a long road, in which Israel was not spared any of the suffering undergone by other peoples.

And it is because of this that the question becomes even more urgent—how can Israel have such a certain conviction about the positivity of reality after its entire history was rife with suffering, tribulations, and torments of every kind?

This attitude of the ancient people of Israel toward reality is even more surprising if we put it in the cultural context of the neighboring peoples. In fact, the experience of pain had brought the others to a very different conviction—that is, that reality is not entirely positive; on the contrary, that there are two types of reality, one positive and one negative. It is what is expressed by Manichaeism—there are two principles, one good and one bad, that are reflected in a good creation and a bad one. Why did this Manichaean vision not gain the upper hand in Israel, as well?

Because of its history. The experience that the Israelites had of God, even in the midst of their trials, was so positive that they could not but affirm his goodness. God revealed himself with all of his salvific power. And from this experience, they concluded that he, the Savior, is also the Creator. There is one good principle at the origin of everything. Everything that comes from God, who is good, is equally good. Therefore, reality is positive. It was the presence of God among his people that educated the Jews to look at reality in its truth, to the point of not letting themselves be determined by the various tribulations that could have impeded them from having an authentic gaze toward reality.

An example comes to mind that I used to give to my high school students. If two parents bring their child to Disneyland, we can easily imagine that the child will be amazed by all of the attractions with which he can have fun. If we are attentive to his reactions, one after another, we will also be struck by the fascination that reality is able to provoke in him. Everything is perceived as positive. But if, by chance, the child is separated from his parents and gets lost in the middle of the crowd, everything changes. The reality is the same as before, but the perception of it has changed. Radically. He doesn't feel it to be friendly, but threatening, hostile. And only when he finds his parents can the true perception of reality be restored.

But what is most striking is that the people of Israel truly came to understand this positivity of reality in a moment of crisis. With the loss of the temple, the monarchy, and their land, going into exile, Israel had been stripped of everything that it identified as the foundation of its faith. "Why, O Jacob, do you say, and declare, O Israel,

'My way is hidden from the Lord, and my right is disregarded by my God'?" It seems to them that they have been abandoned, "disregarded," by the God who once chose them. To respond to this question, Israel is constrained to find a foundation that is even more solid. God sends Isaiah to aid his people, to help them to look carefully at the reality before them: "Lift up your eyes on high and see who has created these [that is, the waters of the sea, the immensity of the heavens, the dust of the earth, and the mountains]. . . . Do you not know or have you not heard? The Lord is the eternal God, creator of the ends of the earth."[2] When everything collapses, there is something that remains—reality.

We want to help each other to look at reality starting from our experience. The cornerstone of our position can be summed up in the sentence, reality is positive. All of us feel the shock of this statement, because we instantly react with the question, is it really true that reality is positive? This is an arduous challenge for us, because we, too, like the ancient Manichaeans, believe that there is a good reality and an evil one. We are immersed in a situation that clouds us, so that we cannot look at reality clearly. We feel shocked by the claim contained in this judgment that reality is positive, to the extent that it clashes with our mentality.

With this judgment about the positivity of reality, we are not offering something that is valid only for Catholics, as if to say that "for us" reality is positive, because the companionship, our being together, "convinces" us to think like this, to console ourselves like this. Our claim is that we are dealing with a piece of evidence that everyone can recognize. Even at this level, Giussani comes to help us: "A positivity toward life, toward reality, is not induced by companionship—it would be of little consolation—but is dictated by our nature; the companionship makes it easier for us to accept this, even when going through bad conditions, complex situations."[3]

Reality can be *perceived* as positive because it *is* positive. We are not talking about "baptizing" reality starting from a religious preconception, a "pious" vision, but about recognizing it in its ultimate nature. Reality is ontologically positive. Why? Reality is positive because it exists. *Everything that exists* is there because the Mystery permitted it to happen (everything, in fact, has an origin in a mysterious Something; nothing makes itself); it provokes and sets the person in motion, it represents an invitation to change, an occasion to take a step toward one's own destiny. Every circumstance is the path and the instrument of our journey—it is a *sign*. Insomuch as it is there, reality is a provocation, and therefore the occasion for the reawakening of the "I" from its inertia. Even the crisis, because it raises pressing questions.

"A crisis," says Hannah Arendt, "forces us back to the questions themselves and requires from us either new or old answers, but in any case direct judgments. A crisis becomes a disaster only when we respond to it with preformed judgments, that is, with prejudices. Such an attitude not only sharpens the crisis but makes us forfeit the experience of reality and the opportunity for reflection it provides."[4]

The Work of Reason

But the irreducible positivity that we are talking about does not reveal itself mechanically, but rather only to those who accept the challenge of reality, who take its questions seriously, who do not retreat in front of life's urgency. Only those who accept this kind of challenge will be able to find adequate reasons to give to themselves and others for dealing with a crisis. How many witnesses there are of people for whom difficulties became occasions for change! This is the greatness of the "I" that we have to wield in front of the crisis; otherwise, we are already defeated, even if the financial situation is resolved, defeated in our person because we have allowed ourselves to be reduced to a cog in the wheel of circumstances. For so many people, situations of suffering have made possible their liberation from a dull life; so many unexpected and surprising fruits have been born from pain that was accepted or defeats through which they let themselves be called into question! How many witnesses there are of people who, because of the change and the intensity that they experienced, are grateful for what happened to them, though they would never have wished for it to happen! What happened was the mysterious means for a reawakening of the "I" and a deeper comprehension of the nature of reality, which they thought they already knew.

Reality is positive because of the Mystery that dwells in it. But what is needed to grasp this positivity? What is required for a recognition of reality like this? Reason, or, better, a use of reason according to the true nature of knowledge of reality in all of its factors. Reason, in fact, can grasp reality as a "given" that vibrates with activity and attraction, as a provocation, and thus as an invitation. "To be reasonable means to recognize what emerges in experience," says Fr. Giussani. "And in experience, reality emerges as positivity [this is the challenge that Fr. Giussani launches at our way of judging—in experience, reality emerges as positivity]. Reality emerging in experience is so positive that it appears inexorably as attraction."[5]

And yet, if we look around, we see that this use of reason is very rare; indeed, it seems almost impossible to find. If reason does not grasp this mystery that constitutes the heart of reality, its most precious value, man yields to the temptation to understand the affirmation "Reality is positive" in a sentimental or moralistic way, as if it meant that reality is desirable and pleasant. How does this happen?

Because of our fragility (a profound weakness that is in us) and the conditioning of the cultural and social context, the power that surrounds us, this use of reason is often extraneous to us. Because of this fragility and this conditioning, when we come upon a reality that shows a negative and contradictory face, reason—which is originally open to reality—backs off, trembles, becomes confused. All it takes is the appearance of an inconvenience on the horizon of daily life to cast doubt on its positivity. We see it in our lives—as soon as something does not go according to our desires, we waver. Just imagine what happens, then, when we are faced with an economic crisis like the current one. And reality goes from being a sign that opens to being a tomb in which we all, many times, suffocate.

The Mystery, entering into history, came into this dramatic situation in order to bring its decisive contribution, as the history of the people of Israel demonstrates. The Judeo-Christian tradition is the source of this human position in which reality is recognized and affirmed in its original positivity: because of its very nature, in fact, faith is an event that is capable of reawakening each person's religious sense and reason, and of sustaining and fulfilling the capacity of man to stay in reality and treat everything according to its true nature; faith allows us to perceive reality in its positivity. Christ came at the culmination of the history of the people of Israel for this: to reawaken our "I" so that we could face any challenge. Christ did not promise to spare us anything, but to make us capable of facing anything—which is very different—and to accompany us to victory. Christ comes now, since we, like the Jewish people in their moment of crisis, are also in a situation of fragility that is insurmountable for us in our own strength. Christ did not become incarnate to spare us the work of our reason, our freedom, or our engagement, but to make it possible—because this is what makes us become human beings, what makes us live life like a fascinating adventure, even in the midst of all its difficulties, even and above all in times of crisis, when everything becomes a question of life and death. Christ became our companion in order to reawaken all of the potential of reason to recognize reality, so we lose neither our heads nor our souls. He came to reawaken the religious sense, so that we are "more" human—putting us in optimal conditions to look at reality according to its true nature—and not to make us "visionaries."

"The dominant culture of today has abandoned reason as knowledge, as recognition of the evidence with which reality proposes itself in experience, that is, as positivity. And it has given up on affection for reality, love for reality. It has given up on love, because in order to recognize reality as it emerges in experience, it is necessary to accept the shock that one feels. Man does not accept reality as it appears, and he wants to invent it in the way that he wants [these are words that acquire additional weight now, in the current financial situation; they are not empty words], he wants to define it in the way that he wants, he wants to give it the face that he wants."[6]

In this situation we can understand the momentous relevance of the battle, carried forward despite general indifference, by Pope Benedict XVI, for the defense of the true nature of reason, to "broaden reason," for a "reason open to the language of being," that is, for an "I" that is equipped to deal with any challenge.

The Steps and Elements of Recovery

Fr. Giussani briefly describes the path for a "recovery" in the following way. To follow this path will mean

> to perceive *existence as need* to construct and, therefore, need for a destiny, for a goal—to construct means to collaborate in achieving a goal, to collaborate in developing and carrying out a plan; *rationality*, loved reason, true guide of man, light of experience; *affection* as the heart of man, fire and heat of experience; and *freedom*, which, in its possibility to choose, ought not to become a blade, a knife that cuts through the balance of knowledge and affection, originally mysterious and effectively constructive and fascinating, but is the embrace of experience in the totality of its factors, without losing anything that is there, that emerges before our eyes and touches our heart. The "recovery" comes from having our feet firmly on the ground of *nature*, as it appears in experience, as it places itself in experience, as it imposes itself in the plumbed depths of experience in its original factors.[7]

It is at this level that Christ demonstrates his exceptionality—giving man back to himself. Therefore, a religious sense that is alive is the verification of faith; at the same time, a true and complete use of reason is a verification of faith: it is the powerful and unmistakable proof that the relationship with Christ, who is contemporaneous with each one of us, is recognized and lived. Christianity does not add itself on from the outside, like a superstructure, like a pietism, to the life of man, but clarifies, educates, and saves the very nature of man, which was wounded but not destroyed by original sin.

"And the first consequence . . . is an inexorable hope as the ultimate sense of the relationship with things, as the ultimate sense of the journey among things. It is a positivity that defeats every adversity that we experience. Indeed, Saint Paul says, in the most revolutionary phrase in all of universal literature: *omnis creatura bona*, every creature is a good. . . . Because of this, Saint Paul concludes, *omnia cooperantur in bonum*, all things cooperate for the positivity of your life, for good."[8] Shortly before he was martyred, Saint Thomas More consoled his daughter with these words: "Nothing can come but that that God will. And I make me very sure that whatsoever that be, seem it never so bad in sight, it shall indeed be the best."[9]

Reality is sign. It is not we who determine that it is like this. It *is* like this. The crisis invites everyone—us and the others—to verify its truth. How?

The crisis is the circumstance that the Mystery did not spare us—in the same way that it did not spare the Jewish people their trials—so that we carry out the verification of our faith in it, so that we experience in it the capacity for change, for positive impact in life; circumstances, in fact, are an essential, and not secondary, part of our vocation as human beings. If, faced with the current context, we do not live reality in its true nature, it means that faith is not lived in its authenticity, that is, as the recognition of a Presence that exalts our original humanity. Then faith becomes useless because it cannot make us live now, in this situation. But a faith like this becomes part of the problem and not of the solution. Instead, paradoxically, the crisis can represent the possibility to verify the human expediency of faith, its reasonableness.

Insomuch as we accept this challenge and personally carry out the verification, we will be able to give reasons for the experience that we live, to offer a way, a suggestion, to stand before others with a cultural identity, to offer something more than everyone's complaints—there are already enough of those—because, as we have repeated many times, "the contribution of Christians can be effective only if knowledge of faith becomes knowledge of reality."[10] So, if we accept this work, we will be able to fill ourselves with such a richness of experience that we will be able to share it in dialogue with everyone, and we will discover what constitutes the historical influence of Christians.

The crisis marks the beginning and the urgency of a cultural battle, first of all with ourselves, that concerns the experience of faith as it was communicated to us. It is a battle to affirm the human. It is the attempt to communicate to co-workers, friends, and anyone whom we encounter the hope that is in us. But it would be an illusory hope, without foundation, if it were not sustained by a verification in experience, by a true use of reason. Christians will not be more believable by becoming more "pious," but by using their reason adequately, challenging everyone with a different, fuller use of reason.

Only in this way will we be able to give a truly decisive contribution. Otherwise we will be insignificant for our fellow human beings, even if we get all fired up like everyone else, and we will fail at a historic duty—to reawaken hope within the crisis. And we Christians can do this—even though we are fragile like everyone else—because of the gift that we have received and that we cannot keep for ourselves.

Our view of the crisis is dictated by a judgment: the impetus of each person is a good for all; the energy of the "I" is not used up in itself, but constructs a people. The history of Italy is a striking example; faced with situations that were much worse than ours—think of the postwar era, with Italy destroyed—people who were moved by a positive impetus got together, took the initiative, and rebuilt the country.

Fr. Giussani pointed out what it is that constitutes the originality of this cultural battle. These are words pronounced prophetically in 1986, during the glorious 1980s, when the world seemed to navigate toward a bright future and the crisis had not yet come. "The solution," he said then,

> is a battle to save—not the battle to stop the shrewdness of civilization, but the battle to rediscover, to testify, man's dependence on God. What has been, throughout time, the true meaning of the human struggle, that is to say, the struggle between the affirmation of the human and the instrumentalization of the human by those in power, has now reached an extreme. . . . The greatest danger today is not the destruction of peoples, killing, murder, but the attempt by the reigning power to destroy the *human* [our true resource]. And the essence of the human is freedom, i.e., the relationship with the infinite. Therefore, it is above all in the West that the great battle must be fought by the person who feels that they are a

person [together with all the other people who feel this way]: the battle between authentic religiosity and power. The limit of power is true religiosity—the limit of any power: civil, political, or ecclesiastic.[11]

———•◦•———

CHAPTER 16

In Politics, Too, the Other Is a Good

In trying to live Easter in the context of the most recent events in the Church, from Pope Benedict XVI's resignation to the dramatic entrance of Pope Francis, I could not help but think about Italy's dramatic situation, and the difficulty of escaping from the paralysis that has been created.

Much has been written about this by people whose expertise in politics makes them far more qualified than I to speak. I have no strategic solution to suggest, but would like to offer a few thoughts in the attempt to collaborate for the good of a nation to which I feel a bond for many reasons.

It seems to me that the situation of deadlock is the result of the perception of the political adversary as an enemy whose influence must be neutralized or at least reduced to the minimum. The European history of the last century has given us sufficient documentation of analogous attempts by the various ideologies to eliminate each other, causing immense suffering to entire populations.

But the outcome of these efforts has led to a clear conclusion: it is impossible to reduce the other to zero. This evidence, together with the desire for peace that cannot be erased from the heart of each person, suggested the first steps of the miracle called a united Europe. What enabled the fathers of Europe to find the willingness to speak to each other, to build something together, even after the Second World War? The awareness of the impossibility of eliminating the adversary made them less presumptuous, less impermeable to dialogue, aware of their own need; they began to give space to the possibility that the others, in their diversity, could be perceived as a resource, a good.

Now, thinking of the present, I say that unless we accept the elementary experience that the other is a good and not an obstacle to the fulfillment of our "I," in politics as well as in human and social relations, it will be difficult to emerge from the situation in which we find ourselves.

Acknowledging the other is the true victory for each of us and for all. The first to be called to travel this road, as happened in the past, are precisely the Catholic politicians, whatever their party. But unfortunately, they too often seem more defined by party alignments than by self-awareness of their ecclesial experience and the desire for the common good. Yet precisely their experience of being "members of each other" (Saint Paul)[1] should enable them to view the other as part of the definition of self and thus as a good.

These days many have watched the Church and been surprised at how she was willing to change, the better to respond to the challenges of the present. In the first place, we have seen a pope who, at the apex of his power, made an absolutely unheard-of gesture of freedom, amazing everyone, so that another man with more energy could guide the Church. Then we witnessed the arrival of Pope Francis, who from the first moment has surprised us with gestures of disarming simplicity that are capable of reaching each person's heart.

In recent years, the Church has been hit by more than a few difficulties, beginning with the pedophilia scandal; she seemed disoriented and adrift, and yet even in facing these difficulties, her fascinating difference shone out.

How can the life of the Church contribute to facing the current situation in Italy? I do not believe it is by intervening in the political arena as one of the many competing parties and opinions. The contribution of the Church is much more radical. If the substance of those who serve this great work that is politics lies only in politics, there is not much to hope for. Lacking any other sure foundation, they will necessarily grasp at politics and personal power and, in the concrete, will see conflict as the only chance for survival. But politics is not sufficient unto itself. This has never been as clear as it is today.

In her poverty as an entity full of limitations, the Church continues to offer people, precisely in these days, the one true contribution, the one for which she exists, and Pope Francis reminds us of it constantly: the annunciation of the risen Christ. He is the only one who fully answers the expectations of the human heart, to the point of making a pope free enough to resign for the good of his people.

Without a real experience of positivity, able to embrace everyone and everything, it is not possible to start anew. This is the testimony that all Christians are called to give, beginning with those engaged in politics, together with every person of goodwill, as their contribution to unblock the situation: the affirmation of the value of the other and the common good above any partisan concerns.

Conclusion:
How Does a Presence Come to Be?

For the feast of Saint Mary Magdalene the liturgy offers two texts that clearly reveal how the Church wants to introduce us to looking at this woman, according to all her expectant waiting and all her yearning. The first is a passage from the Song of Songs, which describes what life was like for a person like Mary: "On my bed at night I sought him whom my heart loves—I sought him but I did not find him. I will rise then and go about the city; in the streets and crossings I will seek him whom my heart loves. I sought him but I did not find him. The watchmen came upon me as they made their rounds of the city: Have you seen Him whom my heart loves?"[1] How I would like to have something of this passion! Mary testifies to us the heart that we would like to have in our innermost being, because the "I" is this search for a love that holds up against the challenges of living.

In the gospel text that tells the story of Mary Magdalene at the tomb, one could trace the answer to two questions that are decisive for life: "How can one live?" and "What are we Christians called to do here in the world?"

"On the first day of the week, Mary of Magdala came to the tomb early in the morning, when it was still dark"—What was it that pushed that woman to the point that she could no longer stay in bed, and that drove her to set out early in the morning, when it was still dark?—"and saw the stone removed from the tomb. So she ran and went to Simon Peter and to the other disciple whom Jesus loved, and told them, 'They have taken the Lord from the tomb, and we don't know where they put Him.'"[2]

Then Mary went back and "stayed outside the tomb weeping." This is life. So how can we live? Without finding that beloved presence, the love of our soul, every morning would be a reason for weeping. Then, we can distract ourselves during the day, but life remains something to weep about, if we do not find the love of our soul, that love that fills life with meaning, intensity, and warmth. The gospel story goes on: "And as she wept, she bent over into the tomb and saw two angels in white sitting there, one at the head and one at the feet where the body of Jesus had been. And they said to her, 'Woman, why are you weeping?' She said to them, 'They have taken my Lord, and I don't know where they have laid Him.' When she had said this, she turned around and saw Jesus there, but did not know it was Jesus. Jesus said to her, 'Woman, why are you weeping? Whom are you looking for?'" This is the link: "Whom are you looking for?" "I am looking for the love of my heart. I am looking for that presence that can fill my life." This is why the Church shows us how to look at Mary Magdalene with this passage of the Song of Songs, which speaks to us of a woman searching for the love of her heart. "She thought he was the gardener and said to him, 'Sir, if you carried Him away, tell me where you laid Him, and I will take Him.' Jesus said to her, 'Mary!' She turned and said to Him in Hebrew, 'Rabbouni,' which means Teacher. Jesus said to her, 'Stop holding on to Me, for

I have not yet ascended to the Father. But go to My brothers and tell them, 'I am going to My Father and your Father, to My God and your God.' Mary of Magdala went [right away] and announced to the disciples, 'I have seen the Lord,' and what He told her."[3]

In this passage, we have the answer to both questions: "How can we live?" and "What are we called to do here in the world?" For Mary, only by responding to the first question (put to her by Christ with the words "Woman, why are you weeping? Whom are you looking for?") and finding the presence she was seeking that answered her weeping, did she have something to communicate to the others: "I have seen the Lord!"

It is a great consolation for each of us that this happened to someone unknown like Mary Magdalene, because it helps us understand that no precondition or standard must be met, no particular gift is required to seek him. This search can even be nearly hidden in the depths of our being, under all the detritus of our evil or forgetfulness, but nothing can eliminate it, just as nothing can stop that woman from seeking. To discover this striving in ourselves, we need only that "original morality," that total openness with which we are created, that deep-down coincidence-with-self, that not-remoteness-from-self that leads Mary to say, "On my bed at night I sought him whom my heart loves," and "Have you seen him whom my heart loves?" This is the original openness we see in other characters of the gospel, all poor wretches like us, but whom nobody could stop from seeking him, like Zacchaeus, who climbed the tree, full of curiosity to see Jesus, or the Samaritan woman, full of thirst and desirous of the one water that could quench her thirst. Looking at these gospel figures, we have no excuses, because they are all poor wretches like us, but are striving to seek him, defined by the search for him and by the passion for him that disarms all our worries, all our moralistic reasoning to justify not seeking him. None of us finds it difficult to imagine what happened inside them when Jesus, bending over their nothingness, called them by name. How amazed they must have been! How much more inflamed they must have been with the passion for him, the desire to seek him!

"Mary!" How all of Jesus' humanity must have vibrated in being able to say her name with such a tone, accent, intensity, and familiarity that Mary recognized him immediately, when just an instant before she had mistaken him for the gardener. "Mary!" It is as if all the tenderness of the Mystery reached that woman through the vibration of the humanity of the risen Jesus, now unveiled, but not for this reason any less intense; rather, with all the humanity of the risen Jesus vibrating with the fact that that woman existed. "Mary!" So then, you can understand how in that moment she realized who he was. She was able to realize who he was because he made all his humanity vibrate to the point of making her feel such an intensity, fullness, and overabundance that she could never have imagined before, and that she could experience only in the relationship with him. Without him, she would never have known who she was or what life could be and become, what intensity of fullness life could reach.

What is Christianity if not that presence, all vibrating for the destiny of an unknown woman—that presence that made her understand what he brought, what he is for life? What newness entered history through the modality with which Christ communicates it! Jesus made us understand what Christianity is by saying to a woman, "Mary!" This communication of being, of "more being," of "more Mary," revealed to that woman who Jesus is. It is not a theory or speech or explanation, but an event that turned the lives of all those who entered into a relationship with him upside down, in one way or another, and that the Gospels, in their disarming simplicity, communicate in the simplest, the most naive way, simply saying the name: "Mary!," "Zacchaeus!," "Matthew!," "Woman, do not weep!" What communication of himself must have happened in them to mark their lives so powerfully, to the point that they could no longer look at reality, at themselves, without being bowled over by that Presence, by that voice, by that intensity with which their name was spoken.

One can understand the upheaval that runs through every page of the gospel in the face of an experience like this. Unfortunately, we are already used to the repercussion and often no longer feel it; everything is taken for granted, already known! But it is not necessarily this way, and we see this when a man like Pope Francis testifies to us his wonder today: "The best summary, the one that comes more from the inside and I feel most true, is this: 'I am a sinner whom the Lord has looked upon. . . . I am one who is looked upon by the Lord.'"[4]

The power of that event, that unique way of relating to the other, of an "I," Jesus, who enters into relationship with a "you," Mary, making her become herself, the exceptionality of that "Mary!" that causes an upheaval in that woman, the heart-melting yearning that filled her, is seen in the way she answers: "Rabbouni! Teacher!" In the austere language of the gospel, Saint John comments, "She turned" upon hearing her name. This is conversion: it is anything but moralism! Conversion is a recognition: "Teacher!" It is the response to the love of One who, saying our name with an affective intensity never before seen, makes us discover who we are, allows us to be ourselves. Acknowledging him is the answer to his passion that reawakens all her affective capacity, because One called her by name in a way that generated a new relationship with things, called "virginity." "Stop holding on to Me," Jesus says to Mary Magdalene. There is no need to hold on. Any other thing is nothing compared to an instant of this affective intensity that Mary experienced with Jesus.

Under the pressure of this incomparable surge of emotion she turns to Jesus with the passion with which she says, "Rabbouni! Teacher!" Indeed, Mary's answer was entirely the fruit of the way she heard herself called by name, entirely flowing from that unique upheaval that Jesus provoked in her. This is anything but moralism! Not in your wildest dreams! The powerful movement of emotion she felt at the communication of being, through Jesus, is what moved her to say "Teacher!" with all her affection.

The Event Every Person Unknowingly Awaits

A yearning for the destiny of man, of each human being, a yearning that that woman felt, was present first in the humanity of Jesus, entirely vibrating with passion for her: this is the newness that entered history with Christ, that is communicated through his flesh, his being moved, his gaze, his way of speaking, the tone of his voice, and that today, as in the past, the human person, each of us, awaits. "Man today expects perhaps unconsciously the experience of the encounter with people for whom the fact of Christ is such a present reality that their life is changed. What will shake today's man is a human impact, an event that echoes the initial event, when Jesus raised His eyes and said, 'Zacchaeus, hurry down. I mean to stay at your house today.'"[5]

This is the event that has bowled us over, too. This event, the echo of the initial event, reached us through the person of Fr. Giussani, through his humanity and his vibration for Christ to which we are witnesses, so much so that many of us would not be here if we had not met him, if we had not been bowled over by the way he communicated Christ to us. We will become more aware of what happened to us in this encounter with Fr. Giussani when we read his biography.[6] Through him, the same vibration that touched Mary reaches us today, not "like" the one then, but "the one" then, the same as then, that same event that reached Mary. And each of us must look at her or his own experience, must go back to the origin, to that original move, to see the first dawn break precisely there, the first desire to belong to Christ. There is no other source of belonging but the experience of Christianity lived as event. This alone was enough for us to feel an irrepressible desire to be "his."

The Beginning of a New Knowledge

"What is Christianity if not the event of a new man who by his nature becomes a new protagonist on the world scene?"[7] The basic issue of life is the appearance of this new creature, this new creation, this new birth.

Only if the presence of Christ permeates our life are we spared the need to raise our arms in front of our face to defend ourselves from the blows of circumstances, so that we can live. And yet many times we are so wounded by the repercussion of circumstances that the journey of knowledge is impeded, and then everything becomes truly suffocating, because it is as if we see reality only in terms of our wounds. Like Mary, who looked at reality through her weeping and could no longer see anything else—she could not even recognize Jesus! Then he appears, calls her by name, and everything begins anew; he enables her to recognize him, to begin to look at reality differently. Because his presence is more powerful than any wound, and so her gaze is thrown wide open again, to be able to see reality in its truth. "He was seen, and he saw," Saint Augustine said of Zacchaeus.[8] How different life would be for each of us if we let that gaze enter, no matter what wounds we bear!

Jesus entered history to educate us to a true knowledge of reality. We think we already know what reality is, but without him we are assailed by fear, we freeze and then we suffocate in the circumstances. With Jesus, on the other hand, everything opens up again, as if he were telling us, "Look, I came to educate you to have the true relationship with reality, to have the right position that enables you to have a new gaze on reality." But if we do not continually let in his gaze, his presence, we live reality like everyone else; we do not experience the newness. Only if Jesus enters and makes the new knowledge possible in us will we be able to experience and bring to the world a different way of staying in reality. All circumstances are given to us for this, to provoke us to this new knowledge, to see what Jesus is: a Presence that enables us to live reality in a different, new way. This shows us that all circumstances—all, with no exceptions—are not obstacles, as we so often see them. We are unable to see the provocation they contain, the attraction they exert, so defined are we by the wound. We have already reduced them because we think we already know what the circumstance is. We think we already know there is nothing new to discover within it, that it is simply to be borne and that we can only try moralistically to rise to the level of enduring it.

Only if the Presence that happened to Mary Magdalene happens again can our journey of knowledge continue and our gaze be thrown wide open. We have much more than "answers" to all the objections or challenges: we have "the answer." However, the answer does not consist, as we think, in having the instruction manual for living, because the instruction manual became flesh, is a Presence, is the Word; the content of the answer is a Presence, a You, the You who reached Mary. If truth is disconnected, if it is not relationship, you do not understand. As Pope Francis wrote to Eugenio Scalfari: "Truth, according to the Christian faith, is the love of God for us in Jesus Christ. Therefore, truth is a relationship."[9] It is like a child who realizes she does not know many things, but one thing she does know: she has her mother and father, and they know, so what is the problem? If I am certain of this Presence that invades life, I can face any circumstance, any wound, any objection, any repercussion, any attack, because all this opens me up to awaiting the way the Mystery will become present, to suggest the path to me, to accompany me even in entering darkness, according to a design that is not mine.

What a difference in the way of staying in reality, when you have questions, when you have open questions: when you pray Lauds or when you observe silence, or when you listen to a friend, or when you have a coffee, or when you read the newspaper, you are poised to discover, to intercept any crumb of truth that you may come across. This way, everything becomes interesting, because if I did not have the question, if I did not have the wound, if I did not have a total openness, I could not even recognize truth, I would not even realize it. This is why ours is a "very human journey," not made of hallucinations or visions, but of participation in an "adventure of knowledge" that enables us to discover more and more the attraction that lies within any limitation, within any difficulty, because any challenge or any circumstance, even a painful one, always has within it something true; otherwise it would not exist.

What Are We Called to Do in the World?

It is starting from this experience of living that we can respond to the question, "What are we called to do here in the world?" We are understanding more and more what our task is, not in spite of the circumstances but through them. It has always been this way in the life of the movement. Now we can understand much better what Fr. Giussani said in 1976, that there are two possibilities for being present in reality: either being a "reactive presence," determined by some reaction of ours, or being an "original presence," born from what has happened to us.

"Reactive means determined by the moves made by others, not our own." This means placing ourselves in reality with "initiatives, using ways of speaking, creating instruments that are not generated as an all-embracing method by our new personality, but suggested by the use of words, the creation of instruments, the attitude and behavior of our adversaries." Since we are "playing on their home field, a reactive presence cannot help falling into two errors. Either it becomes a reactionary presence, i.e., attached to its own positions as 'forms,' without the contents—the motives, the roots—being so clear as to come alive . . . ; or [it is only an] *imitation* of others." On the other hand, "an original presence [is] a presence in accord with our originality";[10] that is, it comes from what we are. To live an original presence right where we are is above all, therefore, the realization of communion with Christ and among ourselves. Mary, Matthew, and Zacchaeus bring to reality a position defined by that communion with him that was generated by his being moved, communicated in saying their names. When this happens to each of us, the communion among us is expressed as presence according to our originality.

An Original Presence

"A presence is original when it springs forth from the consciousness of one's own identity and one's affection for it, and finds its consistence in this."[11] If it finds its consistence, this is because it also finds its satisfaction, as Thomas Aquinas said: "Man's life consists in the affection which sustains him most, for there he finds his greatest satisfaction."[12] The substance of life is there, where we find the greatest satisfaction.

So then, what does it mean to have an identity? "Identity is knowing who we are and why we exist, with a dignity that gives us the right to hope for 'something better' for our life and the life of the world because of our presence." And who are we? "Through faith you are all children of God in Christ Jesus. For all of you who were baptized into Christ have clothed yourselves with Christ. There is neither Jew nor Greek, there is neither slave nor free person, there is not male and female; for you are all one in Christ Jesus."[13] What happened in baptism became perceptible for us in our history and in our awareness through the encounter with the movement; only then did we understand the importance of what happened, of that battle Christ began with us in baptism to win us over, as *vir pugnator*. We became aware of it when, encountering the movement, we were won over through the way our name was called. Then we understood what Saint Paul meant when he wrote, "You have been seized and made one with Christ."[14]

We have been seized. "You did not choose Me, but I chose you,"[15] Jesus says. "This is an objective choice that we can never rid ourselves of again; it is a penetration of our being that does not depend on us and that we can no longer erase."[16] This is our identity. This choice defines who we are and introduces into the world an incomparable newness. "For all of you who were baptized into Christ have clothed yourselves with Christ. . . . For you are all one in Christ Jesus."[17] Fr. Giussani continues, "There is nothing culturally more revolutionary than this conception of the person, whose meaning, whose substance is unity with Christ, with an Other, and through this, a unity with all those whom He seizes, with all those whom the Father puts into His hands."[18] This conception of our person—which is such only because there is One who speaks our name again; otherwise we would still be there weeping at the fact of living—is not an abstraction. It is an experience, not a notion, and precisely from this having-been-seized, having-been-chosen, flows a self-awareness of ourselves like the one born in Mary, who could no longer look at herself as before, but as entirely defined by that "Mary!"

We have to grasp well what we have just said, that is, what gives solidity to our identity. "Our identity is to be one with Christ. Being one with Christ is the constitutive dimension of our person. If Christ defines my personality, you, who have been seized by Him, necessarily enter into the dimension of my personality." So emerge the features of a *new creature* in the world, which does not depend on the favor of the quality of the circumstances. "Whether I am alone in my room, or three of us are together studying at the university, or twenty of us eating together in the cafeteria, everywhere and in any case, this is our identity. The problem is, therefore, our self-awareness, the content of the consciousness of ourselves: 'It is no longer I who live, but it is You who live in me.'" The emergence of our identity depends, then, on the flourishing in us of this new self-awareness; therein lies its root. "This is the true *new man* in the world—the new man who was Che Guevara's dream and the lying pretext for cultural revolutions by which people in power have tried and still try to take the people into their hands, in order to subjugate them according to their ideology; and this new man is born above all not out of being consistent, but as a *new self-awareness.*"[19]

How is our new identity manifested? What form does it take? In what concreteness does it take shape? "*Our identity manifests itself in a new experience* within us [in the way we live any circumstance and any challenge of reality] and among us: the experience of *affection for Christ and the Mystery of the Church, which finds its closest concreteness in our unity.* The identity is the living experience of affection for Christ and for our unity."[20] An affection that is very far from the image we normally have that places it in the category of easy sentimentality, in the changeable and impermanent category of feelings. "The word 'affection' is the greatest and most comprehensive of all our ways of expressing ourselves. It indicates much more an 'attachment' that is born out of a value judgment—the acknowledgment of what there is in us and among us—than a sentimental, ephemeral facility as fleeting as a leaf at the mercy of the wind. And in faithfulness to the judgment, that is, in faithfulness to the faith, as one grows older this attachment increases and becomes more sturdy, vibrant, and powerful."[21]

Sinking in a Fact

What is this living experience of Christ for each of us and whoever becomes involved, this experience of unity?

> [It] is the locus of *hope*, therefore of the welling forth of the *gusto* of life and the possible blossoming of *joy*—which does not have to leave out or deny anything in order to affirm itself; and it is the locus of the recovery of a *thirst to change one's life,*

the desire that one's life be consistent, that it change by virtue of what it is at bottom, that it may be worthier of the Reality it carries. The passion to change one's life [not the justification of our mistakes!] lives within the experience of Christ and our unity. And it is the opposite of moralism: not a law to which we conform, but a love to which we adhere, a presence to follow more and more with all of ourselves, a fact within which we can truly sink.[22]

Inside us, as fragile and mistake-prone as we may be, there is an irresistible desire to be wrapped up in this bottomless and limitless love, to "sink" without resistance in the fact of Christ: the desire to be his, to belong even more to him, to seek him ceaselessly, bursts out in us. "The serene, well-balanced, and at the same time passionate desire to change oneself thus becomes a daily reality—without any shadow of pietism or moralism. It becomes a love for the truth of one's being [a seeker of the beloved], a desire as wonderful and as uncomfortable as thirst."[23]

However, all this must mature in us. If this small kernel of a beginning does not grow and become mature, the first storm will crush it. We cannot endure—Giussani said in 1976, but it is still true today—"unless that initial ring of truth ripens to maturity; we can no longer bear, as Christians, the enormous mountain of work, responsibility, and toil to which we are called. For people are not brought together by initiatives [this is not what gives substance and attracts]; what brings them together is the ring of truth of a presence, which is given by the Reality that is among us and which we 'carry'—Christ and His Mystery made visible in our unity."[24]

"Pursuing more deeply the idea of presence," continues Fr. Giussani, "we must then redefine community. The community is not a cluster of people to carry out initiatives; it is not the attempt to construct a party organization. *The community is the place of the effective construction of our person*, i.e., of a mature faith." So the purpose of the community is to "*generate adults in the faith*. What the world needs is the presence of adults in the faith, not capable professionals or competent workers, for society is full of these but all of them can be contested profoundly in their capacity to create humanity."[25]

But how can a person reach maturity of faith? What is the method by which the community becomes the place of the person's construction of a mature faith? Giussani's answer is always clear: following. "To *follow* means to become one with persons who live the faith more maturely, to *become involved in a living experience*, that 'passes' (*tradit* in Latin, which gives us 'tradition') its dynamism and its *gusto* into us. This dynamism and this *gusto* pass into us not through our reasoning, not at the conclusion of a logical process, but, as it were, by osmosis: it is a new heart that communicates itself to ours; it is the heart of another that begins to move inside our own life."[26] Following has nothing to do, therefore, with obeying user instructions or doing what others tell us to do. It is engagement with a living event, which causes another person's heart to start vibrating within our own.

From this conception of following "arises the foundational idea of our pedagogy of *authority*: truly authoritative for us are the persons who draw us in with their hearts, their dynamism, and their gusto, born out of faith. *True authoritativeness, then, is the definition of friendship*."[27] Indeed, Giussani continues, "True friendship is the *profound companionship to our destiny*." I always think of Burnand's image of Peter and John running to the tomb with eyes wide open, together striving toward destiny. Each of us can compare this with the usual concept of friendship we live. Striving together toward destiny. "And it is not a question of temperament. . . . True friendship is felt in the heart of the word and the gesture of presence." Friends are those people who help us go forward towards destiny, who live their faith more maturely, and with whose experience we can identify. Because we have but one urgent need: "to take faith seriously as a 'reagent' on concrete life, so that we are led to see the identity between faith and what is more truly human—in faith, our humanity becomes more true." All this must "become true in us, and this is why time has been given to us." This verification must take place more and more frequently; otherwise we yield to the "temptation of utopia," that is, "placing our hope and our dignity in a 'project' generated by us."[28]

In relation to this point, Fr. Giussani recalled the early days of the movement, that is, the beginning of his adventure with young people: "We did not come into the schools trying to formulate an alternative project for the schools. *We came in with the consciousness of bringing What saves man also into the schools.*" We can say the same of any sphere of life. Then he recounts when this awareness began to dim in 1963 and 1964, and then in 1968. What did those who went away, who were not loyal, faithful to that original beginning—what did they betray? The presence. What do we betray? The presence! "The project had taken the place of presence."[29] This is very clear to us now. We have seen what we have gained by going along with certain alignments, but only now do we begin to realize how much we have lost, in terms of presence, of original presence. We have to decide whether to become a faction or an original presence. This does not mean that in order to be "for" everyone we must belong to no one. No, it means the opposite. To be for everybody, it is necessary to belong to One, to him who alone can give us that satisfaction that makes us free to be truly ourselves, to be an original presence and not a reactive presence.

What are we called to do in the world? Fr. Giussani repeats the answer to this second question. The goal of our action is not to carry out a project of social action, but to be a presence, to make Christ present where we are called to live. "*What is new is presence* as awareness of carrying something definitive—a definitive judgment on the world, the truth of the world and the human—that is expressed in our unity. What is new is presence as awareness that our unity is the instrument for the rebirth and liberation of the world."[30] We cannot replace this with any idea or project we have in our minds. As Cardinal Scola wrote in one recent pastoral letter, "It is not a matter of a project, much less a calculation. Full of gratitude, Christians intend to 'give back' the gift they have unworthily received and that therefore asks to be communicated with the same gratuitousness."[31]

Why are we tempted to replace faith—presence—with a project? Because we think that faith, the Christian community as a presence, does not have enough of an impact, is unable to change reality. We believe that faith, in order to be concrete, is missing something that we believe we have to add, not as an expression of what we are, but in order to fix something faith is lacking by nature (as if Jesus lacked something and should have added something else to his testimony to himself). This was the thought of all those who believed that Christianity, lived according to tradition, was insufficient for being present. But on the contrary: "*What is new* is the presence of this event of new affection and new humanity; it is the presence of this *beginning of the new world* that we are. What is new is not the avant-garde, but the Remnant of Israel, *the unity of those for whom what happened is everything* and who await only the manifestation of the promise, the realization of what is inside what happened. What is new is not, then, a future to be pursued; it is not a cultural, social, and political project. What is new is presence." We see it testified to daily by Pope Francis: he needs nothing more than the fact of standing, unarmed, before everyone, because "being a presence does not mean not expressing oneself; presence, too, is expression."[32] But it is something very different from reactiveness.

The difference between pursuing a utopia, a project, and being a presence, bringing the seed of something new wherever we are, lies in the diversity of our method of expression. "Utopia uses as its method of expression speech, projects, and the anxious search for instruments and organizational forms. Presence has as its method of expression an operative friendship, gestures revealing a different way of being a protagonist, one that enters everything, making of everything (school desks, studies, the attempt at university reform, etc.) gestures that are, above all, gestures of real humanity, i.e., of charity. A new reality is not built by speeches or organizational projects, but by living gestures of new humanity in the present." We should each of us reflect on this: how we can enter reality with gestures of real humanity, that is, of charity. Therefore, it is not "the abolition of a responsibility," but a different way of conceiving of responsibility. "I indicated what has to happen so that we may work more and have a greater impact on reality, and do so with ever greater gladness, not in exhaustion and bitterness that divide us from each other. The task that awaits us is the expression of an aware presence, capable of being critical and systematic. This task implies a job. *This job is to put our identity into the materialness of life. My identity*, in as much as it penetrates the materialness of life, that is to say, in *as much as it is inside* the condition of existence, works and makes me react."[33]

Fr. Giussani said all these things in 1976, and in the 1990s he insisted again, even more radically:

> Since the 1976 Equipe, entitled, *From Utopia to Presence*, we have made a journey that now pushes us to explore and reach the core of the word "presence": we need to explore it and reach the core . . . because presence is in the person, exclusively in the person, in you [that is, in the new creature]. Presence is a topic that coincides with your "I." Presence is born and consists in the person. . . . And what defines the person as an actor and protagonist of a presence is clarity of faith [we see this well in Pope Francis], that clarity of awareness that is called faith, that clarity of awareness that naturally is called intelligence, because faith is the ultimate aspect of intelligence. It is intelligence that reaches its ultimate horizon, that identifies its destiny, identifies that of which everything consists, identifies the truth of things, identifies where is justice and the good, identifies that great presence, the great presence that enables the transfiguring manipulation of things, through which things become beautiful, things become just, things become good, and everything organizes itself in peace. Presence consists entirely in the person, is born and consists in the person, and the person is intelligence of reality to the point of touching the ultimate horizon.[34]

Now we can clearly see that the two questions—"How can one live?" and "What are we called to do in the world?"—go together. The factor that unites them is the person. We could deceive ourselves into thinking that what is truly important is something else, filling life with initiatives to avoid converting to Christ. But how different it is when the initiatives are the expression of this conversion, of our belonging to him. "The presence of Christ, in day-to-day living, increasingly involves the beating of the heart: being moved by his

presence becomes being moved in daily life and illuminates, beauti-
fies, softens, and makes sweet the tenor of daily life, more and more.
Nothing is useless, nothing is extraneous, because nothing is extraneous to your destiny, and therefore there is nothing of which you cannot become fond [not endure, but become fond of!]. You can become
fond of everything, affection is born for everything, everything, with
its magnificent consequences of respect for the thing you do, preci-
sion in the thing you do, loyalty with your concrete work, tenacity in
pursuing its goal; you become more tireless."[35] As this passage from
the prophet Isaiah says: "Though young men faint and grow weary,
and youths stagger and fall, they that hope in the Lord will renew
their strength, they will soar as with eagles' wings; they will run and
not grow weary, walk and not grow faint."[36]

A Generative Gladness

When his presence penetrates to our innermost being, it fills our life
with gladness. This is the ultimate litmus test that Fr. Giussani leaves
to us. How many truly glad people do we know? Without gladness,
there is no generation, no presence. Gladness is what links the two
questions, "How can one live?" and "What are we called to do in the
world?"—because without an answer for the first, there is no answer
for the second either. Without the gladness introduced by the Presence that gives us life, there is no presence, no generation of anything
new. Gladness is the condition for generating.

When are we glad? What makes us glad? "Gladness is the rever-
beration of the certainty of happiness, of the Eternal, and it comes
from certainty and the will to journey on, from awareness of the journey one is making." We are glad because we have a certainty that
launches us on a journey. "'With this gladness it is possible to look at
everything with fondness,'" Giussani stressed, quoting one of the col-
lege students. And he added: "Looking with sympathy at someone
you find unpleasant is to generate a new thing in the world, is to generate a new event. Gladness is the condition for generation. Joy is the
condition for fruitfulness. Being joyful is the indispensable condition

for generating a different world, a different humanity. But we have a figure in this regard who should be of consolation for us, or of consoling sureness: Mother Teresa of Calcutta. . . . Hers is a generative gladness, fruitful: she does not move a finger without changing something. And her gladness is not a forced, artificial laugh, no, no, no! It is entirely, profoundly lined by the sadness of things, like the face of Christ." A self-aware human being, just as they are aware of the people they have alongside them in the world around them, "cannot be other than profoundly lined by sadness." But sadness is not in contradiction with gladness. Sadness is a "transitory condition, a condition of the journey," and it leaves "intact the vibration that, coming from the Eternal . . . communicates itself to this world . . . as clarity and certainty in our journey." Therefore, "even our wickedness does not take gladness [away from us]. . . . Gladness is like a cactus flower, that in a plant full of thorns generates something beautiful."[37]

NOTES

Foreword

Javier Prades is rector of San Dámaso University in Madrid, Spain.

1. John Paul II, *Fides et Ratio*, September 14, 1998, 83. Unless otherwise noted, all citations and quotations from papal documents are taken from w2.vatican.va.

2. Thomas Aquinas, *Summa Theologiae*, prologue, q. 2, a. 3.

3. Luigi Giussani, *L'io rinasce in un incontro (1986–1987)* [The "I" Is Reborn in an Encounter] (Milan: BUR, 2010), 181. Translation ours. See also chapter 5 in the present book, p. 56.

4. T. S. Eliot, "Choruses from 'The Rock,'" VII, in *Complete Poems and Plays: 1909–1950* (New York: Harcourt, Brace & World, 1971), 106.

5. John Paul II, "To Participants in the National Congress of the Ecclesial Movement for Cultural Commitment" (Rome, January 16, 1982).

6. Angelo Scola, *Buone ragioni per la vita comune* [Good Reasons for Sharing Life] (Milan: Mondadori, 2010), 37–38.

7. Cf. Pope Francis, *Evangelii Gaudium: On the Proclamation of the Gospel in Today's World* (November 24, 2013), 7.

8. Giussani, *L'io rinasce in un incontro*, 300.

9. Cf. Benedict XVI, *Porta Fidei* (October 11, 2011), 2.

10. Cf. John Paul II, *Fides et Ratio*, 73.

11. Pope Francis, *Message of His Holiness Pope Francis Signed by the Cardinal Secretary of State to the Participants in the Meeting for Friendship among Peoples*, Rimini (August 24, 2014), http://w2.vatican.va/content/fran cesco/it/messages/pont-messages/2014.index.2.html.

12. Josef Zvérina, "Letter to the Christians of the West," in *Generating Traces in the History of the World*, by Luigi Giussani, Stefano Alberto, and Javier Prades, trans. Patrick Stevenson (Montreal and Kingston: McGill-Queen's University Press, 2010), 111.

Chapter 1. Is a New Beginning Possible?

1. Luigi Giussani, *The Religious Sense*, trans. John E. Zucchi (Montreal and Kingston: McGill-Queen's University Press, 1997), 90; see also Gaius, *Institutionum Commentarii quattuor*, II, 12–17.

2. Joseph Ratzinger, *Christianity and the Crisis of Cultures*, trans. Brian McNeil (San Francisco: Ignatius Press, 2006), 50–51.

3. Ibid., 51.

4. Ibid., 41, 42, 36, 43–44.

5. Ibid., 48.

6. Benedict XVI, "Address of His Holiness Benedict XVI to the Roman Curia Offering Them His Christmas Greetings" (Rome, December 22, 2005).

7. Benedict XVI, interview for the documentary film *Campane d'Europa*, October 15, 2012.

8. "True Religiosity and Power: Notes from a Conversation between Luigi Giussani and a CL Group in New York, March 8, 1986," *Traces* 7, no. 2 (2005): 18–19; for the full text, see *Traces* 4, no. 2 (2002): i–xii.

9. Benedict XVI, "Address of His Holiness Benedict XVI" (Reichstag Building, Berlin, September 22, 2011).

10. Ratzinger, *Christianity and the Crisis of Cultures*, 47–48.

11. Angelo Scola, "Remarks after the Homily on the Ninth Anniversary of the Death of Fr. Giussani and the Twenty-Second Anniversary of Pontifical Recognition of the CL Fraternity" (Milan, February 11, 2014). For the full remarks in English, see A. Scola, "Responsible for a Gift," *Traces* 16, no. 3 (2014): 36–39.

12. Hannah Arendt, *Between Past and Future* (New York: Penguin, 1968), 174–75.

13. Benedict XVI, *Spe Salvi* (2007), 24.

14. Rainer Maria Rilke, "Second Elegy," in *Duino Elegies*, translated by Stephen Mitchell (Boulder, CO: Shambhala, 1992), lines 42–44.

15. Mauro Magatti and Chiara Giaccardi, *Generativi di tutto il mondo, unitevi!* [Generatives of the World, Unite!] (Milan: Feltrinelli, 2014), 14. Translation ours.

16. Giacomo Leopardi, "Night Song of a Wandering Shepherd in Asia," in *Canti*, trans. J. Galassi (New York: Farrar, Straus & Giroux, 2010), 199, line 89.

17. Cesare Pavese, *The Business of Living: Diaries, 1935–1950* (New Brunswick, NJ: Transaction Publishers, 2009), 180.

18. Benedict XVI, *Message to the Participants in the Meeting for Friendship among Peoples*, Rimini (August 19, 2012)

19. T. S. Eliot, "Choruses from 'The Rock,'" VI, in *The Complete Poems and Plays: 1909–1950* (New York: Harcourt, Brace & World, 1971), 108.

20. Benedict XVI, *Spe Salvi*, 24–25.

21. Luigi Giussani, *L'io, il potere, le opere: Contributi da un'esperienza* [The "I," Power, Works: Contributions from an Experience] (Genoa-Milan: Marietti, 2000), 166.

22. Luigi Giussani, quoted by Alberto Savorana in his biography of Giussani, *Vita di don Giussani* (Milan: Rizzoli, 2013), 489. Translation ours.

23. Giussani, *L'io rinasce in un incontro*, 253–54, 182.

24. Ibid., 182.

25. Ratzinger, *Christianity and the Crisis of Cultures*, 52.

26. Quoted in Benedict XVI, "Lecture by the Holy Father Benedict XVI at the University of Rome 'La Sapienza'" (undelivered address prepared for January 17, 2008):

> In my opinion, Jürgen Habermas articulates a vast consensus of contemporary thought when he says that the legitimacy of a constitutional charter, as a basis for what is legal, derives from two sources: from the equal participation of all citizens in the political process and from the reasonable manner in which political disputes are resolved. With regard to this "reasonable manner," he notes that it cannot simply be a fight for arithmetical majorities, but must have the character of a "process of argumentation sensitive to the truth" (wahrheitssensibles Argumentationsverfahren).

27. Francis, *Letter to a Non-Believer* (September 4, 2013).

28. Francis, *Evangelii Gaudium* (November 24, 2014), 199.

29. Benedict XVI, *Spe Salvi*, 24.

30. See Rémi Brague, *Europe: La voie romaine* [Europe: The Roman Way] (Paris: Criterion, 1992).

31. Wlodzimierz Redzioch, ed., *Stories about Saint John Paul II Told by His Close Friends and Co-Workers* (San Francisco: Ignatius Press, 2015), 19.

32. Ratzinger, *Christianity and the Crisis of Cultures*, 51.

33. *Dignitatis Humanae*, Second Vatican Council Declaration on Religious Freedom, December 7, 1965, 1.

34. *Dignitatis Humanae*, 2.

Chapter 2. Truth and Freedom: A Paradigm

1. Joseph Ratzinger, *Truth and Tolerance: Christian Belief and the World Religions* (San Francisco: Ignatius, 2004), 140.

2. Joseph Ratzinger, *Christianity and the Crisis of Cultures*, 50–51.

3. Ibid., 51.

4. Romano Guardini, *The End of the Modern World* (Wilmington, DE: ISI Books, 1998), 97–98.

5. Ibid., 98.

6. Ibid.

7. Mk 2:12.

8. Luigi Giussani, *At the Origin of the Christian Claim*, trans. Viviane Hewitt (Montreal and Kingston: McGill-Queens University Press, 1998), 84.

9. Guardini, *End of the Modern World*, 98.

10. Ibid., 98–99.

11. Enzo Jannacci, "Caso Eluana, parla l'ateo Jannacci: Allucinante fermare le cure," interview by Fabio Cutri, *Corriere della Sera*, February 6, 2009, 3. Eluana Englaro (1970–2009) had been living in a vegetative state for seventeen years as a result of a car accident when the family asked for and obtained judicial permission to stop force-feeding her. The incident sparked a long debate in Italy on end-of-life issues.

12. Benedict XVI, "Address of His Holiness Benedict XVI" (Berlin, September 22, 2011).

13. Pope Francis, "A Big Heart Open to God," interview by Antonio Spadaro, S.J., *America*, September 30, 2013, www.americamagazine.org/pope-interview.

14. Ratzinger, *Christianity and the Crisis of Cultures*, 34.

15. Ratzinger, *Truth and Tolerance*, 231.

16. Phlm 1:10–17.

17. "Letter to Diognetus" 6. The Greek text is found in *Patrologia Graeca* 2.1167–86.

18. For a closer look at this issue, see Gabrio Lombardi, *Persecuzioni, laicità, libertà religiosa: Dall'Editto di Milano alla "Dignitatis Humanae"* [Persecutions, Secularity, and Religious Freedom: From the Edict of Milan to *Dignitatis Humanae*] (Rome: Studium, 1991); Gerardo Del Pozo Abejón, *La Iglesia y la libertad religiosa* [The Church and Religious Freedom] (Madrid: BAC, 2007); Angelo Scola, *Let's Not Forget God: Freedom of Faith, Culture, and Politics* (New York: Image, 2014).

19. Augustine, Letter 93, 5.17, in *The Letters of St. Augustine*, trans. Rev. J. G. Cunningham (North Charleston, SC: Createspace, 2015), 185.

20. A major schismatic movement that troubled the Church in Africa beginning in the fourth century. Augustine had contact with the Donatists in Hippo and began to struggle against them through a long series of writings.

21. "You now see therefore, I suppose, that the thing to be considered when any one is coerced, is not the mere fact of the coercion, but the nature of that to which he is coerced, whether it be good or bad: not that any one can be good in spite of his own will, but that, through fear of suffering what he does not desire, he either renounces his hostile prejudices, or is compelled to examine truth of which he had been contentedly ignorant; and under the influence of this fear repudiates the error which he was wont to defend, or seeks the truth of which he formerly knew nothing, and now willingly holds what he formerly rejected. Perhaps it would be utterly useless to assert this in words, if it were not demonstrated by so many examples. We see not a few men here and there, but many cities, once Donatist, now Catholic, vehemently detesting the diabolical schism, and ardently loving the unity of the Church; and these became Catholic under the influence of that fear which is to you so offensive by the laws of emperors, from Constantine, before whom your party of their own accord impeached Cæcilianus, down to the emperors of our own time, who most justly decree that the decision of the judge whom your own party chose, and whom they preferred to a tribunal of bishops, should be maintained in force against you." Augustine, Letter 93, 5.16, in Cunningham, *Letters of St. Augustine*, 184–85.

22. Massimo Borghesi, *Critica della teologia politica: Da Agostino a Peterson; La fine dell'era costantiniana* [Critique of Political Theology: From

Augustine to Peterson; The End of the Era of Constantine] (Genoa-Milan: Marietti, 2013), 43. Translation ours.

23. For more, see Scola, *Let's Not Forget God*, 47–48.

24. *Dignitatis Humanae*, I, 2.

25. Nikolaus Lobkowicz, "Pharaoh Amenhotep and Dignitatis Humanae," *Oasis*, no. 8 (2008): 9.

26. Pope Benedict XVI, "Address of His Holiness Benedict XVI" (Rome, December 22, 2005).

27. Ibid.

28. Ibid.

29. Joseph Ratzinger, *Church, Ecumenism, and Politics: New Endeavors in Ecclesiology* (San Francisco: Ignatius Press, 2008), 218.

30. Ratzinger, *Christianity and the Crisis of Cultures*, 47–49.

31. *Dignitatis Humanae* II, 12.

32. Benedict XVI, *Spe Salvi*, 24. Benedict stresses the following point: "Naturally, new generations can build on the knowledge and experience of those who went before, and they can draw upon the moral treasury of the whole of humanity. But they can also reject it, because it can never be self-evident in the same way as material inventions. The moral treasury of humanity is not readily at hand like tools that we use; it is present as an appeal to freedom and a possibility for it." The rest of the paragraph offers precious observations:

> This, however, means that:
> a) The right state of human affairs, the moral well-being of the world can never be guaranteed simply through structures alone, however good they are. Such structures are not only important, but necessary; yet they cannot and must not marginalize human freedom. Even the best structures function only when the community is animated by convictions capable of motivating people to assent freely to the social order. Freedom requires conviction; conviction does not exist on its own, but must always be gained anew by the community.
> b) Since man always remains free and since his freedom is always fragile, the kingdom of good will never be definitively established in this world. [Remember the parable of the weeds.] Anyone who promises the better world that is guaranteed to last forever is making a false promise; he is overlooking human freedom. Freedom must constantly be won over for the cause of good. Free assent to the good never exists simply by itself. If there were structures which could

irrevocably guarantee a determined—good—state of the world, man's freedom would be denied, and hence they would not be good structures at all."

33. Lobkowicz, "Pharaoh Amenhotep and Dignitatis Humanae," *Oasis*, no. 8 (2008): 9.

34. Onorato Grassi, "Movimento, 'regola' di libertà" [Movement, a "Rule" of Freedom], *CL Litterae Communionis*, no. 11 (1978): 44. Translation ours.

Chapter 3. In the Collapse of the Self-Evident, a Subject Is Generated

1. See Savorana, *Vita di don Giussani*, 130, 145.

2. Luigi Giussani, *The Risk of Education* (New York: Crossroads, 2001), 11.

3. Giussani, *L'io rinasce in un incontro*, 181–82.

4. Ratzinger, *Truth and Tolerance*, 140.

5. G. K. Chesterton, *Orthodoxy* (London: William Clowes and Sons, Ltd., 1934), 64.

6. Luigi Giussani, "By Grace, Always," in *He Is If He Changes*, supplement to *30 Days*, no. 7–8 (1994): 57–59.

7. Ibid., 32.

8. *Catechism of the Catholic Church*, no. 1960.

9. International Theological Commission, *In Search of a Universal Ethic: A New Look at the Natural Law*, para. 52, http://www.vatican.va/roman _curia/congregations/cfaith/cti_documents/rc_con_cfaith_doc_20090520 _legge-naturale_en.html.

10. Angelo Scola, "Il no ai divorziati resta, ma non è un castigo e sugli omosessuali la Chiesa è stata lenta," interview by Paolo Rodari, *La Repubblica*, October 12, 2014, 19.

11. Luigi Giussani, "The Long March to Maturity," *Traces* 10, no. 3 (2008): 25–27.

12. Ibid., 26, 23.

13. Luigi Giussani, *Uomini senza patria (1982–1983)* [People without a Homeland] (Milan: BUR, 2008), 96–97. Translation ours.

14. Giussani, *L'io rinasce in un incontro*, 182.

15. Savorana, *Vita di don Giussani*, 489.

16. Giussani, *At the Origin of the Christian Claim*, 97–98.

17. Luigi Giussani, "La gioia, la letizia e l'audacia: Nessuno genera, se non è generato" [Joy, Gladness, and Audacity: No One Generates Unless He Has Been Generated], *Tracce-Litterae Communionis*, no. 6 (1997): iv.

18. Pope Francis, *Message of His Holiness Pope Francis Signed by the Cardinal Secretary of State to the Participants in the Meeting for Friendship among Peoples*, Rimini (August 24, 2014).

19. Luigi Giussani, *Dall'utopia alla presenza: 1975–1978* [From Utopia to Presence: 1975–1978] (Milan: BUR, 2006), 66.

Chapter 4. The Challenge of True Dialogue after the Charlie Hebdo Attacks

1. On January 7, 2015, two masked and armed men broke into the offices of the satirical weekly newspaper *Charlie Hebdo*, in the heart of Paris, shouting, "Allah is great." Their intention was to "avenge the Prophet" after the publication of cartoons they deemed offensive. The terrorists killed twelve people: journalists and cartoonists who worked in the newspaper and two policemen.

2. Pope Francis, "Address to Participants in the Meeting Sponsored by the Pontifical Institute for Arabic and Islamic Studies" (Rome, January 24, 2015).

3. Pope Francis, "Address to Participants in the Plenary Assembly of the Pontifical Council for the Laity" (Rome, February 7, 2015).

Chapter 5. Christianity Faced with the Challenges of the Present

1. Cf. Fyodor Dostoevsky, *Notebooks for "The Possessed,"* ed. Edward Wasiolek (Chicago: University of Chicago Press, 1968), 237.

2. Luigi Giussani, *L'uomo e il suo destino: In cammino* [Man and His Destiny: On the Road] (Genoa: Marietti, 1999), 63. Translation ours.

3. Pope John Paul II, *Ecclesia in Europa* (June 28, 2003), 47.

4. Benedict XVI, "Homily at Terreiro do Paço" (speech, Lisbon, May 11, 2010).

5. *Gaudium et Spes* (December 7, 1965), 21.

6. Ratzinger, *Truth and Tolerance*, 137.

7. Giussani, *At the Origin of the Christian Claim*, 6.

8. Augustine, *Confessions*, Trans. F. J. Sheed (Indianapolis: Hackett, 2006), 3.

9. Giussani, *L'io rinasce in un incontro*, 181.

10. Pietro Citati, "Questa generazione che non vuol crescere mai" [This Generation That Never Wants to Grow Up], *La Repubblica*, August 2, 1999, 1.

11. Eugenio Scalfari, "Quel vuoto di plastica che soffoca i giovani" [That Plastic Void That Suffocates the Youth], *La Repubblica*, August 5, 1999, 1.

12. Augusto Del Noce, "Lettera a Rodolfo Quadrelli (1984)" [Letter to Rodolfo Quadrelli (1984)], *Tracce-Litterae Communionis*, no.1 (2007): 86.

13. See Ernest L. Fortin, "The Regime of Separatism: Theoretical Considerations on the Separation of Church and State," in *Ernest Fortin: Collected Essays*, ed. J. Brian Benestad (Lanham, MD: Rowman & Littlefield, 1996), 3:8.

14. Antonio Machado, "Has My Heart Gone to Sleep?," *Solitudes*, no. 16, in *Selected Poems*, trans. Alan S. Trueblood (Cambridge, MA: Harvard University Press, 1982), 93.

15. Antonio Machado, "To a Dry Elm," in *Fields of Castilla*, repr. in *Border of a Dream: Selected Poems of Antonio Machado*, trans. Willis Barnstone (Port Townsend, WA: Copper Canyon Press, 2004), 229.

16. Eugenio Montale, "Prima del viaggio" [Before the Trip], in *Tutte le poesie* (Milan: Mondadori, 1990), 390. Translation ours.

17. Cf. Mt 19:29.

18. John Henry Newman, *An Essay in Aid of a Grammar of Assent* (New York: Catholic Publication Society, 1870), 53. As Henri de Lubac stressed, part of Catholic theology had also fallen into this error. "While wishing to protect the supernatural from any contamination, people had in fact exiled it altogether—both from intellectual and from social life—leaving the field free to be taken over by secularism. Today that secularism, following its course, is beginning to enter the minds even of Christians. . . . The last word in Christian progress and the entry into adulthood would then appear to consist in a total secularization which would expel God not merely from the life of society, but from culture and even from personal relationships." Henri de Lubac, *The Mystery of the Supernatural*, trans. Rosemary Sheed (New York: Herder and Herder, 1967), xi–xii.

19. Pierre Rousselot, *The Eyes of Faith*, trans. Joseph Donceel, S.J. (New York: Fordham University Press, 1990) 65.

20. H. Schlier, *Linee fondamentali di una teologia paolina* [Basic Outlines of Pauline Theology] (Brescia: Queriniana, 2004), 12–13. Translation ours.

21. Cf. Benedict XVI, "Meeting with the Parish Priests and the Clergy of the Diocese of Rome" (speech, Rome, February 26, 2009).

22. Mt 7:29.

23. Mk 2:12.

24. Benedict XVI, *Deus Caritas Est* (December 25, 2005), 12.

25. Jn 3:16.

26. Augustine of Hippo, *Answer to the Pelagians, III: Unfinished Work in Answer to Julian*, trans. Roland J. Teske, S.J. (Hyde Park, NY: New City Press, 1999), 226 (bk. 2, 146).

27. Immanuel Kant, *Religion within the Boundaries of Mere Reason*, trans. and ed. Alan Wood and George di Giovanni (Cambridge: Cambridge University Press, 2003).

28. Pope John Paul I, quoted in *Humilitas*, no. 3 (2001): 10.

29. Benedict XVI, "Interview with Father Eberhard von Gemmingen," Vatican Radio, August 15, 2005, English translation at http://www.asianews .it/news-en/(Vatican,Social-Doctrine-of-the-Church)-The-first-interview -with-Benedict-XVI:-Youth,-it's-beautiful-to-be-Christians!-3913.html.

30. Benedict XVI, "Meeting with the Bishops of Portugal" (speech, Fátima, Portugal, May 13, 2010).

31. Luigi Giussani, *L'avvenimento cristiano* [The Christian Event] (Milan: BUR, 2003), 23–24. Translation ours.

32. Giussani, Alberto, and Prades, *Generating Traces in the History of the World*, 17–18.

33. Benedict XVI, *Deus Caritas Est*, 1.

34. "At the origin of our life of faith there is an encounter, unique in kind, which discloses a mystery hidden for long ages (cf. 1 Cor 2:7; Rom 16:25–26) but which is now revealed." John Paul II, *Fides et Ratio*, 7.

35. For a comparison of the Synoptic narratives and that of John relating to the calling of the disciples, see Raymond Brown, *The Gospel according to John I–XII*, Anchor Bible 29 (New York: Doubleday, 1966), 55–81.

36. Pierre Grelot, *Jésus de Nazareth* (Paris: Cerf, 1997), 260. Translation ours.

37. To see such a search at work, in its many forms, we should go back to all the encounters of the gospel. It is the Samaritan woman's search for a happiness that her five husbands had been unable to give her (Jn 4:11–17). It is the expectation of the chief tax collector of Jericho district, named Zacchaeus, that not even all the money accumulated, not always in an honest way ("He was very rich," says the gospel), had been able to fulfill (Lk 19:1–10). It is the need for healing of the blind man of Jericho, who kept

shouting even when they tried to shut him up to prevent him from harassing the Master (Mk 10:46–52). Without this searching, Christianity would not make sense, nor could it be encountered. "Nothing is so incredible as an answer to an unasked question." Reinhold Niebuhr, *The Nature and Destiny of Man: A Christian Interpretation* (New York: Charles Scribner's Sons, 1955), 2:6.

38. Giussani, *L'avvenimento cristiano*, 14–15. Translation ours. In another text Giussani insists,

> Christianity is an event. There is no other word to indicate its nature, neither the word *law*, nor the words *ideology, concept*, or *plan*. Christianity is not a religious doctrine, a series of moral laws or a collection of rites. Christianity is a fact, an event. All the rest is a consequence. The word "event" is therefore crucial. It indicates the method chosen and used by God to save man: God became man in the womb of a fifteen- to seventeen-year-old girl named Mary, in "the womb . . . where our desire did dwell," as Dante says. The manner in which God entered into relationship with us to save us is an event, not a thought or a religious sentiment. It is a fact that took place in history, a fact that reveals who God is and points out what God wants from man, what man must do in his relationship with God. As a way of communicating Himself to man, God could have chosen direct enlightenment, so that each individual would have to follow what God suggested to him in his thoughts and in his heart. This would have been by no means an easier or safer road, since it would be constantly exposed to the fluctuation of feelings and thoughts. But the way God chose to save us is an event, not our thoughts! (Giussani, Alberto, and Prades, *Generating Traces in the History of the World*, 9)

39. Søren Kierkegaard, *Practice in Christianity*, ed. and trans. Howard V. Hong and Edna Hong (Princeton, NJ: Princeton University Press, 1991), 62.

40. Lk 24:19–21.

41. As the Protestant theologian Peter Stuhlmacher wrote: "As the night of Good Friday falls over Jesus, who died on the tree of ignominy and whom friends hurriedly laid in a rocky tomb, every Jew opposed to Jesus could—indeed had—to say with Deuteronomy 21:22–23: This one who has been hung on the cross has suffered his just punishment; he died 'cursed of God'! His disciples, gripped by fear and doubt, are all to recover from this logical and dreadful interpretation of Jesus' death on the cross (cf. John

19:31; Acts 5:30; 10:39; Justin, *Dialogue with Trypho* 89:2; 90:1) only when the crucified one appears to them in divine life on Easter morning." *Jesus of Nazareth—Christ of Faith*, trans. Siegfried Schatzmann (Peabody, MA: Hendrickson, 1993), 35–36.

42. "To deny [the appearance of the Risen One] . . . would render inexplicable the development of early Christianity and its mission." Ibid., 36.

43. *Catechism of the Catholic Church* (New York: Doubleday, 1995), 788.

44. John Paul II, *Veritatis Splendor* (August 6, 1993), 25.

45. Gal 3:27–28.

46. Second Vatican Council, *Lumen Gentium* (November 21, 1964), 7.

47. *Catechism of the Catholic Church*, 1265: "Baptism not only purifies from all sins, but also makes the neophyte 'a new creature.'"

48. Benedict XVI, "Address, International Airport of Santiago de Compostela" (speech, Santiago de Compostela, Spain, November 6, 2010). In his homily at the dedication of the basilica of the Sagrada Familia cathedral in Barcelona the next day, Benedict XVI said, "The Church of herself is nothing; she is called to be the sign and instrument of Christ, in pure docility to his authority and in total service to his mandate."

49. Luigi Giussani, "Something That Comes First," *Traces* 10, no. 10 (November 2008), www.traces.com/archive.

50. John Paul II, *Redemptor Hominis* (March 4, 1979), 10. "The name for that deep amazement at man's worth and dignity is the Gospel, that is to say: the Good News. It is also called Christianity. This amazement determines the Church's mission in the world and, perhaps even more so, 'in the modern world.' This amazement, which is also a conviction and a certitude—at its deepest root it is the certainty of faith."

51. Marius Victorinus, "In epistolam ad Ephesios," in *Marii Victorini Opera exegetica*, Liber secundus, Corpus Scriptorum Ecclesiasticorum Latinorum 83 (Vienna: Österreichische Akademie der Wissenschaften, 1986), chap. 4, verse 14.

52. John Henry Newman, "Personal Influence, the Means of Propagating the Truth," sermon 5, para. 34, in *Fifteen Sermons Preached before the University of Oxford between A.D. 1826 and 1843*, ed. J. D. Earnest and G. Tracey (Oxford: Oxford University Press, 2006).

53. 2 Cor 5:14–15.

54. "For the Church, charity is not a kind of welfare activity which could equally well be left to others, but is a part of her nature, an indispensable expression of her very being." Benedict XVI, *Deus Caritas Est*, 25a.

55. Benedict XVI, homily (Plaza del Obradoiro, Santiago de Compostela, Spain, November 6, 2010).

56. Benedict XVI, "Address to the 24th Plenary Session of the Pontifical Council for the Laity" (Rome, May 21, 2010).

57. "Tragically, above all in nineteenth century Europe, the conviction grew that God is somehow man's antagonist and an enemy of his freedom." Benedict XVI, homily (Plaza del Obradoiro, Santiago de Compostela).

58. Benedict XVI, "Meeting with the Bishops of Portugal."

59. The method of testimony through which the Christian truth is offered certainly does not violate the freedom of those who are touched by beauty, nor does it abandon them to fate, but provokes them, calling them to get to the depths of their nature, through the acceptance of that same beauty in which the heart finds its fulfillment. John Paul II, in the *Redemptoris Missio*, 42, writes, "The witness of a Christian life is the first and irreplaceable form of mission: Christ, whose mission we continue, is the 'witness' *par excellence* (Rv 1:5; 3:14) and the model of all Christian witness. The Holy Spirit accompanies the Church along her way and associates her with the witness he gives to Christ (cf. Jn 15:26–27)." See Pope Paul VI, *Evangelii Nuntiandi*, 21, 41; Second Vatican Council, *Ad Gentes*, 11–12; John Paul II, *Redemptor hominis*, 11.

60. In Joseph Ratzinger, "The Beauty and Truth of Christ: Message to the CL Meeting in Rimini, August 24–30, 2002," *L'Osservatore Romano*, weekly edition in English (November 6, 2002), 6.

Chapter 6. The Religious Sense, Verification of the Faith

1. Giacomo Leopardi, "Night Song of a Wandering Shepherd in Asia," in *Canti*, p. 199, lines 84–89.

2. Giussani, *Religious Sense*, 45. The religious sense is "man's natural movement towards his First Beginning and Final End; a vague intuitive awareness that he is both responsible and at the same time dependent on Another; a natural, inchoate utterance of the soul about its mysterious relationship with the Supreme Being; a spontaneous gesture by human nature, in an attitude of adoration and supplication; the soul's urgent longing for a personal Infinite Being, like the eye's longing for light or a flower's need of the sun." It was in 1957 when, in his pastoral letter for Lent, then-archbishop of Milan Giovanni Battista Montini used these words. A few months later, Luigi Giussani published the first edition of his text *The Religious Sense*; ex-

actly forty years later, Fr. Giussani completed his last and definitive version of the work (which is also the first volume of his fundamental trilogy).

3. Joseph Ratzinger / Pope Benedict XVI, *Dogma and Preaching: Applying Christian Doctrine to Daily Life*, ed. Michael J. Miller, trans. Michael J. Miller and Matthew J. O'Connell, unabr. ed. (San Francisco: Ignatius Press, 2011), 77.

4. Niebuhr, *Nature and Destiny of Man*, 2:6.

5. Luigi Giussani, *Un avvenimento di vita, cioè una storia* [An Event of Life, That Is, a History] (Rome and Milan: Edit-Il Sabato, 1993), 38.

6. Luigi Giussani, *L'attrattiva Gesù* [The Attraction That Is Jesus] (Milano: BUR, 1999), 287. Translation ours.

7. Luigi Giussani, *Letter to the Fraternity* (October 7, 1997), in *The Work of the Movement: The Fraternity of Communion and Liberation* (Milan: Cooperativa Editoriale Nuovo Mondo, 2005), 278–80.

8. Giussani, *Religious Sense*, 97; emphasis original.

9. Ibid., 117.

10. Ibid., 97.

11. Ratzinger, *Truth and Tolerance*, 136.

12. Giussani, *Religious Sense*, 10.

13. Giussani, *L'io rinasce in un incontro*, 162.

14. Luigi Giussani, *"Il tempo si fa breve": Esercizi della Fraternità di Comunione e Liberazione* [Time Is Short: Spiritual Exercises of the Fraternity of Communion and Liberation] (Milan: Cooperativa Editoriale Nuovo Mondo, 1994), 23–25. Translation ours.

15. Ibid.

16. Luigi Giussani, *L'autocoscienza del cosmo* [The Self-Awareness of the Cosmos] (Milan: BUR, 2000), 17. Translation ours.

17. Giussani, *L'io rinasce in un incontro*, 182.

18. Ibid., 206–7.

19. Giussani, *L'autocoscienza del cosmo*, 17–18.

20. Luigi Giussani, *Why the Church?* (Montreal: McGill-Queen's University Press, 2001), 6–7.

21. Ibid., 7.

22. Ibid., 7.

23. Giussani, *L'attrattiva Gesù*, 286–87.

24. Giussani, *Why the Church?*, 147.

25. Benedict XVI, "Address on the Occasion of Christmas Greetings to the Roman Curia" (speech, Rome, December 20, 2010).

26. Lk 6:44.

27. 2 Cor 5:17.

28. Jacopone da Todi, "Lauda XC," in *Le Laude* (Florence: Libreria Editrice Fiorentina, 1989), 313. Translation ours.

29. Luigi Giussani, *L'uomo e il suo destino*, 117.

30. Giussani, *Religious Sense*, 106.

31. Giussani, Alberto, and Prades, *Generating Traces in the History of the World*, 15–16.

32. Ibid.

33. Luigi Giussani, *Is It Possible to Live This Way?*, vol. 2, *Hope* (Montreal: McGill-Queen's University Press, 2008), 105.

34. Giussani, Alberto, and Prades, *Generating Traces in the History of the World*, 22–23.

35. Ibid., 23.

36. Luigi Giussani, *Tutta la terra desidera il tuo volto* [All the Earth Desires Your Face] (Cinisello Balsamo: San Paolo, 2000), 124. Translation ours.

37. Luigi Giussani, *La familiarità con Cristo* [Familiarity with Christ] (Cinisello Balsamo: San Paolo, 2008), 135. Translation ours.

38. Mt 18:3.

39. Mt 5:3.

Chapter 7. The "Eternal Mystery of Our Being"

1. Luigi Giussani, *Alla ricerca del volto umano* [In Search of the Human Face] (Milan: Rizzoli, 1995), 9–10. Translation ours.

2. Philip Roth, *The Counterlife* (New York: Vintage Books, 1986), 324–25.

3. Abraham Joshua Heschel, *Who Is Man?* (Stanford, CA: Stanford University Press, 1965), 27.

4. Giussani, *Alla ricerca del volto umano*, 10.

5. George Bernanos, *Un uomo solo* [A Man Alone] (Vicenza: La Locusta, Vicenza, 1997), 41. Translation ours.

6. Giussani, *L'io rinasce in un incontro*, 364–65.

7. Luigi Giussani, *The Journey to Truth Is an Experience* (Montreal: McGill-Queen's University Press, 2006), 54.

8. Olivier Rey, *Itinéraire de l'égarement: Du rôle de la science dans l'absurdité contemporaine* [Directions from Bewilderment: The Role of Science in Contemporary Absurdity] (Paris: Seuil, 2003), 17. Translation ours.

9. Giussani, *Why the Church?*, 34.

10. Giussani, *L'io rinasce in un incontro*, 173–74.

11. Benedict XVI, *Jesus of Nazareth: Holy Week; From the Entrance into Jerusalem to the Resurrection* (San Francisco: Ignatius Press, 2011), 153.

12. Giussani, *L'io rinasce in un incontro*, 365.

13. Hannah Arendt, *Responsibility and Judgment* (New York: Random House, 2003), 37.

14. See Luigi Giussani, "The Religious Sense: Its Nature," in *The Religious Sense*, 45–48.

15. Giussani, *L'io, il potere, le opere*, 24.

16. Giussani, *Alla ricerca del volto umano*, 9.

17. Jn 4:15.

18. Giussani, *Religious Sense*, 45.

19. Ibid., 46.

20. Heschel, *Who Is Man?*, 55.

21. Giacomo Leopardi, "The Dominant Idea," in *Canti*, 213, lines 19–20.

22. Ibid., 213, line 3.

23. Giacomo Leopardi, "To Himself," in *Canti*, 235, line 16.

24. Giussani, *Religious Sense*, 47.

25. Giussani, *L'io rinasce in un incontro*, 385. See Clemente Rebora, "Sacchi a terra per gli occhi" [Sacks on the Ground for the Eyes], line 15, in *Le Poesie* (Milan: Garzanti, 1988), 141; and Eugenio Montale, "L'agave sullo scoglio—Maestrale" [The Agave on the Reef—Mistral], in *Collected Poems*, trans. Jonathan Galassi (New York: Farrar, Straus and Giroux, 1998), 94.

26. Giacomo Leopardi, *Pensieri*, LXVIII, trans. W. S. Di Piero (Baton Rouge and London: Louisiana State University Press, 1981), 113.

27. Giussani, *Religious Sense*, 48.

28. Giacomo Leopardi, "On the Portrait of a Beautiful Woman," in *Canti*, 257, lines 22–23.

29. Giussani, *Religious Sense*, 51.

30. Ibid., 52.

31. Fyodor Dostoevsky, *The Devils*, trans. David Magarshack (Middlesex: Penguin Books, 1971), 54.

32. Giussani, *Religious Sense*, 52–53. See Dostoevsky, *The Devils*, 656.

33. Cesare Pavese, *Business of Living*, 180.

34. Ibid., 267.

35. Giussani, *Religious Sense*, 54.

36. Giussani, *Journey to Truth Is an Experience*, 55.

37. Alfred N. Whitehead, *Religion in the Making* (New York: Macmillan, 1927), 16.

38. Giussani, *Religious Sense*, 56.

39. M. Luzi, "Di che è mancanza" [What Is It That You Are Missing?], lines 1–5, in *Sotto specie umana* [Under Human Species] (Milan: Garzanti, 1999), 180. Translation ours.

40. Pär Lagerkvist, "My Friend Is a Stranger," in *Evening Land: Aftonland*, trans. W. H. Auden and Leif Sjöberg (Detroit: Wayne State University Press, 1975), 119.

41. Giussani, *Religious Sense*, 58.

42. Ps 63:2–9.

43. Ps 42:2–3.

44. Mt 5:6.

45. Luigi Giussani, *L'Alleanza* (Milan: Jaca Book, 1979), 106. Translation ours.

46. Is 26:8.

Chapter 8. Broadening Reason

1. Pope Benedict XVI, "Meeting with the Representatives of Science" (University of Regensburg, Regensburg, Germany, September 12, 2006).

2. Giussani, *Religious Sense*, 97.

3. Political philosophy since Aristotle has always acknowledged this fact: "Only in the ambit framework of a people can an individual man live as a man amongst men." Hannah Arendt, *The Jew as Pariah: Jewish Identity and Politics in the Modern Age* (New York: Grove Press, 1978), 90.

4. Romano Guardini, *Persona e libertà: Saggi di fondazione della teoria pedagogica* [The Person and Freedom: Essays from the Foundation for Pedagogical Theory] (Brescia: Editrice La Scuola, 1987), 50. Translation ours.

5. Giussani, *Religious Sense*, 7.

6. Giussani, *L'io, il potere, le opere*, 36.

7. Ratzinger, *Truth and Tolerance*, 64–65.

8. *The Religious Sense*, Arabic translation (Cairo: Tawasul Centre, 2011).

9. Alain Finkielkraut, *Nous autres, modernes* (Paris: Gallimard, 2011), 17–18. Translation ours.

10. "There is no possessing, only an existing, only an existing that yearns for its final breath, for asphyxiation." Franz Kafka, *Aphorismen The Zurau* [Aphorisms] (New York: Schocken Books, 2006), no. 3435.

11. Finkielkraut, *Nous autres, modernes*, 32.

12. Alain Finkielkraut, "Tirerò Péguy fuori dal ghetto" [I'll Get Péguy out of the Ghetto], interview by S. M. Paci, *30 Giorni* 6 (June 1992): 58–61.

13. Finkielkraut, *Nous autres, modernes*, 33.

14. See Jean Guitton, *Nouvel art de penser* (Paris: Aubier, 1946), 87. Translation ours.

15. See María Zambrano, *Hacia un saber sobre el alma* [Towards a Knowledge of the Soul] (Madrid: Alianza Editorial, 2000), 104.

16. Hannah Arendt, *The Origins of Totalitarianism* (New York: Schocken Books, 2004), 605.

17. Luigi Giussani, *In cammino (1992–1998)* [On the Road (1992–1998)] (Milan: BUR, 2014), 311. Translation ours.

18. Martin Heidegger, *Off the Beaten Track*, trans. Julian Young and K. Haynes (New York: Cambridge University Press, 2002), 139.

19. Cf. Luigi Giussani, *Si può (veramente?!) vivere così?* [Is It (Really?!) Possible to Live This Way?] (Milan: BUR, 1996), 79. Translation ours.

20. See Agostino Gemelli, *L'anima dell'insegnamento* [The Heart of Teaching] (Milan: Società Editrice Vita e Pensiero, 1930), 69. Translation ours.

21. Giussani, *Religious Sense*, 24.

22. Luigi Giussani, *L'uomo e il suo destino: In cammino*, 117.

23. Martin Heidegger, *Nietzsche*, vol. 4, *Nihilism*, trans. F. A. Capuzzi (San Francisco: Harper & Row, 1982), 201.

24. Benedict XVI, "Address to the Participants in the IV Congress of the Italian Church" (Verona, December 19, 2006).

25. Giussani, *In cammino*, 257.

26. Xavier Zubiri, *Inteligencia y razón* [Intelligence and Reason] (Madrid: Alianza Editorial, 1983), 95–96. Translation ours.

27. Hans Urs von Balthasar, *The Glory of the Lord: A Theological Aesthetics*, vol. 1, *Seeing the Form*, trans. E. Leiva-Merikakis (San Francisco: Ignatius Press, 1998), 450.

28. Giussani, *Religious Sense*, 101.

29. Ibid., 110.

30. Eugenio E. Montale, *Cuttlefish Bones (1920–1927)*, trans. William W. Arrowsmith (New York: W.W. Norton and Co., 1992), 31.

31. William Shakespeare, *Romeo and Juliet*, ed. Brian Gibbons (London: Methuen & Co. Ltd., 1980), 1.1.94.

32. Giussani, *Religious Sense*, 117.

33. Ibid., 139.

34. Benedict XVI, "Meeting with the Representatives of Science."

35. Ibid.

36. Ibid.

37. Giussani, *Religious Sense*, 27.

38. For more on this, see Edmund Husserl, *The Crisis of European Sciences and Transcendental Phenomenology: An Introduction to Phenomenology*, trans. David Carr (Evanston, IL: Northwestern University Press, 1970), § 9.

39. Benedict XVI, "Meeting with the Representatives of Science."

40. Giussani, *Religious Sense*, 97.

41. Ibid., 17.

42. Erwin Schrödinger, "Science and Humanism: Physics in Our Time," in *Nature and the Greeks and Science and Humanism* (New York: Cambridge University Press, 1996), 155.

43. Edmund Husserl, *La crisi delle scienze europee e la fenomenologia trascendentale* [The Crisis of European Sciences and Transcendental Phenomenology: An Introduction to Phenomenological Philosophy] (Florence: G. C. Sansoni Editore, 1953), 60–61. Translation ours.

44. Ibid., 35.

45. John D. Barrow, "La vita è 'impossibile' senza Dio" [Life Is 'Impossible' without God], interview by Luigi Dell'Aglio, *Avvenire*, October 10, 2006, 29. Translation ours. For more on this, see John D. Barrow, *Impossibility: The Science of Limits and the Limits of Science* (Oxford: Oxford University Press, 1998); Barrow, *New Theories of Everything: The Quest for Ultimate Explanation* (Oxford: Oxford University Press, 1992).

46. See John I. Jenkins and Thomas Burish, "Reason and Faith at Harvard," *Washington Post*, October 23, 2006, www.washingtonpost.com.

47. Francesco Severi, *Dalla scienza alla fede* (Assisi: Edizioni Pro Civitate Cristiana, 1959), 103. Translation ours.

48. Chancellor of the University of Florence from 2000 to 2009.

49. Augusto Marinelli, "C'è un capitale umano che vuole crescere," *Il Riformista*, December 4, 2006, 6. Translation ours.

50. Giussani, *Religious Sense*, 131.

51. Luisa Muraro, "Il Papa? È dalla parte di noi donne" [The Pope? He's with Us Women], *Tempi*, October 12, 2006. Translation ours.

52. Dante Alighieri, *Paradiso*, trans. Robert and Jean Hollander, Princeton Dante Project (Princeton, NJ: Princeton University, 1997–98), canto 22, line 151, etcweb.princeton.edu/dante.

53. "A context such as the academic one invites [us] in its peculiar way to enter anew the theme of the crisis of culture and identity, which in these decades dramatically places itself before our eyes. The University is one of the best qualified places to attempt to find opportune ways to exit from this

situation. In the University, in fact, the wealth of tradition that remains alive through the centuries is preserved—and especially the Library is an essential means to safeguard the richness of tradition— . . . and can be illustrated in the fecundity of the truth when it is welcomed in its authenticity with a simple and open soul. In the University the young generations are formed who await a serious, demanding proposal, capable of responding in new contexts to the perennial question on the meaning of our existence. This expectation must not be disappointed." Benedict XVI, "Visit to the Pontifical Lateran University" (speech, Rome, October 21, 2006).

Chapter 9. Freedom Is the Most Precious Gift Heaven Gave to Humanity

1. Miguel de Cervantes, *Don Quixote*, trans. Edith Grossman (New York: HarperCollins, 2003), 832.

2. Ratzinger, *Truth and Tolerance*, 231.

3. Gustave Janouch, *Conversations with Kafka*, trans. Goronwy Reese (New York: New Directions, 1971), 23.

4. Paul Gilbert, "Libertà e impegno" [Freedom and Commitment], *La Civiltà Cattolica* 3505 (1996): 147, 22. Translation ours.

5. For a concise summary of this journey see Ratzinger, *Truth and Tolerance*, 236–44; Gilbert, "Libertà e impegno," 17–20.

6. In the dominant mind-set, "institutions, tradition, authority as such appear as the opposite pole of freedom. The anarchistic trait in the demand for freedom is growing stronger, because people are not satisfied with the ordered forms of social freedom. The great promises of the dawn of the modern era were not redeemed, yet their fascination is unbroken. Nowadays the democratically ordered form of freedom can no longer be defended just by this or that reform of the law. The foundations are being called into question. It is a matter of what man is and of how he, as an individual as a whole, can live the right life." Ratzinger, *Truth and Tolerance*, 243.

7. According to Ratzinger, Sartre is emblematic of this position: "Sartre regards the freedom of man as being his damnation. . . . Man has no nature but is simply freedom. He has to live his life in some direction or other, yet it runs out into nothingness even so. His meaningless freedom is man's hell. . . . The absolute anarchic freedom of man constituted by his self-determination is revealed, for any who tries to live it out, not as the most sublime exaltation of existence, but as a life of nothingness, of absolute emptiness, as the definition of damnation. In this extrapolation of a radical

concept of freedom, which was for Sartre his experience of life, it becomes clear that being freed from truth does not engender pure freedom; rather it abolishes it. The anarchistic freedom, taken to a radical conclusion, does not redeem man; rather, it makes him into a faulty creation, living without meaning." Ratzinger, *Truth and Tolerance*, 244–45.

8. The same boredom denounced by Dostoevsky in *The Demons*: "Everything has become so boring there is no need to be punctilious about entertainment, as long as it's diverting," says one of his characters on the way to view the body of a young suicide victim. Another asks, "Why have we got so many people hanging or shooting themselves—as if we jumped off our roots, as if the floor had slipped from under everyone's feet?" Trans. Richard Pevear and Larissa Volokhonsky (New York: Vintage Classics, 1994), 326–28.

9. As Abraham Heschel writes, "Man to his own self becomes increasingly vapid, cheap, insignificant. Yet without the sense of ultimate significance and ultimate preciousness of one's own existence, freedom becomes a hollow phrase." Abraham Joshua Heschel, *The Insecurity of Freedom* (New York: Farrar, Straus & Giroux, 1967), 18.

10. Giussani, *Religious Sense*, 87–88. See also Romano Guardini, *Persona e libertà*, 57–58: "Freedom is in no way a 'problem.' Rather, it is a fact. The awareness of being free is not the result of a demonstration, but the immediate content of experience."

11. Giussani, *Religious Sense*, 88.

12. "What will satisfy the soul?" *The Little Flowers of St. Francis*, ed. Valentine Long (Totowa, NJ: Catholic Book Publishing Corp., 2015), ch. 8.

13. Lawrence Smith, *Cesare Pavese and America: Life, Love and Literature* (Amherst: University of Massachusetts Press, 2008), 29.

14. Leopardi, *Pensieri*, LXVIII, 321.

15. Luigi Giussani, *Il senso di Dio e l'uomo moderno* [The Sense of God and Modern Man] (Milan: BUR, 1994), 19. Translation ours.

16. Thus the Second Vatican Council insisted that the attitude leading to atheism is never an original one, but rather a secondary one (*Gaudium et Spes*, 19–20). No one is born atheist. A person must become so by eliminating some factors of her human experience. She is not deprived of freedom, although the same Council also uses very measured language to point out that there are many other factors that might lead one to not recognize reality as a sign within one's life that attracts and opens one up to the Mystery.

17. Romano Guardini observes, "I experience my freedom when I experience belonging, when I experience my action as originating in me, not

passing through me and thus needing another urging, but originating in me, and therefore mine in a unique way. In this way I am my own." *Persona e libertà*, 101. On the "fact" of freedom as basic to the human being, see Cornelio Fabro, *Il libro dell'esistenza e della libertà vagabonda* [The Book of Existence and Idle Freedom] (Casale Monferrato: Piemme, 2000), 282: "Freedom is the first existential certainty"; translation ours. Also Henri Bergson: "Freedom is thus a fact and among the facts that one affirms, none is clearer." In Suzanne Guerlac, *Thinking in Time: An Introduction to Henri Bergson* (Ithaca, NY: Cornell University Press, 2006), 93. See also Hans Urs von Balthasar, *Theo-Drama*, vol. 2, *Dramatis Personae: Man in God* (San Francisco: Ignatius Press, 1990); Adriano Bausola, *Libertà e responsabilità* (Milan: Vita e Pensiero, 1995), 9–82.

18. The weakening of our capacity to judge is one of the most obvious signs of the fragility of the self we have spoken of. Georges Bernanos made the following comment on the matter:

> If someone were to ask me what is the most general symptom of this spiritual anemia, I would surely reply: indifference to both truth and falsehood. Today, propaganda proves whatever it wants to, and people more or less passively accept whatever it suggests. Of course this indifference hides a weariness, something like a disgust with the faculty of judgment. But the faculty of judgment cannot be exercised without a certain interior pledge. Anyone who pledges, pledges himself. Modern man does not pledge himself any more, because he no longer has anything to pledge. . . . Modern man is still capable of judging, since he is still capable of reasoning. But his judgment doesn't function any more than a motor functions without fuel: not part of the motor is missing, but there is no gas in the tank. To many people, this indifference to truth or falsehood seems more comic than tragic. I find it tragic. It implies a frightful detachment, not only of the mind but of the entire person, even of the physical part of the person. Anyone who is indifferently open to truth or falsehood is ripe for any kind of tyranny. The passion for truth goes along with the passion for liberty. (*Last Essays of Georges Bernanos*, trans. Joan and Barry Ulanov [New York: Greenwood, 1968], 116–17)

19. See Juan Ramón Jiménez, *Alerta* (Salamanca: Universidad de Salamanca, 1983).

20. Giussani, *Religious Sense*, 91.

21. Ibid.

22. See Hannah Arendt, "What Is Existenz Philosophy?," *Partisan Review* 13, no. 1 (1946): 53. She continues: "The That of Being as the given—whether as the reality of the world, as the incalculability of one's fellow men, or the fact that I have not created myself—becomes the backdrop against which man's freedom emerges, becomes at the same time the stuff which kindles it. That I cannot resolve the real to the object of thought becomes the triumph of possible freedom."

23. Bernanos, *Last Essays*, 72–73.

24. María Zambrano, *El hombre y lo divino* [Man and the Divine] (Madrid: Siruela, 1991), 40. Vasily Grossman, a man who bore unspeakable suffering for freedom, gives us these striking words:

> Life is freedom and, therefore, dying is a gradual denial of freedom. Consciousness first weakens and then disappears. The life-processes—respiration, the metabolism, the circulation—continue for some time, but an irrevocable move has been made towards slavery; consciousness, the flame of freedom, has died out. . . . What constitutes freedom, the soul of an individual life, is its uniqueness. The reflection of the universe in someone's consciousness is the foundation of his or her power, but life only becomes happiness, is only endowed with freedom and meaning, when someone exists as a whole world that has never been repeated in all eternity. Only then can they experience the joy of freedom and kindness, finding in others what they have already found in themselves. (*Life and Fate*, trans. Robert Chandler [New York: New York Review Books, 2006], 555)

25. Pope Benedict XVI observes, "I think of the 'Prodigal Son' who thought his father's house was boring, who thought he needed to take life on by the full, to seize hold of it and to enjoy it—until he noticed that it is really empty, and that he was free and great when he lived in his father's house." "Benedict XVI on Youth, the Faith and More: Interview with Vatican Radio," *Zenit*, August 16, 2005, https://zenit.org/articles/benedict-xvi-on-youth-the-faith-and-more/.

26. Charles Péguy, "The Mystery of the Holy Innocents," in *The Mystery of the Holy Innocents and Other Poems*, trans. Pansy Pakenham (London: Harvill Press, 1956), 76–77.

27. Giussani, *Tutta la terra desidera il tuo volto*, 116.

28. Giussani, *At the Origin of the Christian Claim*, 86. "Man's greatness and his freedom derive from a direct dependence on God, a condition by which man realizes and affirms himself. Dependence on God is the primary condition for what truly interests man." Ibid., 87.

29. Ludwig Wittgenstein, *Movements of Thought: Diaries, 1930–32, 1936–37*, as quoted in J. C. Kagge and A. Nordmann, *Public and Private Occasions* (Lanham, MD: Rowman & Littlefield, 2003), 175, 177, 197.

30. Carlo Betocchi, *Dal definitivo istante: Poesie scelte e inediti* [From the Definitive Instant: Selected and Unpublished Poems] (Milan: BUR, 1999), 146. Translation ours.

31. Benedict XVI, "Message On the Occasion of the 26th Meeting for Friendship among Peoples" (Rimini, August 21–27, 2005).

32. Guardini writes, "God is he who gives to those who approach him definitive fullness and thus the definitive solution. This is fulfilled in Revelation, in Christianity." Romano Guardini, *Persona e libertà*, 113.

33. William of Saint-Thierry, *On Contemplating God*, trans. Sr. Penelope, C.S.M.V. (Spencer, MA: Cistercian Publications, 1971), 37.

34. See *Gaudium et Spes*, 22.

35. Tertullian, *De carnis resurrectione* 8 (PL 2:806).

36. See Gal 4:4–7.

37. Charles Péguy, "The Mystery of the Holy Innocents," 99–100.

38. Luigi Giussani, *La libertà di Dio* [God's Freedom] (Genoa-Milan: Marietti, 2005), 36. Translation ours.

39. "Where there is faith, there is freedom." Saint Ambrose, "To Clementianus," Letter 69. In *The Fathers of the Church: A New Translation*, vol. 26, *Saint Ambrose: Letters*, trans. Sister Mary Melchior Beyenka, O.P. (Washington, DC: Catholic University of America Press, 1954), 411.

40. Hannah Arendt, *On Revolution* (London: Penguin, 1965), 35. Here Arendt is referring to the revolutionary spirit of recent centuries.

41. Giussani, "Il 'potere' del laico, cioè del cristiano" [The 'Power' of the Laity, i.e., of Christians], in *Un avvenimento di vita*, 38–39.

42. Giussani, *La libertà di Dio*, 17.

43. See von Balthasar, *Theo-Drama*, vol. 2; Angelo Scola, Gilfredo Marengo, and Javier Prades, *La persona umana: Antropologia teologica* [The Human Person: Theological Anthropology], Amateca 15 (Milan: Jaca Book, 2000), 104–96.

Chapter 10. Introduction to Total Reality

1. Pietro Citati, "Questa generazione che non vuol crescere mai" ("This Generation That Never Wants to Grow Up"), *La Repubblica*, August 2, 1999, 1.

2. Giussani, *L'io rinasce in un incontro*, 181–82.

3. Ibid.

4. Cesare Pavese, "A Rosa Calzecchi Onesti" [To Rosa Calzecchi Onesti], in *Lettere, 1926–1950* [Letters, 1926–1950] (Turin: Einaudi, 1968), 2:655. Translation taken from Giussani, *Religious Sense*, 56.

5. Jorge Mario Bergoglio, *La bellezza educherà il mondo* [Beauty Will Educate the World] (Bologna: Emi, 2014), 8. Translation ours.

6. Ibid., 14–15.

7. Ibid., 12–13.

8. Massimo Recalcati, *Il complesso di Telemaco* [The Telemaco Complex] (Milan: Feltrinelli, 2013), 114. Translation ours.

9. Bergoglio, *La bellezza educherà il mondo*, 17.

10. Zambrano, *Hacia un saber del alma*, 140.

11. Pope Francis, "Address to Students and Teachers from Schools across Italy" (Rome, May 10, 2014).

12. Josef Andreas Jungmann, *Christus als Mittelpunkt religiöser Erziehung* (Freiburg im Breisgau: Herder & Co. G.M.B.H., 1939), 5. Translation ours.

13. Pope Francis, "Address to Students and Teachers."

14. Bergoglio, *La bellezza educherà il mondo*, 23.

15. Ibid., 24.

16. Ibid., 24–25.

17. Recalcati, *Il complesso di Telemaco*, 136, 141.

18. Bergoglio, *La bellezza educherà il mondo*, 32–33.

19. Pope Francis, "Address to Students and Teachers."

20. Bergoglio, *La bellezza educherà il mondo*, 7–8.

21. Ibid., 42–44.

22. Ibid., 46–48.

Chapter 11. The "Hot Point"

1. Antonio Polito, *Contro i papà: Come noi italiani abbiamo rovinato i nostri figli* (Milan: Rizzoli, 2012), 16. Translation ours.

2. Ibid., 21.

3. Ibid., 12, 23, 12–13.

4. Ibid., 20.

5. Ibid., 21.

6. Luigi Giussani, "Don Giussani: Il potere egoista odia il popolo" [Egoist Power Hates People], interview by Gianluigi Da Rold, *Corriere della Sera*, October 18, 1992, now in Giussani, *L'io, il potere, le opere*, 214–19.

7. Eugenio Scalfari, "Quel vuoto di plastica che soffoca i giovani," 1.

8. Leopardi, "On the Portrait of a Beautiful Lady," in *Canti*, 259, lines 50–52.

9. Polito, *Contro i papà*, 26–28. See R. Ardrey, *The Social Contract* (New York: Storydesign.ltd, 2014).

10. Polito, *Contro i papà*, 26, 22.

11. Ibid., 67.

12. Ibid., 68.

13. Ibid., 131–33.

14. Ibid., 143–44.

15. Pope Benedict XVI, *Light of the World: The Pope, the Church, and the Signs of the Times; A Conversation with Peter Seewald* (San Francisco: Ignatius Press, 2010), 26.

16. See Pope Paul VI, "Address to Members of the Pontifical Council for the Laity" (Rome, October 2, 1974).

17. Giussani, *Risk of Education*, 64.

18. Ibid., 64, 67, 9–10.

19. Ibid., 80–81.

20. Ibid., 83.

21. Rabindranath Tagore, "Free Love," in *Gitanjali* (Mineola, NY: Dover Publications, 2000), 33.

Chapter 12. A Communication of Yourself

1. Charles Péguy, *Lui è qui: Pagine scelte*, ed. D. Rondoni and F. Crescini (Milan: BUR, 2007), 39. Translation ours.

2. See Augustine, *Tractate on the Gospel of John* (Washington, DC: Catholic University of America Press, 1988), 258 (26.5).

3. Giussani, *Why the Church?*, 34.

4. Giussani, *Journey to Truth Is an Experience*, 95.

5. Ibid., 142.

6. Ibid.

7. Romano Guardini, *L'essenza del cristianesimo* [The Essence of Christianity] (Brescia: Morcelliana, 2007), 12. Translation ours.

8. Luigi Giussani, "Viterbo 1977," in *Il rischio educativo* [*The Risk of Education*; Italian ed.] (Turin: SEI, 1995), 61. Translation ours.

9. Ibid.

10. Ibid., 73.

11. 2 Cor 5:17; Gal 6:15.

12. Giussani, "Viterbo 1977," 73.

13. Nikolai Berdjaev, *Pensieri controcorrente* [Counter Current Thoughts] (Milan: La casa di Matriona, 2007), 59. Translation ours.

14. Giussani, "Viterbo 1977," 89.

15. Luigi Giussani, *Certi di alcune grandi cose (1979–1981)* [Certain of a Few Great Things] (Milan: BUR, 2007), 155–56. Translation ours.

16. See Giussani, *At the Origin of the Christian Claim*, 86.

17. Giussani, *Journey to Truth Is an Experience*, 94.

18. Giussani, "Viterbo 1977," 84.

19. Ibid., 62.

20. Ibid., 86.

21. Ibid., 75–76.

22. Ibid., 76.

23. Giussani, *Journey to Truth Is an Experience*, 100.

24. Ibid.

25. Ibid., 101.

26. Giussani, "Viterbo 1977," 88.

Chapter 13. "Lady, Your Beauty Was a Ray of Heavenly / Light to My Thinking"

1. Benedict XVI, *Spe Salvi*, 25.

2. Benedict XVI, "Opening of the Congress of the Diocese of Rome on Family and Christian Community" (speech, Rome, June 6, 2005), 11.

3. Pavese, *Business of Living*, 180.

4. Benedict XVI, *Deus Caritas Est*, 2.

5. "The Greeks—not unlike other cultures—considered *eros* principally as a kind of intoxication, the overpowering of reason by a 'divine madness' which tears man away from his finite existence and enables him, in the very process of being overwhelmed by divine power, to experience supreme happiness. All other powers in heaven and on earth thus appear secondary: *'Omnia vincit amor,'* says Virgil in the *Bucolics*—love conquers all—and he adds: *'et nos cedamus amori'*—let us, too, yield to love." Benedict XVI, *Deus Caritas Est*, 4.

6. Benedict XVI, *Deus Caritas Est*, 5.

7. Giacomo Leopardi, "Aspasia," in *Canti*, 239, lines 33–34.

8. Ibid., lines 44–48.

9. C. S. Lewis, *Surprised by Joy* (San Diego: Harcourt Brace, 1955), 220.

10. See Rainer Maria Rilke, "Fourth Elegy," in *Duino Elegies*, 23, lines 11–20.

11. See Giacomo Leopardi, "To His Lady," in *Canti*, 145, lines 45–47: "Whether you are the one and only / eternal idea that eternal wisdom / disdains to see arrayed in sensible form . . ."

12. See Luigi Giussani, *Le mie letture* [My Readings] (Milano: BUR, 1996), 30. In this book the theme is dealt with more thoroughly.

13. Giussani, *At the Origin of the Christian Claim*, 64–65.

14. Mt 10:34–37, 39–40.

15. Mt 19:11–12.

16. John Paul II, general audience (Rome, April 28, 1982). Available in Italian, Spanish, and Portuguese at www.vatican.va. Translation ours.

17. Luigi Giussani, *Il tempo e il tempio: Dio e l'uomo* [Time and the Temple: God and Man] (Milan: BUR, 1995), 20–21. Translation ours.

18. John Paul II, general audience (Rome, May 5, 1982). Available in Spanish, Italian, and Portuguese at www.vatican.va. Translation ours.

19. John Paul II, *Familiaris Consortio* (November 22, 1981), 16.

20. Luigi Giussani, *Affezione e dimora* [Affection and home] (Milan: BUR, 2001), 250. Translation ours.

21. Benedict XVI, "Address at the Vigil of Prayer at the Conclusion of the Fifth World Meeting of Families" (Valencia, July 8, 2006).

22. Giussani, *Journey to Truth Is an Experience*, 72.

23. 2 Cor 4:7.

24. See Jn 4:18.

25. Jn 4:15.

Chapter 14. With the Audacity of Realism

1. Dante Alighieri, *Purgatory*, trans. Robert and Jean Hollander, Princeton Dante Project (Princeton, NJ: Princeton University, 1997–98), canto 17, lines 127–29, etcweb.princeton.edu/dante.

2. Pope Benedict XVI, general audience (Rome, November 21, 2012).

3. See Thomas Aquinas, *Super Secundam ad Corinthios*, commentary on 2 Cor 5:5–10, para. 165.

4. Luigi Giussani, *Un avvenimento di vita*, 308.

5. Ibid.

6. Established in 1986, the Company of Works (CdO) is a not-for-profit business association at the national level that aims at promoting the spirit of mutual collaboration and support among its members, for an

optimal utilization of human and economic resources. The association has headquarters in Italy and several other countries.

7. Luigi Giussani, *Il movimento di Comunione e Liberazione (1954–1986): Conversazioni con Robi Ronza* [The Communion and Liberation Movement (1954–1986): Conversations with Robi Ronza] (Milan: BUR, 2014), 155. Translation ours.

8. Giussani, *Religious Sense*, 131.

9. Giussani, *Il rischio educativo*, 63.

10. Ibid., 64.

Chapter 15. Crisis: A Challenge to Change

1. Gn 1:4, 10, 12, 18, 21, 31.

2. Is 40:12, 26–28.

3. Giussani, *Si può (veramente?!) vivere così?*, 292–93.

4. Hannah Arendt, *Between Past and Future* (New York: Viking Press, 1968), 174–75.

5. Luigi Giussani, *Realtà e giovinezza: La sfida* [Reality and Youth: The Challenge] (Turin: SEI, 1995), 98. Translation ours.

6. Ibid., 100.

7. Ibid.

8. Giussani, *Si può (veramente?!) vivere così?*, 293–94.

9. Letter of Margaret Roper to Alice Alington after the meeting with her father in prison. From *The Last Letters of Thomas More*, ed. Alvaro De Silva (Grand Rapids, MI: Eerdmans, 2000), 72–89.

10. Pope Benedict XVI, "Address to the 24th Plenary Session of the Pontifical Council for the Laity" (Rome, May 21, 2010).

11. Luigi Giussani, "Christ, All We Have," *Traces: Litterae Communionis*, no. 2 (2002): v.

Chapter 16. In Politics, Too, the Other Is a Good

1. Rom 12:4–5.

Conclusion: How Does a Presence Come to Be?

1. Sg 3:1–4.

2. Jn 20:1–2.

3. Jn 20:11–18.

4. Pope Francis, "A Big Heart Open to God."

5. Cf. Lk 19:5. Luigi Giussani, "From Baptism, a New Creature," in *Traces* 8, no. 6 (June 2006): 23 (excerpt from *L'avvenimento cristiano*, 24).

6. Savorana, *Vita di don Giussani*.

7. Giussani, *L'avvenimento cristiano*, 23.

8. Augustine, *Sermons on Selected Lessons of the New Testament* (Oxford: John Henry Parker, 1844–45), 2:893 (124.4).

9. Pope Francis, *Letter to a Non-Believer*, 2.

10. Luigi Giussani, "From Utopia to Presence," *Traces* 4, no. 11 (December 2002): ii.

11. Ibid.

12. Aquinas, *Summa Theologiae*, IIa, IIae, q. 179, a. 1.

13. Gal 3:26–28.

14. See Gal 3:27.

15. Jn 15:16.

16. Giussani, "From Utopia to Presence," ii.

17. Gal 3:27–28.

18. Giussani, "From Utopia to Presence," ii.

19. Ibid.

20. Ibid., iii; emphasis original.

21. Ibid.

22. Ibid.

23. Ibid.

24. Ibid., iv.

25. Ibid.

26. Ibid., v.

27. Ibid., vi; emphasis original.

28. Ibid., vii–viii.

29. Ibid., vii.

30. Ibid., viii.

31. Angelo Scola, *Il campo è il mondo* [The Field Is the World], pastoral letter (Milan: Centro Ambrosiano, 2013), 40. Translation ours.

32. Giussani, "From Utopia to Presence," viii–ix.

33. Ibid., ix.

34. Luigi Giussani, *Un evento reale nella vita dell'uomo (1990–1991)* [A True Event in the Life of Man (1990–1991)] (Milan: BUR, 2013), 142–43.

35. Ibid., 103–4.

36. Is 40:30–31.

37. Giussani, *Un evento reale nella vita dell'uomo*, 240–41.

SOURCES

This book presents essential reflections by Fr. Julián Carrón from 2005 to 2015. The various texts, prepared for different occasions, have been extensively revised and organized by the author to provide an organic presentation of the elements of his journey with Communion and Liberation during the past decade.

Damian Bacich translated the foreword and chapters 2, 5, and 9; Sheila Beatty, chapters 3, 4, 6, and 16, and the conclusion; Sheila Beatty and Suzanne Tanzi, chapters 7, 12, 14, and 17; Jennifer Cottini, chapters 1, 11, and 15; Rachel McNamara and Valentina Oriani, chapter 10; Patrick Stevenson, chapter 13; and Patrick Stevenson and Suzanne Tanzi, chapter 8. Particular thanks are due to Mariangela Sullivan, who reviewed all the texts.

PART I. THE CONTEXT AND THE CHALLENGES

1. Is a New Beginning Possible?
The text is taken from a talk given on April 9, 2014, at *MiCo Milano Congressi*, in the context of a public conference on the topic of Europe, on the occasion of the European parliamentary elections. An earlier version was published in *Tracce: Litterae Communionis*, no. 5 (May 2014).

2. Truth and Freedom: A Paradigm

The text elaborates on a lecture delivered on July 29, 2014, in La Thuile, during the Spiritual Exercises for the *Memores Domini* (unpublished).

3. In the Collapse of the Self-Evident, a Subject Is Generated

This text was drawn from a lecture delivered on November 5, 2014, in Pacengo del Garda, at the conclusion of the annual spiritual exercises for CL priests. An earlier version was published in *Tracce: Litterae Communionis*, no. 11 (December 2014).

4. The Challenge of True Dialogue after the Charlie Hebdo Attacks

This text was drawn from an article printed in the *Corriere della Sera* on February 13, 2015, one month after the January 13 attacks in Paris.

PART 2. AN EVENT OF REBIRTH

5. Christianity Faced with the Challenges of the Present

This text was taken from and further elaborates upon a presentation given on November 19, 2010, in Madrid, as part of the Congress entitled "Catholics and Public Life," organized by the Fundación Universitaria San Pablo CEU (unpublished).

6. The Religious Sense, Verification of Faith

The text was drawn from remarks given on January 26, 2011, at PalaSharp in Milan, as part of the presentation of Luigi Giussani's book *The Religious Sense*. An earlier version appeared in *Tracce: Litterae Communionis*, no. 2 (February 2011).

7. The "Eternal Mystery of Our Being"

The text is a partial reproduction of the contents of the first lesson delivered in Rimini on April 30, 2011, during the annual Spiritual Exercises for the Fraternity of Communion and Liberation (published in the supplement to *Tracce: Litterae Communionis*, no. 5 [May 2011]).

8. Broadening Reason

The text elaborates on the contents of two talks, one delivered on October 26, 2006, at the Catholic University of the Sacred Heart of Milan at an event marking the publication of the Arabic-language edition of Luigi Giussani's *The Religious Sense* (published in *Allargare la Ragione*, ed. Alessandro Gamba [Milan: Vita e Pensiero, 2007], 21–38, and as a supplement to *Tracce-Litterae Communionis*, no. 1 [January 2007]), and the other on December 18, 2006, at the Università degli Studi of Florence on the topic "university and education" (unpublished).

9. Freedom Is the Most Precious Gift Heaven Gave to Humanity

The text is drawn from a presentation given on August 22, 2005, in Rimini during the 26th Meeting for the Friendship amongst Peoples, entitled "La libertà è il bene più grande che i cieli abbiano donato agli uomini" (Freedom Is the Greatest Good the Heavens Have Given to Humanity). An earlier version was published as a supplement to *Tracce: Litterae Communionis*, no. 9, special issue (2005).

PART 3. AN EDUCATIONAL EMERGENCY

10. Introduction to Total Reality

The text presents the contents of a talk delivered on May 12, 2014, at the Salone del Libro in Turin, on the occasion of the presentation of Jorge Mario Bergoglio's book *La bellezza educherà il mondo* (Beauty Will Educate the World). An earlier version appeared in a booklet by the same author entitled *La bellezza educherà il mondo* (Bologna: EMI, 2014), 49–63, annexed to the *Tracce-Litterae Communionis* magazine.

11. The "Hot Point"

The text is taken from the contents of a talk delivered on January 25, 2013, at the Hall on Via Sant'Antonio in Milan, as part of an event coorganized by Rizzoli and the Centro Culturale di Milano (Milan Cultural Center) for the presentation of Antonio Polito's book *Contro i papà* (Against Fathers). An earlier version was published in the form of notes on the Communion and Liberation website, clonline.org, in February 2013.

12. A Communication of Yourself

The text reproduces the contents of a lecture delivered on October 14, 2007, in Milan, to a group of teachers belonging to Communion and Liberation, as part of a conference entitled "Viterbo 1997–Milano 2007: Trent'anni di presenza nella scuola" (Viterbo 1977–Milano 2007: Thirty Years of Presence in Schools). An earlier version appeared in *Tracce Quaderni* as a supplement to *Tracce-Litterae Communionis*, no. 10 (November 2007).

PART 4. A NEW PROTAGONIST ON THE WORLD SCENE

13. "Lady, Your Beauty Was a Ray of Heavenly / Light to My Thinking"

The text is drawn from the contents of a presentation held on July 5, 2006, in Valencia, as part of the "Fifth World Meeting of Families with Pope Benedict XVI," on "the transmission of faith in the family." An earlier version was published in *Tracce-Litterae Communionis*, no. 9 (October 2006).

14. With the Audacity of Realism

The text is a reelaborated version of a talk delivered on November 25, 2012, in Milan at the National Assembly of the organization Compagnia delle Opere (Company of Works). An earlier version was published in *Tracce: Litterae Communionis*, no. 11 (December 2012).

15. Crisis: A Challenge to Change

The text is a reworking of the contents of two presentations, the first from November 4, 2011, at the Mediolanum Forum in Assago, and the second from November 17, 2011, at the Capranica theater in Rome, during a public conference on the topic "the crisis: a challenge to change" (unpublished).

16. In Politics, Too, the Other Is a Good

The text reproduces an article published in *La Repubblica* on April 10, 2013.

Conclusion: How Does a Presence Come to Be?

The text is drawn from the contents of a lecture delivered on September 28, 2013, at the Mediolanum Forum in Assago for Beginning Day, the first day of Communion and Liberation's social year. An earlier version was published in *Tracce: Litterae Communionis*, no. 9 (October 2013).

INDEX

abortion, 5, 10, 29
academy. *See* university, the
adolescents. *See also* young people
  "eternal," 137
  needs of, 154
adults
  abdication of role by, 146
  curiosity discouraged by, 160
  education as problem of, 162
  responsibilities of, 156, 191–92,
    194, 221–22
  as witnesses, 153–54
affection, 128, 166, 202, 203, 218,
    226–27
  for Christ, 83, 128, 182, 214, 220
  for the Church, 220
  freedom and, 63, 68, 182
  lack of, 56, 138, 202
  for reality, 202
  reason and, 76, 83, 86, 108
African women, encounter with, 25

Alberti, Rafael, 125
Alighieri, Dante, 115, 189
Ambrose, Saint, 131, 251n39
anarchistic freedom, 247nn6–7
Andrew the Apostle, 77–79, 85
anthropological drift, 18
apathy, 108, 157–62. *See also*
  nihilism
appearance, reality reduced to, 75,
    109–10, 141–42
Ardrey, Robert, 149
Arendt, Hannah, 125, 131, 250n22,
    251n40
  on crisis, 9, 200
  on culture, 244n3
  on ideologies, 91, 107
atheism, 55, 248n16
attraction
  of an authority, 61, 153–54
  of Christ, 18, 69, 71, 83, 128–30,
    182–83

of new rights, 11–12
of a presence, 26, 44, 63, 71
of reality, 123–24
reawakening, 143, 153–54,
    163–65
Augustine, Saint, 80, 159, 216
    on freedom of religion, 29–30,
        232nn20–21
    heresy confronted by, 29–30, 61,
        232nn20–21
    on restlessness, 56, 58, 108, 138
authority, 153–54, 173, 222
autonomy, 22, 23, 118–19, 154–55
    attraction overcoming, 129
    as illusory, 119

baptism, 66, 218–19
Barrow, John, 113
Barthes, Roland, 104–6
beauty, 240n59, 255n11
    of changed life, 71
    of Christ, 71, 83, 180
    of Christian event, 18, 26, 50,
        182–83
    of reality, 110, 123, 142
    rejection of, 123
    as sign of God, 181, 182–83
belonging
    freedom as, 131, 193–94, 248n17
    test of, 194
Benedict XVI, Pope, 12, 63, 66, 70,
        83, 178
    on Christ, 61
    on the Church, 239n48, 239n54
    on dialogue, cross-cultural, 103
    on the Enlightenment, 4–6, 27
    on Europe, 6–7, 230n26, 240n57
    on faith, 15–16, 55–56, 75
    on families, 186

on freedom, 9–10, 13, 17, 108–9,
    116, 233n32, 247nn6–7
on marriage and love, 179, 180,
    254n5
on moralism, 62, 71
on the prodigal son, 250n25
on reason, 75, 101, 114, 152, 202
on relativism, 21–22, 25–26, 58
resignation of, 207
on science, 112
on sleepy faith, 90
on the university, 111, 246n53
on values, collapse of, 21–22
on Vatican II, 6, 31–35
on witnesses to Christian truth,
    15–16
Berdjaev, Nikolai, 166
Bergoglio, Jorge Mario. See Francis,
    Pope
Bergson, Henri, 248n17
Bernanos, George, 89, 249n18
Betocchi, Carlo, 128
biological reductionism, 124–25
blind man of Jericho, 237n37
bodies, 129, 184–85
bonds, freedom as absence of,
    117–20, 129, 193, 247n6,
    250n25
boredom, existential, 57–58,
    138–40, 157–62, 248n8
Brague, Rémi, 18

Carrón, Julián, 25, 167–68
    Giussani and, 167–68
    painter friend of, 121–22
Catechism of the Catholic Church, 66
    creation of soul in, 125
    knowledge of God in, 41
Catholic Reformation, 62

celibacy, 183–85

Cervantes, Miguel de, 116

Charlie Hebdo attacks, 48–50,
235n1

"Chernobyl effect," 56, 137–38

Chesterton, G. K., 39

children

early Christians and, 29

fear of having, 8–9

marriage as educative for, 187

relationship with, 150–52

understanding of, 151

Christ. *See also* incarnation

affection for, 83, 128, 182, 214,
220

answering human need, 56,
59–64, 67–69, 71, 82, 184,
189

attraction of, 18, 69, 71, 83, 128,
182–83

belonging to the Father, 129–30

on celibacy, 183–85

and the Church, love between,
185–87

the Church as sign of, 239n48

"come and see" (Christ's words),
63–64

as companion, 128–30

contemporaneousness of, 64–69,
82, 83–85

encountering, 43–46, 47, 63–69,
77–80, 129, 163–64, 211–17,
220–22, 237n34

as historical fact, 85

freedom made possible by,
128–30

fulfillment deriving from, 63–64,
67, 71, 83, 183, 187, 214–15

humanity of, 18

in the "I," 45–47, 67–68, 78–80,
130, 219

as master-witness, 143

newness of, 214–15

parables of, 27, 93, 117–20, 126,
233n32, 250n25

and the Pharisees, 39

presence of, in suffering, 132–34

real presence of, 64–69, 74, 76,
78, 95, 215–17, 218–20

reduction of, 62, 84

religious sense clarified by, 77–86

seeing, 63–64, 85

as unexpected, 59

unity with, 219–20

values activated by, 24

Christianity. *See also* testimony,
Christian

beauty of, 18, 26, 50, 182–83

"Christianist," 18

as condition for being human,
127

early, 19, 28–30, 32, 83

Enlightenment originating in, 4,
6–7, 34–35

in Europe, 3–20

as event, 17–18, 26, 61, 63–65,
130–31, 170, 213, 214–15,
238n38

as freedom, 131–32, 251n39

as incomprehensible, 61

modernity challenging, 53–71

as new life, 70, 165, 167

"notional," 82–83, 170

reactionary positions of, 54

reasonableness of, 76, 187

reduced versions of, 42–43, 55,
60–62, 70–71, 73, 82–83,
236n18

relevance of, 58–59

resurrection central to, 239n42

spiritualization of, 164

and the state, 5, 7–8, 30, 31,
33–34

truth of, 18, 60

values rooted in, 4, 6, 22–23,
24–25

Church, the

affection for, 220

charity in, 239n54

and Christ, love between, 185–87

Christ's body as, 66

continuity and discontinuity in,
31–32, 33

education in, 82, 131

event of Christ continuing in,
131

freedom found in, 131

and Italy, 208–9

persecution of, 29, 33

pluralism and, 28–30, 54

power rejected by, 35, 206

schismatics and, 29–30,
232nn20–21

as sign of Christ, 239n48

social doctrine of, 18

unity of, 131, 221, 223, 224

willingness to change, 208–9

witnesses formed in, 68–69

Citati, Pietro, 57, 58, 137

The City of God, 30

civilization, end of, 87–88

civis romanus, 3

Clément, Olivier, 160

coercion

Church's role in, 29–30, 34,
232n21

and fear of freedom, 49

freedom from, 19–20, 27–28,
29–30, 32

communication

education as, 162, 164, 168–69

of faith, 18, 19–20, 26, 41–42

of ourselves, 157–73, 213

Communion and Liberation (CL)
movement, 219, 223

Common Fund of, 193

Company of Works (CdO) of,
190, 192–93, 255n

education as goal of, 191

Giussani inspiring, 37

and verification of faith, 167–68

work of, 191–92

community, 193–94, 221–22. *See
also* Church, the

companion, Jesus as, 128–30

companionship, true, 97–98, 133

Constitution on the Church in the
Modern World, 34

Contro i papà (Polito), 145–47

conversion

to Christ, 86, 225–26

of life, 220–21, 225–26

vs. moralism, 214, 221

as recognition, 214

scientific study leading to, 114

creation, God's, 125, 197–99

crisis, 9

change prompted by, 197–206

of culture, 246n53

economic, 188–89

of Europe, 3–20, 48–50, 53–71,
147–48, 205–6, 207–9

recovery from, 203–6

and self-discovery, 189

cross, scandal of, 65

crucifixes, Strasbourg ruling on, 6

crucifixion, the, 238n41
culture, 244n3
  clash, 102
  definition of, 101–2
  dialogue beyond, 48–50, 101–15
  as false source of security, 43
  friendship and, 102–3
  reality mediated by, 102
  void in, 49

Darwinism, 149–50
debates, futility of, 39, 41, 45,
  70–71
Del Noce, Augusto, 58
desire. *See also* fulfillment, yearning
  for
  confused, 129
  education and, 139, 154, 156
  for happiness, marriage and, 180,
    181–83
  as infinite, 121–22, 124, 126,
    127, 180–83, 187
  for love, 221
  for meaning, 160–62
  nihilism suppressing, 161–62
  for truth, 156, 217
despair, 96, 143–44
detachment, 185, 214
Deus Caritas Est, 63, 180
dialogue
  beginning in encounter, 50, 115
  religious liberty and, 49–50
Dignitatis Humanae, 30–31, 34, 35
dignity, 30–31, 33–34, 70, 122
  amazement at, 67–68, 239n50
  reductionism taking away, 152
Diognetus, Letter to, 29
doctrine, experience separated
  from, 37, 61
Donatists, 29–30, 232nn20–21

Dostoevsky, Fyodor, 53–54, 55, 96,
  248n8
dualism, 169–70

Edict of Milan, 29
Edict of Thessalonica, 19, 29
education
  as adults' problem, 162
  authority and, 153–54, 173, 222
  conformity in, 76
  crisis in, 137–44, 145–46, 157–62
  in criticism, 154
  desire and, 139, 154, 156
  despair having no place in,
    143–44
  in the faith, 55, 74, 82
  freedom and, 155, 156
  independence fostered by,
    154–55
  vs. instruction, 146
  marriage and, 186–87
  in reality, 110–15, 137–44,
    154–55, 157–62, 168
  of the religious sense, 80–82, 86
  renewal of, 165–73
  the university's task of, 110–15
  verification in, 154–55
  witnesses required for, 55, 69,
    142–44, 155, 171, 186–87, 192
Egidi Morpurgo, Valeria, 149
egotism, 40–41
"elementary experience" (Giussani),
  152
Eliot, T. S., 13, 19
Emmaus, disciples of, 65
encounter, 15–16, 35, 46–47,
  195–96
  with Christ, 43–46, 47, 63–69,
    77–80, 129, 163–64, 211–17,
    220–22, 237n34

faith (*cont.*)
  friendship and, 222
  vs. human works, 223–26
  "I" reawakened by, 74, 165–66,
    201–2, 225
  making life more human, 70
  maturing, 55, 189, 192, 194,
    221–22
  reason linked to, 56–57, 75,
    111–12, 141, 160–61
  and the religious sense, 84
  revivifying, 55–56, 82–84,
    170–71, 201–2
"Faith and Reason" courses, 113–14
family
  debate over, 177–78, 179
  strife, 181, 182–83
  supporting, 186
Farouq, Wael, 102, 106
fear
  vs. audacity, 190
  after *Charlie Hebdo* attacks, 48
  existential, 43
  of freedom, 8–9, 15, 48–49, 117,
    139
  vs. freedom, 9, 105
  orthodoxy enforced through,
    231n11
Finkielkraut, Alain, 103–6
First Vatican Council, 41
Fortin, Ernest, 58
Francis, Pope, 21, 213, 225
  on Church's purpose, 209
  education and, 137, 138, 140,
    141, 142–44
  election of, 207, 208
  on "essentials," 18, 26, 46
  on pastoral ministry, 26, 50
  on presence, 46, 213, 216, 224
  on truth as relationship, 17, 216

freedom, 8–9, 27–35, 117–20, 131,
    203, 248nn8–10. *See also*
    religious liberty
  as absence of bonds, 117–20,
    129, 193, 247n6, 250n25
  anarchistic, 247nn6–7
  as belonging, 131, 193–94,
    248n17
  to be ourselves, 117, 171
  as capacity for satisfaction, 121
  Christianity meeting desire for,
    131–32, 251n39
  in the Church, 131
  community and, 115, 193–94
  of conscience, 29
  and conviction, 16, 17
  as criterion of other values, 4–5,
    27
  vs. death, 250n24
  definition of, 5, 120–22
  dogmatism of, 5
  education as invitation to, 155,
    156
  Europe and, 3–10, 16–17, 19–20,
    48–50, 53
  vs. fear, 9, 105
  fear of, 8–9, 15, 48–49, 117, 139
  as filial, 120
  as gift, 27, 116–34
  God as enemy of, 240n57
  and infinity of desire, 121–22
  Jesus making possible, 128–30
  lack of, 116–17, 125–26
  meaningless, 247n7
  and mystery, 124–28
  vs. nihilism, 49–50, 109, 122
  and permissiveness, 12
  reality and, 27–28, 83–84, 109,
    117–20, 122–24, 156, 161,
    190, 250n22

God
  communicating through the "I,"
    165
  death of, 58
  emotion inspired by, 99–100
  exclusion of, from Enlighten-
    ment thinking, 4, 6
  face of, 64, 99, 128–29
  freedom as gift of, 27, 116–34
  freedom as relationship with, 7,
    134, 166–67, 205–6, 250n28
  goodness of, 198
  Guardini on, 251n32
  knowledge of, 41
  life as gift from, 70
  love of, 109, 129, 164, 182–83,
    221
  making credible, 15–16
  plan of, 171–73, 204
  present in the Church, 131
  refusing, 86, 126–27
goodness
  of the other, 16–20, 207–9
  of reality, 197–200, 201–6
Gospel, the
  encounters in, 237n37
  experiencing, 43–44
  human dignity in, 68, 239n50
  taken for granted, 213
grace, 41, 190, 196
Grelot, Pierre, 63
Grossman, Vasily, 250n24
Guardini, Romano
  on culture, 101–2
  on freedom, 248n10, 248n17
  on God, 251n32
  on personhood, 25
  on values, Christian origin of,
    22–23, 24–25
Guitton, Jean, 106

Habermas, Jürgen, 16, 230n26
hegemony, temptation of, 29–30
Heidegger, Martin, 107, 108
Heschel, Abraham Joshua, 88, 93,
    248n9
history
  reason conditioned by, 5, 6
  and the self-evident, 21–26
Holy Spirit, 17, 240n59
hope, 59, 97, 203, 204–5, 220
"hot point," 138, 145–56. *See also*
    "I," the
humanity
  as "capable of God," 125
  crisis of, 7, 58, 159–60
  devotion of, 80–82
  elimination of, 22, 88
  exaltation of, 70, 86, 204–6
  freedom of, as gift, 27, 116–34
  limitations of, discomfort with,
    11–13
  new, 18, 203, 214–15, 219–20
  reduction of, 8–10, 12–14, 43–44,
    108–9, 112, 148–52, 205
  religious sense of, 14, 55–56
  response of, to God, 172–73
  at risk, 7
  singleness of, 103
  ultimate questions of, 72–73
  vocation of, 54, 125, 204, 217–18,
    225–26
human rights, conflict between, 5
Husserl, Edmund, 113

"I," the, 12, 43–45, 104, 165
  annihilation of, 151–52
  Christ's presence in, 45–47,
    67–68, 78–80, 130, 219
  communicating, 157–73, 213
  confusion of, 87–91

crisis and, 200–202
definition of, 72–73
economic troubles and, 188–89
encountering the other, 40–41,
    43–44, 46–47, 213–14
estrangement from, 138
faith and, 74, 165–66, 201–2,
    225
fragility of, 88, 165, 201–2, 205,
    249n18
God communicating through,
    165
and lack of self-knowledge,
    89–90
marriage and, 94–95, 179–81,
    186–87
mystery of, 67, 74–75, 87–100
the other necessary to, 43, 143
power's effect on, 38–39, 40, 89,
    90
reality and, 41–42, 72–75, 106,
    122–24, 160–61, 164, 200–202
reason and, 107–8, 113
reawakening of, 14–16, 43–45,
    72, 138, 153–55
reduction of, 12–13, 38–41,
    88–89, 109, 148–52
religious sense and, 97–98
resurrection, principle of, 165
self-giving and, 69
true nature of, 12, 44–45, 72–73,
    91–98, 179–81, 194–95
vocation of, 69–71, 180, 204,
    217–18, 223–26
and the "You," 98–99, 124,
    179–80, 208, 214
identity, 165, 218–20, 225
    in Europe, 16
    of Europe, 6
    freedom and, 50

as "heart," 103
    loss of, and nihilism, 147–48
    of young people, 147–48
ideology, nature of, 107
idolatry, 195
incarnation
    beauty of, 182–83
    as event, 17–18, 61, 170, 238n38
    reason for, 81–82, 201–2, 203,
        216
individualism, futility of, 77
International Theological Com-
    mission, 41
Isaiah, 199, 226
Israel, ancient, 197–99
Italy, 147, 193, 205, 207–9, 231n11

Jacopone da Todi, 83
James, William, 150
Jannacci, Enzo, 25
Jesus Christ. See Christ
Jiménez, Juan Ramón, 124
Jobs, Steve, 146
John Paul I, Pope, 62
John Paul II, Pope, 67–68, 89
    on celibacy, 183–84
    on Christianity, cultural, 55, 60
    on Christian testimony, 240n59
    on the Church, 66
    on encounter, 237n34
    on the Gospel, 239n50
John's Gospel, 63–64, 77–79
John the Baptist, 77–79, 85
joy, 45–46, 220, 226–27
judgment, importance of, 123–24,
    249n18
Jungmann, Josef Andreas, 141

Kabasilas, Nicolas, 71
Kafka, Franz, 104, 117, 244n10

reality as, 167, 203

the religious sense as, 72–86, 203

witnesses requiring, 50, 189, 204–5

Victorinus, Marius, 68

violence

coercion and, 49

in marriage, 181, 182

nihilism giving rise to, 49, 248n8

Virgil, 254n5

virginity, 183–85, 214

vocation

gladness crucial to, 226–27

as presence, 225–26

relationship as, 125, 129–30, 179–80, 186–87

wars of religion (post-Reformation), 22, 30, 62

Whitehead, Alfred North, 98

wholeness, 92, 93, 113, 115, 159–60, 226

William of Saint-Thierry, 129

witnesses. *See* testimony, Christian

Wittgenstein, Ludwig, 128

work, persons' responsibility for, 188–96

"the world," idea of, 88–89

"You," the, 98–99, 124, 179–80, 208, 213–14. *See also* "I," the

young people

avoiding maturity, 57, 137

fearfulness of, 8–9, 15, 49

freedom of, 153, 155, 156

lethargy of, 56–58, 137–38, 147–48, 161

meaning and, 140–44, 145

overprotection of, 146–48

reality introduced to, 139–40, 154–55, 173

relationship with, 150–52

teaching, 73–74, 154–55, 164, 223

Zacchaeus, 212, 216, 237n37

Zambrano, María, 106, 125–26, 140

Zubiri, Xavier, 109

JULIÁN CARRÓN

is a Catholic priest and theologian from Spain.
He is president of the Fraternity of Communion and Liberation
and professor of theology at the Catholic University of the Sacred Heart
in Milan. He is the editor of *Christ, God's Companionship with Man*
by Luigi Giussani.